The Executive S...
in Europe

International Administrative and Secretarial Procedures

Carolyn Maclay and
John Harrison

PITMAN
PUBLISHING

PITMAN PUBLISHING
128 Long Acre, London WC2E 9AN

A Division of Longman Group UK Limited

First published in Great Britain 1994

© Longman Group UK Limited 1994

A CIP catalogue record for this book is available on request from the British Library.

ISBN 0-273-60311-6

Typeset by Avocet Type, Bicester, Oxon
Printed in Great Britain by Clays Ltd, St Ives plc

The Publishers' policy is to use paper manufactured from sustainable forests.

CONTENTS

Appendix

Case study and questions from the French Ministry of Education Brevet de Technicien Supérieur Examination for Trilingual Secretaries

Index

PREFACE

The Executive Secretary in Europe is a comprehensive textbook and essential reference source for executive secretaries and personal assistants, designed for the following purposes:

1 To prepare students for advanced level secretarial examinations such as:

- NVQ Level 3 Administration Awards;
- PEI Level 3 Administration and Secretarial Procedures;
- LCCI Private and Executive Secretary's Diploma;
- Equivalent examinations in other countries, such as the French Ministry of Education Brevet de Technicien Supérieur Examination for Trilingual Secretaries;
- European Diploma for Business Education (Secretarial), to be offered in France, Germany and the UK (by the RSA).

2 To introduce office staff to the international environment and international sources and provide a book which can be used by secretaries of any nationality working anywhere in Europe – the EU's single market with its free movement of employees should extend such opportunities for staff to work abroad. The book has been prepared specifically to help secretarial staff at all levels who have varying degrees of foreign-language ability. The contents are as relevant for a temporary secretary as for a permanent employee.

3 To show the benefits, both for the individual and the company, of having secretarial and support staff with an ability to communicate effectively in more than one language. In addition, to make clear the benefits of recruiting secretaries and personal assistants with at least an understanding of and familiarity with foreign cultures, and with competent management techniques and skills in new technology.

4 To develop management skills for senior secretaries – an area so far neglected. It makes good business and economic sense for executive secretaries to be established members of the management team, playing a crucial role in the administration of their organisations.

5 To provide a practical workbook for advanced students and those already in employment who aspire to top-level secretarial positions by including:

- work tasks for assessment of the UK NVQ Level 3 competences, geared to the requirements of executive secretaries;
- a good selection of relevant past examination questions based on realistic case studies and scenarios for exercise purposes;
- checklists and *aides-mémoire* with pointers to essential secretarial tasks;
- personal action plans for self-assessment (which may be set against NVQ outcomes when required), challenges to enhance potential;

- a reading list with suggestions for further reading in preparation for examinations;
- an assessment reference chart for NVQ Level 3 competences listing:

  - the elements of competence
  - the chapters of this book which provide relevant knowledge for the competences
  - the work tasks and personal action plans for assessment of the competences

  Further information on NVQ assessment and guidelines is given in the NVQ Administration Standards Level 3 booklet supplied by the Administration Lead Body, 16 Park Crescent, London W1N 4AH.

A special feature of the book is the information bank, with its comprehensive selection of useful material, much of it written in the foreign language concerned. It is based on five major European markets: France, Germany, Italy, Spain and the United Kingdom.

The three sections of the information bank cover:

- abbreviations and acronyms
- glossary of key business vocabulary
- international business information sources

These will prove valuable for both personal and professional development. The intention is to provide 'signposts' pointing the way for the reader to acquire more detailed and up-to-date data whenever and wherever required.

Executive secretaries will find the information within this book helpful in their day-to-day liaison with international partners. The material has been selected to support them as they take the initiative in displaying high levels of professionalism and inter-cultural understanding within the context of Europe. This will contribute to personal success and enhance the competitive advantage of the enterprise they represent.

CM
JH

ACKNOWLEDGEMENTS

The authors wish to record their appreciation for the valuable advice and assistance given by many individuals and organisations, including, in some cases, their permission to reproduce photographs and other illustrations. These include:

Valerie Bell
British Telecommunications plc
British Telecommunications plc (Tymnet)
David Broucher of the British Embassy in
  Bonn
Sheila Burgess of Sheila Burgess
  International
Cave Tab Ltd
Cranfield School of Management
Sophie Grinspan of Longman France
Martha Handeyside of Alhambra
  Longman Spain
Sarah Harrison, for text production
Kevin Hughes of Longman Italia
IBM United Kingdom Ltd
The Italian Trade Centre
LaserMaster Europe Ltd
Marion Leishman
John Lidstone

Mark Maclay
Her Majesty's Stationery Office
Herman Miller Ltd
Hewlett-Packard Ltd
Karen Parrott of Parcelforce International
Paul Phillips of Ogilvy & Mather
  Advertising
Prima Magazine
The Institute of Public Relations
The Public Relations Consultants
  Association
Trevor Roberts of the British Embassy in
  Madrid
Mike Rogers
Roderick Stuart
Margaret Thevenot
Waiko UK Ltd
Woodcon Products Ltd

Carolyn Maclay would also like to extend her thanks and appreciation to the Winston Churchill Memorial Trust for permission to reproduce material and for the support it has given with its fellowship award. Long may the Trust flourish, to offer opportunity and responsibility to people of all ages and from all walks of life.

The NVQ performance criteria (pages xvi and xvii) are Crown copyright and are reproduced by kind permission of the National Council for Vocational Qualifications and the Administration Lead Body. The illustration on page 183 is also Crown copyright and is reproduced by kind permission of the Controller of Her Majesty's Stationery Office.

We are also grateful to the French Ministry of Education, the London Chamber of Commerce and Industry and the Pitman Examinations Institute Examinations Boards for permission to reproduce case studies and questions set in recent examinations. These are indicated in the book by the abbreviations:

LCCI PESD (LCCI Private and Executive Secretary's Diploma).

PEI ASP (PEI Administration and Secretarial Procedures Level 3 Examination).

Finally, we should like to thank the secretaries, personal assistants and employers who have been involved in the research for this book. Their input has been invaluable.

CASE STUDIES

CASE STUDY 1

Comlon International plc
Comlon House, West Street, London SW1Y 2AR

Comlon International plc has been a diamond supplier worldwide for 30 years.

The Chief Executive, Gregory Norton, was appointed six years ago and has extended the interests of the Company by acquiring a group of three gem laboratories and a small company which uses precious metals in the production of dental crowns and fillings.

Last year Comlon purchased Oriental Pearls, with branches in Singapore and Tokyo. Over the previous five years Oriental Pearls trebled its business, specialising in high-quality pearls. Over 50 per cent of the white and cream pearls are exported to Italy: the grey and pink pearls are sent to France. In these countries subsidiary companies of Oriental Pearls design and manufacture jewellery for export worldwide.

A review of Oriental Pearls is under way and a report will be made to the Board at its August meeting.

The Diamond Division provides almost 60 per cent of the world's industrial diamonds. Mary Foreman has recently begun to investigate possible links with Brazilian producers.

The stones chosen by two designers, Emica and Norina, who are under contract with the major fashion houses to produce jewellery to complement each season's clothes, must be of high quality and have some unusual aspect such as colour, shape or size.

Efforts have been made since the acquisition of Oriental Pearls to persuade the two designers to use Comlon as a supplier of high-quality pearls but they continue to purchase only diamonds from Comlon International.

The Chairman has during the last ten years purchased examples of fine jewellery from all over the world. The Comlon Museum was opened in 1980 in Amsterdam; three examples of designs by Emica and Norina are sent each year to Head Office. The Board chooses one of the three for Comlon to purchase for display in the Museum.

The Museum has become a popular tourist attraction. The new extension, to be called the Brantwood Gallery, will be opened formally on Friday 30 October.

You are PA/Secretary to Mrs Catherine Walsh, Director and Head of Administration (as in the organisation chart, *see* Fig 1).

LCCI Private and Executive Secretary's Diploma

You will be using this information for some of the assessment tasks in this book.

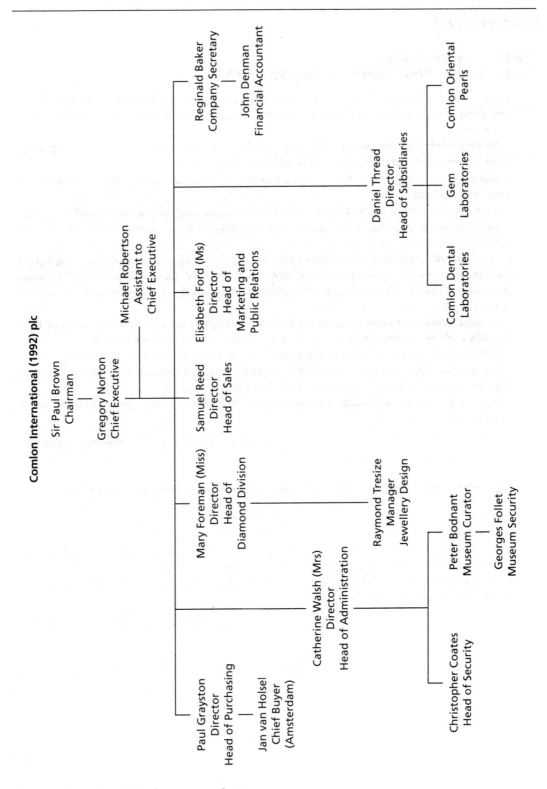

Fig 1 Organisation chart for case study 1

CASE STUDY 2

Comlon International plc
Comlon House, West Street, London SW1Y 2AR

Comlon International plc is an international news gathering organisation. The Head Office is in London and there are main branches in the capital cities of all European and many Asian countries.

North America is organised into three main branch areas – west, mid, east – and South America into three branch areas – north, central and south.

Australasia is a main branch with three sub-branches – Australia (west), Australia (east) and New Zealand.

Each main branch is staffed by a small administrative unit and a number of journalists supplemented at peak times by freelance journalists known as 'stringers' for whose work a flat fee is paid.

The Board of Directors approved the extension of operations from the news gathering agency base to become a worldwide provider of news via satellite TV. Comlon International plc owns a channel and effort is now being concentrated on building up expertise and resources in this new area.

Dwight Jones, a Canadian, whose experience has been in the promotion of satellite TV in Canada and the United States, has been appointed as Marketing and Sales Director. This is a reflection of the importance being placed by the Board on the new venture.

For its news gathering operation Comlon International plc requires communication to be fast and accurate. It relies heavily on both telex and fax.

You are Secretary to Mr Patrick Moreland, Operations Director (as in the organisation chart, see Fig 2).

LCCI Private and Executive Secretary's Diploma

You will be using this information for some of the assessment tasks in this book.

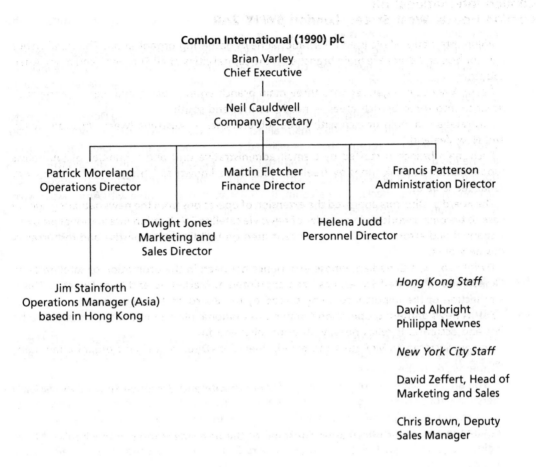

Comlon International (1990) plc
Brian Varley
Chief Executive

Neil Cauldwell
Company Secretary

Patrick Moreland
Operations Director

Martin Fletcher
Finance Director

Francis Patterson
Administration Director

Dwight Jones
Marketing and
Sales Director

Helena Judd
Personnel Director

Jim Stainforth
Operations Manager (Asia)
based in Hong Kong

Hong Kong Staff

David Albright
Philippa Newnes

New York City Staff

David Zeffert, Head of
Marketing and Sales

Chris Brown, Deputy
Sales Manager

Fig 2 Organisation chart for case study 2

CASE STUDY 3

Scenario

You are secretary to Mr Michael Vivoir, Marketing Manager of Sylvan Limited, who manufacture a comprehensive range of hair care products.

The firm is expanding rapidly and Mr Vivoir wishes you to have increased responsibilities. In order to do this, he has agreed to the appointment of a junior secretary to relieve you of some of your more routine duties. In addition, the junior secretary will be responsible for providing a secretarial service to the Marketing Department's Senior Administrator.

You also have responsibility for checking and controlling the Marketing Department's petty cash account. An imprest of £100 is maintained and individual payments may not exceed £20. Andrew Gardner has recently been appointed to fill a vacancy in the Sales Records Office and he has been given the task of administering the petty cash account. He says that he has done it before in a previous job, so you leave him to prepare the account unaided for the first month. If, after checking the account, it is unsatisfactory you agree with Andrew to rewrite it and supply him with a set of instructions to follow in the future.

PEI Administration and Secretarial Procedures

CASE STUDY 4

Scenario

You work as Personal Assistant to Mrs Sylvia Fairbanks, Personnel Manager of DZ Ltd, an engineering company situated on the south coast of England, employing 198 people, 32 of whom work in the offices.

You are involved in all recruitment for DZ Ltd. The company is about to take on additional personnel for both the engineering works and the administrative support areas, and you will be assisting in the preparation of induction programmes for the new employees.

Additionally, you provide full secretarial support for the many meetings in which Mrs Fairbanks is involved. These include the Works Council and the Safety Committee, both of which she chairs.

PEI Administration and Secretarial Procedures

READING LIST

Secretarial and Business Administration

Business Administration, Josephine Shaw

Effective Business Administration and Communication, Desmond Evans

European Business, Richard Welford and Kate Prescott

European Studies, Tony Scott

Information Processing, Elaine Mullins

Human Resources Management, H T Graham and R Bennett

Management Appreciation, Helen Harding

Modern Business Administration, Robert C Appleby

Office Organisation and Secretarial Procedures, Helen Harding

People in Organisations, Valerie Bell and John Harrison

Professional Text Production Plus, Margaret Cashin and Diana Jones

Secretarial Case Studies, John Harrison and Marion Leishman

Secretarial Duties, John Harrison

Secretary's Desk Book, John Harrison

Secretarial Procedures in the Electronic Office, Desmond Evans

Supervisory Management, P W Betts

Training Guides for word processing, databases, spreadsheets, desktop publishing and operating systems

Languages

French for Business Studies, P Taylor and F Delbourgo

German for Business Studies, Susanne Parker and Claire Burke

Franc Exchange: Effective Business Communication in France, J Gladkaw, C Saunders, C Gordon and R Penfound

Business in France, J Szarka

Freut Mich! German for Business, Paul Hartley

Making Your Mark: Effective Business Communication in Germany, M Howarth, M Woodhall and R Penfound

Pronto! Italian for Business, P Durrant and A Lamping

¡Oiga!, Jim Bray and Matias Gomez

All these are published by Pitman Publishing.

See also the Information Bank, Part 3 (pages 229–99) for other sources of information.

ASSESSMENT OF NVQ LEVEL 3 ADMINISTRATION COMPETENCES

Unit/ Element	Competence	Chapter	Work task for assessment of competence page in text	Personal action plan No
1.1	Organise allocation and despatch of mail	4	66	11 24
1.2	Use the telephone system to the full	2	33	4 5
1.3	Transmit and receive information using electronic equipment	3	49	8
2.1	Use and develop manual and computerised filing systems	4	67	9
2.2	Locate and abstract information from unspecified sources	3	50	7
2.3	Organise and present information in a variety of formats	2	34	3
3.1	Receive, screen and assist visitors	10	211	41
4.1	Arrange travel and accommodation	6	115–16	19
4.2	Plan and organise business visits			
5.1	Produce text from oral and written material using an alphanumeric keyboard	6	116–17	17 18
5.2	Present narrative, graphic and tabular information using an alphanumeric keyboard			
5.3	Organise and arrange the copying, collating and binding of documents	4	67	12
6.1	Identify and respond to correspondence for own action	2	34	23
7.1	Manage appointments	6	117	16
7.2	Organise own work schedule	7	137	22 24

CHAPTER 1

The role of the secretary in the international environment

IDENTIFYING THE ROLE

The *Oxford English Dictionary* definition of a secretary is: 'A title applied to various confidential officers . . . one who is employed to conduct correspondence, to keep records and transact other business for a person or society'. For a personal assistant there is no specific definition except a reference to: 'designating an official or employee attached to a person in a subordinate capacity'. Assistant is defined as: 'present to help, aiding, helpful, auxiliary to . . . standing or remaining by, present, accompanying'.

There is no doubt that secretaries and personal assistants do fulfil the type of tasks outlined above. However, the wording does not even *begin* to define the full range of responsibilities and tasks that secretaries and personal assistants may undertake.

The secretarial role has developed tremendously in recent years, and recognition of this complex role has at last begun to be apparent in the scope of job responsibility, career opportunities and financial rewards, and deservedly so. A *good* secretary or PA is highly skilled and indispensable as an 'executive assistant' in the international office environment.

In many ways the secretary/PA has a most frustrating role, with enormous influence but often little *direct* authority. Because of this many turn to other occupations and never realise their potential as executive secretaries. If they were to take or be given a managerial/executive role, as suggested here, they would remain to work for and to the benefit of the organisation. The secretary is at the centre of office life. As a result, secretaries have a *fundamental responsibility to communicate well and effectively* at a domestic level and increasingly at an international level.

The creation of the single market in Europe, the ability to move around the world quickly and easily, and the speed of technological development facilitating business all play their part in reducing barriers to trade and mobility. Differences will, however, always exist between countries in terms of social conventions, language and time zones. The secretary must develop the skills of awareness, flexibility and worldliness required to operate effectively and make a positive contribution in the multicultural, multi-disciplinary arena of an international organisation. The secretary needs to develop more specific management-oriented skills, as described in this book, to complement the technical skills.

Executive secretaries are in the front line of business communication. They must be able to say what needs to be said assertively, but not aggressively, and to demonstrate their managerial skills. Preparation for advanced secretarial examinations and training in personal development are essential if these needs are to be satisfied. May those words 'I am *just* a secretary' be consigned to the past.

This chapter highlights two fundamental building blocks aiding effective communication and raising the profile of the efficient and professional secretary. This in turn should assist in the process of career progression and job satisfaction. These building blocks are:

- understanding the structure and function of an organisation and the way in which it operates;
- developing your own niche within this structure.

By understanding the structure of your organisation, you will be a long way towards understanding 'the business' in which you are working. Developing a niche in an organisation depends on having clear personal goals and an understanding of where personal strengths and weaknesses lie and how best they can be 'tailored' and utilised within a specific organisational structure.

THE STRUCTURE AND FUNCTION OF ORGANISATIONS

Communication systems exist within organisations of every size. These are lines of formal and informal authority and they constitute an organisational structure. They are usually illustrated in the form of an organisation chart or organogram. The size and nature of the chart will vary according to the size of the organisation and the area of business in which it operates. To a certain extent it will also reflect the management style permeating through the organisation from its chief executive officer and/or senior management. The importance of organisational structures is shown in the practice of good recruitment consultancies, which will automatically seek detailed diagrams of structure, organisational background and corporate culture in order to have a full brief. This in turn enables them to seek the most suitable candidate for a job vacancy. Executive search firms or 'head hunters' as a matter of course keep up-to-date organisation charts of companies in specific industry sectors. These are used as starting–points from which to try to access candidates and 'contacts' at comparable levels within suitable organisations.

Some companies, where appropriate, display relevant branches or units of their organisation charts to customers. Others guard theirs closely in the belief that such information may give away hints to market success or business practice.

The organisational structure of a company is the distillation of many different strands that breathe life into a company, such as:

- company strategy;
- company staff and their skills;
- management style;
- company systems and *modus operandi* (the way they work);
- corporate culture, i.e. guiding concepts and shared beliefs, values and hopes.

An organisation chart presents the essential components of the organisation and shows how it is organised and how different departments interrelate.

Two further ingredients are needed to provide a more rounded picture of the organisation. They are:

a a statement of corporate objectives;

b a mission statement.

Corporate objectives

These are common goals which form the guiding principles of an organisation and provide collective objectives which the organisation sets from time to time for overall achievement by its employees. Each employee has a responsibility to contribute towards the achievement of the organisation's corporate objectives. For example, the corporate objectives of a company might include:

- ensure that the company's products/services are more competitive than in previous years;
- enhance the value/quality of the company's products/services;
- increase the company's sales by penetrating emerging markets.

These objectives provide a focus for achievement, goals to 'score' and challenges to overcome. They can keep a complicated enterprise on course. They help provide motivation at a corporate and a personal level. All successful companies have a written set of corporate objectives. We return to the subject of objectives in Chapter 11.

Mission statement

This is usually one or two sentences which outline the overall aims of the organisation. The mission statement is often more general in nature and is supported by the corporate objectives. For example, the mission statement to accompany the above corporate objectives might be:

To secure a major share of the market throughout Europe.

This sits like an umbrella over the corporate objectives and strategies for achieving these objectives. In some organisations, the mission statement is printed over office doorways to remind and motivate staff!

PERSONAL ACTION PLAN 1

▶ **Draw up your own personal career mission statement and career objectives.**

▶ **Why are you a secretary?**

▶ **How would you like to see your career develop in the next five years?**

Organisation charts

The organisation chart in Fig 1.1 shows the London office of *Prima* magazine owned by Gruhner and Jahr, a German publishing company. About 40 people are employed in *Prima*'s head office. The purpose of the chart is to illustrate how the company is organised, showing the composition and relationships between its divisions, departments,

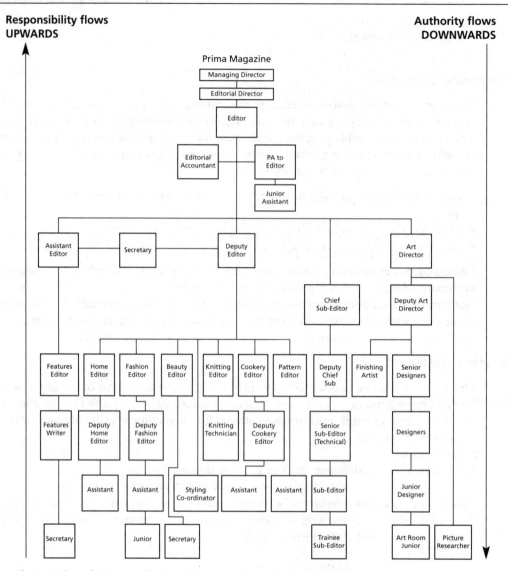

Fig 1.1 Line chart organisation structure for *Prima* magazine

sections and units. Some organisation charts include the names of personnel and their job titles; others give just the titles. The chart also shows lines of communication (vertical and horizontal), levels of authority and responsibility. There are many kinds of organisational structure, such as line, staff or functional organisation; organisation by committee, function or project; and other informal structures. Combinations of organisational structure are normally used. All have their merits and shortcomings.

Each person in the organisation chart in Fig 1.1 is accountable to their immediate superior up the line, so that they know clearly to whom they report and for what tasks they are responsible. It is a typical organisation chart based on a hierarchical principle of authority with responsibility flowing in a direct line from top (proprietors) to bottom (clerical staff). The PA to the editor is responsible to the editor for all the responsibilities outlined in the job description given in Chapter 9.

Advantages of a line organisation

1 Simple, direct and easy to understand.
2 Directness of control simplifies co-ordination of activities within a department.
3 Decisions can be rapidly made as the chain of command is direct.
4 Relatively straightforward delegation and control of work.
5 Clearly defined lines of authority, recognition of responsibility and span of control.
6 Staff discipline should be easier, with clear lines of authority.
7 Easy to understand the position and status of all concerned.

Disadvantages of line organisation

1 Danger of autocracy and co-operation/co-ordination difficulties.
2 Head of the department controls and sets the tone of the department/organisation. Lazy boss, lazy department? Does too much depend on one person?
3 Inflexibility can develop, which causes problems if circumstances force changes in a department or in the organisation.
4 Lack of understanding between departments and limited opportunities to understand or acquire new experience of different disciplines. Demarcation boundaries between areas of work may hamper the smooth running of the organisation.
5 No indication is given of informal relationships.

Vertical communication

Vertical communication usually covers the following spheres of responsibility:

Management line

Managing staff:
- setting objectives, priorities and policies
- issuing instructions
- initiating change
- motivating
- discipline
- delegating
- advice/listening/consulting

General information dissemination:
- progress reports

Of course, communication is a two-way process and communication *upwards* is vital if correct decisions are to be made. Such communication might involve:

Management line

↑

Data transferral:
- general/specific information passing
- progress reports
- problems/grievances
- consultation/requests

Proactive input:
- initiating ideas/suggestions

Reactive input:
- reactions to change
- reactions to instructions

Lateral communication

Communication is not only vertical within an organisation but also lateral. This involves communication across departments, disciplines, sections and colleagues with the common aim of achieving objectives. Lateral communication is often characterised by:

- passing information;
- discussion/requests;
- advice/consultation;
- problems/grievances.

Lateral communication may manifest itself in the following ways:

- meetings (formal and informal);
- documentation (daily, weekly, monthly or quarterly);
- house journals/newsletters;
- in-house presentations;
- computer terminal information link-up;
- social gatherings/office gossip!

Task or project teams

Many companies favour a management approach which results in a different organisational structure. Some companies are run as meritocracies (leadership by merit) and work on a task team basis, although functioning as a meritocracy does not presuppose working on a team basis. This type of structure depends on the nature of the business and the type of corporate culture at play. Task or project teams vary in size and bring together units of staff with different skills, specialisations and expertise as shown in the two team units in Fig 1.2.

PRODUCT TEAM A   PRODUCT TEAM B

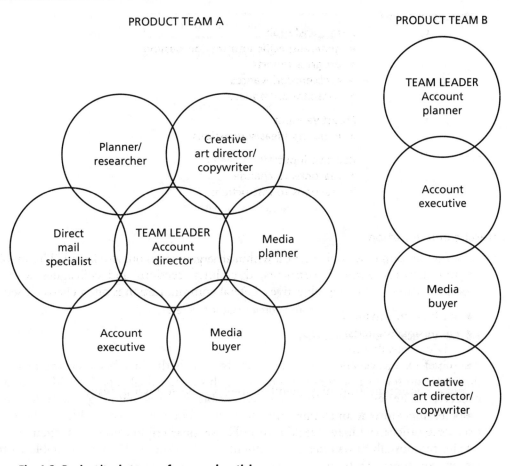

Fig 1.2 Project/task teams for an advertising agency

Within the same organisation a more 'traditional' vertical organisation chart may also figure in different departments, as illustrated in Fig 1.3.

It is also important to remember that any good organisation chart is never carved in stone. It has to be dynamic and create an internal environment which will produce results. A flexible form that can change slightly or substantially according to requirements, whether they are market forces or internal personnel changes, is useful. The human element will always affect the process to a greater or lesser extent.

Levels of responsibility

The following list shows the traditional levels of responsibility within a company:

1 Proprietors   = Shareholders
2 Top management   = Directors
3 Middle management   = Managers/heads of department
4 Supervisors
5 Administrators/secretaries
6 Clerical staff/receptionists

Fig 1.3 Vertical organisation chart

The chief executive officer or managing director is the link between the board of directors and senior management because of his or her dual capacity as director and executive. The senior executives are responsible for implementing and undertaking work to meet policy objectives and decisions. They are accountable to the chief executive officer and managing director. Those involved in middle management are usually responsible for running departments or divisions and are accountable to the senior executive officer.

Each rung on the ladder of seniority usually liaises with the rung immediately above or below itself. However, situations may arise whereby normal communication channels have to be bypassed to avoid delays or problems or to solve sudden crises due to illness, for example.

Span of control

The two models of task teams highlight another element in understanding organisational structure, that is, the area of responsibilities or span of control, otherwise known as 'span of management' or 'span of responsibility'. In Fig 1.2, the team leader for Product A has a greater span of control than that of the team leader for Product B. The span of control is the number of staff or subordinates who can be supervised or managed effectively by one person, whether it is a manager or a supervisor. It is normally recommended that one person should not have direct responsibility for the work of more than six employees, but this depends on the nature of the work undertaken by the subordinates. Where work is routine, this could be increased. Team Leader A has a span of control of six people and Team Leader B three people. This may be due to the size of the advertising account, the seniority of the team leader or the bias of the account. In short, the span of control depends on the abilities of those being supervised, the complexity of the work being done, how effective communication is and the ability and personality of the supervisor. Team leaders bring together the expertise of the different departments and functions, as shown below (again, using the example of Fig 1.2).

Functions of departments

Department	Function
Department	*Function*
Account director	Overall co-ordinator and manager of an advertising account group. A generalist who represents the agency to the client and client requirements to the agency. Daily client liaison, budget control, presentation preparation. Must understand a client's product and market. Liaises with all departments involved in preparing and executing an advertising campaign to produce work on time, correctly, in line with client and budget needs.
Planner/researcher	Talks to the consumer about the product to be advertised. Carries out market research. Prepares a 'creative brief' which encapsulates the advertising message to be promoted. This is based on client requirements, the market place and consumer feedback and trends.
Copywriter/art director	Produces the big idea. Creates advertising that sells and is memorable, based on the execution of the 'creative brief'.
Media planner	Researches cost-effective forms of media to use in a campaign and recommends suitable media for the product to be advertised in line with the advertising budget.
Media buyer	A deal-maker. Buys TV slots or press space at the best possible rates for the client and in line with the budget.
Direct mail specialist	Has access to suitable mailing lists, data and figures supporting direct mail campaigns. Recommends a suitable direct mail activity schedule.
Account executive	A junior version of an account director. A co-ordinating role to ensure the best work comes out of the different departments. A 'nuts and bolts' role dealing with clients on a daily basis and the different departments internally. Writes reports and assists the account director.

DEVELOPING THE ROLE

Organisation charts and organograms present an organisation or department as a totality. However, the totality is made up of *individuals* each with their own areas of responsibility and expertise, their own aspirations, strengths, shortcomings and philosophies – in other words, the human element.

Any secretary or PA who takes their job seriously, will be keen to do well and be recognised as a contributor to the organisation. A secretarial career can be a much more challenging, fulfilling and high-profile role than in the past, due partly to recognition by employers of the secretary's potential and partly to the changing nature of business. There is both the increasing importance of information technology and the rise in demand for secretarial staff with a foreign-language ability.

Taking the language aspect first, as this is highly relevant to improving international communication skills, there has always been a steady requirement for bilingual secretaries, or 'secretary-linguists' as they are called by the Institute of Linguists, particularly in the last five years. Despite a deep recession, the level of recruitment of secretary-linguists has remained relatively unscathed in England when compared with general levels of secretarial recruitment. This is a niche or specialised market in itself.

The magical phrase 'European Single Market' had some effect in galvanising employers to consider the value of retaining secretarial and management staff with foreign languages. This has afforded executive secretaries dramatic increases in job opportunities with languages, provided the language and secretarial skills are good! Traditional language areas such as the diplomatic service; international organisations such as the EC, NATO and UN; multinational organisations such as oil companies and the media have all expanded, and other areas, such as finance, fashion, cosmetics and the legal field, have become growth sectors. Eastern Europe has also opened up crucial new markets for specific language specialists.

English may remain the international language of business but those companies whose staff make the effort to understand the languages and cultures of fellow European business partners are benefiting most. They are developing a niche, be it by engaging a French-speaking receptionist or a chief executive officer's PA with a good working knowledge of, say, Spanish. Employing a secretary with some language ability may clinch a new business deal, reassure a concerned client or establish a special business rapport. Whatever the circumstances, it will make a difference and produce a positive impact in the business arena.

The evidence is clear: language skills are becoming vital to retain a competitive edge and provide a route for a secretary to develop a niche in a company.

So, what does 'developing a niche' really mean?

It means focusing on an area of responsibility, earmarking it as your own, making it your own and performing it better than anyone else. This depends on two things:

1   How positive and proactive the employer is prepared to be.
2   The secretary having clear-cut views on wants and needs, and pinpointing new professional skills to be developed and enhanced.

So, how do you achieve this?

- identify the *role*
- use *initiative*
- be *seen*
- be *heard*

In short, MAKE IT HAPPEN.

Identifying the role

This stage can vary in length. For some it is a straightforward exercise in mapping out responsibilities and homing in on areas that can be developed as special or unique projects. For others the task is not as clear cut. It may take weeks or months to build up a picture of routine tasks and for areas of potential development or real interest to appear. Opportunities do not always present themselves immediately. Flexibility is essential in monitoring this element of your personal action plan.

It is also worth starting from a position of strength by obtaining as broad a base of skills as possible. From a solid foundation more options and ranges of applications appear. Areas of expertise, experience and responsibility can become more specialised as the secretary's career develops. As the pyramid of progress diagram in Fig 1.4 shows, where the more junior role might require basic or superficial abilities in many areas such as those at the base of the pyramid, a senior PA role might call on specialist abilities in the areas of communication, language, information processing or specialist administration. The key lies in retaining a *pool of skills* to be called on as and when necessary.

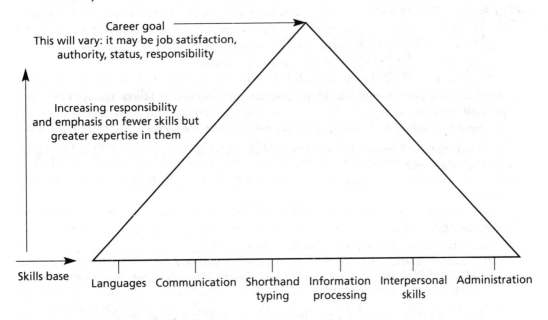

Fig 1.4 The pyramid of progress

Why are skills so important?

This obvious question must be addressed, for in today's job market where many a college leaver seeks a job with 'minimal secretarial content' it is surprising that they contemplate a secretarial career at all.

At the heart of an efficiently-run office are capable managers and secretarial and administrative staff who are equally capable. Each function requires unique skills. The successful executive secretary is both a consummate team player *and* solo performer. Understanding, anticipating and communicating with the boss, colleagues and customers will make the difference between performing a routine role and developing that role.

Once the executive secretary has established a role as a reliable, consistently sound secretary, this will herald the establishment of a good reputation or 'track record'. Secretarial skills are vital because they are at the heart of the task-oriented job function. Personality and 'chemistry' between boss and secretary are key components in a working relationship; however, a 'great personality' does not produce memos or meet deadlines.

Use your initiative

Secretarial, administrative and language skills are main areas where the energies of the executive secretary are channelled. They must, therefore, be good and work for the secretary *as well as* for the boss. During secretarial training, natural abilities and skills become clear and lead to the preference for, say, text processing, financial record keeping or shorthand. Make the most of these indications from the outset, incorporate them into your personal action plan and use such skills to your advantage.

PERSONAL ACTION PLAN 2

▶ **Evaluate your current job specification.**
What are your strengths?
Are they being utilised to their full potential?

▶ **How does your current job differ from the role you would like to see yourself fulfilling?**
Have you discussed this with your boss or personnel officer?

▶ **What skills and personality traits would you consider vital if you were recruiting for your own job?**

Self-management

Remember: SELF-MANAGEMENT IS THE KEY TO SUCCESS – MAKE IT HAPPEN

This means taking control of your life, assessing yourself and finding the right balance. This is not easy, nor does it happen overnight. The key lies in approaching challenges in a positive manner with an 'I can and I will' attitude. Honesty in self-appraisal and goal-setting and -getting are key elements in developing your niche and achieving professional and personal fulfilment.

Begin the process now!

Detailed below are skills that fall into the three main categories of the secretarial domain. Carry out a personal analysis of strengths, weaknesses, opportunities and threats (a SWOT analysis) so that you can set goals to develop strengths further, overcome weaknesses and be aware of threats and opportunities within a professional context. Analysis can be carried out at a purely functional level, and there is a list of skills or functions to assist in that process (*see* page 13). The example sheet of a SWOT analysis shown in Fig 1.5 on page 14 includes other dimensions against which analysis can be carried out. These include personality and office environment variables such as personal qualities, office politics and how general market conditions may be affecting a company or the role the secretary has within that company.

Put down answers in order of priority and, after evaluation, set goals and monitor progress on a monthly basis of the top priority for each dimension in each section.

SKILLS

Secretarial	Administrative	Language
Typing	Financial record-keeping	Oral communications
WP/computing	Travel arrangements	Telephoning
Shorthand	Letter and report writing	Face to face
Audio-typing	Hotel bookings	Written
Correspondence	Organising conferences	Translation
Diary/appointments	Organising meetings	Interpreting
Meetings/minutes	Organising entertainment	Client liaison
Reports	Budget control	Technical translations
Numeracy tasks	Filing	Secretarial duties in a foreign language
Telephoning	Internal liaison	
Reception	Research projects	Interpersonal skills
	Client contact	
	Public relations	
	Interviewing	
	Training	
	Supervision	

Once you have carried out your personal SWOT analysis put it into action.

- Research the opportunity.
- Identify your goal/set your objectives.
- Have a strategy to achieve the objectives – this will involve:
- Being seen and being heard.

At the heart of this strategy will be the concept of: *communication with my boss*. Only then can the business partnership flourish with mutual benefit.

- Review your progress – this will assist in setting new goals and achieving them successfully, and so the process continues.

The benefits of niche-building

- You establish yourself as an individual within the corporate structure.
- You send out positive PR for yourself. Your boss will also benefit as he or she will be seen as the boss who is efficient and who can pick talent.
- There is at least *one* area where you are more highly skilled than anyone else.

SWOT ANALYSIS				
	Strengths	*Weaknesses*	*Opportunities*	*Threats*
Functional ability/skills				
Personality				
Office environment				
General market environment				
Goals				

Fig. 1.5

- You are contributing towards your own job satisfaction, which in turn builds confidence.
- You are fulfilling your potential, taking on more tasks and being delegated more responsibility.
- You are sowing the seeds for career development and promotion.
- You are contributing to improving company performance – nothing succeeds like success!

EXAMINE YOUR KNOWLEDGE

1 (a) Draw your own company, branch or unit organisation chart if you have not already seen it.

  (b) How does your organisation chart reflect the business you are in?

  (c) Consider ways or systems that would help to improve inter- and intra-departmental communication within your organisation.

2 (a) What information does the organisation chart in Case Study 1 give you?

  (b) What are the advantages and disadvantages of this organisational system?

  (c) How does this organisation differ from your own in relation to (i) levels of responsibility; (ii) span of control; (iii) lines of communication?

3 Lack of co-ordination between and within the departments of an organisation is one of the major reasons for inefficiency and low productivity. Consider what factors cause poor co-ordination and suggest ways of overcoming such problems.

4 A head teacher is quoted in your local newspaper as saying that new technology in offices is making secretaries redundant and that a secretarial career is one without a future. Write a letter to the newspaper commenting on this observation and putting forward your ideas on the future role of the secretary in the international environment.

CHAPTER 2

The communication process

Words, when written or spoken, so often prove to be inadequate tools to articulate our thoughts, needs, goals and intentions. The word 'communication' is at the heart of our day-to-day existence. However, many of the problems that arise in personal and professional relationships can be traced to ineffectual communication, that is to say, problems with articulation or comprehension or, indeed, a complete lack of communication.

For the executive secretary or PA working in the international environment, written and spoken communication (perhaps in more than one language) will form the bulk of the workload and provide, at times, double or treble the scope for misunderstanding and 'crossed wires'. Effective communication is essential for the successful secretary/PA and this is based on solid communication systems.

PRINCIPLES OF EFFECTIVE COMMUNICATION

Know yourself and know what you want
This is not as straightforward as it sounds and requires preparation and decision-making; more so when communication is in a foreign language or with a person whose mother tongue is not English.

It is easy to know what you *do not* want rather than what you *do* want. It is easier to have no opinion on a subject than to spend time thinking, assimilating information, developing and modifying points of view, opinions and beliefs.

Communication is most effective when it reflects our intentions for a relationship. In other words, have a specific direction, a plan. There is great power in communication and each person is ultimately responsible for the nature of the relationship which has been created by the act of communication.

Be sensitive
This does not mean that you should be 'hypersensitive' in your reactions to what people say, but rather be aware and pay close attention. Notice changes in a person's behaviour, for relationships change when communication changes. Communication does not always mean talking. Listening and watching 'powerfully' are communication tools. How well an executive secretary listens and takes in information will say much both about the person being listened to and about the secretary. When listening, focus your eyes and full attention on the speaker; concentrate on the content of what is being said; question and clarify when appropriate; do not just interrupt; and take notes if necessary.

Be flexible and keep all options open
People who have the most options will have the greatest chance of securing what

they want from communication, for there is usually more than one choice. This is not purely a manipulative move. Being flexible is so important because it is linked with the real, day-to-day problem of coping with stress and remaining healthy. Confronted with a stressful communication situation, the executive secretary can:

1 run away from it;
2 stand firm and remain inaccessible to another person's argument (this leads to disappointment and failure rather than positive feedback and progress);
3 adapt and find a way of coping with the problem, thus raising the stress threshold and gaining experience so that if a similar situation arises the secretary can cope and communicate effectively.

See the job through with determination

Persistence is required to communicate effectively on a consistent basis or to change a relationship. This you may have to do if you deal with difficult people or with clients who have preconceived ideas regarding the company for which you work or the role of a secretary. Make no excuses. Do what it takes to achieve your objective. This relates to the idea of knowing what you want. Once you know what you want, make a commitment to achieve it with your skills and the help of those around you.

Warning! Beware of the barriers to effective communication (Fig 2.1).

People	Environment
(Usually complex issues)	(Usually more clear-cut physical barriers)
Negative approach/attitude	Organisational structure forcing delay or over-complicated lines of communication forcing a total breakdown in communication
Personal preconceptions regarding abilities	
Negative or contradictory body language	Bad planning in the physical location of work stations
Poor planning, e.g. bad timing in meetings	Noise in the office
	Faulty machinery

Fig 2.1 Barriers to effective communication

METHODS OF COMMUNICATION

A plethora of communication methods and systems are at the disposal of the executive secretary. Of course, many factors must be taken into account when deciding on the appropriate form of communication, factors such as:

- subject matter;
- means available;
- confidentiality;
- urgency, timescale, deadline;
- cost;
- security;
- international time zones;

- foreign language requirements – utilising the services of translation agencies and how this can affect timing;
- 'house style'/house rules;
- legal requirements;
- internal office politics;
- cultural differences/customs which may affect methods of business practice, such as the availability of personnel, bank holidays, forms of address.

Some of these factors are particular only to international business. However, awareness of such possible operational complexities is vital.

The three categories of business communication are written, oral and visual, as follows:

Written	Oral	Visual
letters	face to face (meetings	VDU
memos	and presentations)	video
reports	telephone	graphs
telex	dictation (audio or face	tables
fax	to face)	diagrams
codes	foreign language	charts
cable	interpreting	slide projection
translations of foreign		computer networking
language material		electronic mail
manuals		brochures
directories		maps
		Viewdata

Televisual facilities are also available with special telephone conference facilities (*see* page 29).

Confidentiality

Confidentiality is a vitally important theme at senior level. This can be maintained in communication by the following methods:

a Restricting circulation of confidential information to those involved.
b Choosing the appropriate method of communication dependent on the subject matter.
c Physically controlling security of papers, files and information. Locking away papers when not in use.
d Marking papers 'Confidential'.
e Shredding papers when necessary.
f Being careful when using the telephone.
g Using tact and diplomacy to avoid questioning from unauthorised personnel.
h If communicating in a foreign language, being aware of anyone else not involved directly in the conversation who may understand what you are saying.

CORRESPONDENCE

The executive secretary will devote a significant proportion of time to correspondence – preparation of reports and letters, dictation, supervision of junior secretaries'

Quality	Advantage			Disadvantage		
	Written	*Oral*	*Visual*	*Written*	*Oral*	*Visual*
Permanent	x		x		x[1]	
Reference	x	x[2]	x		x[3]	
Legal contracts	x				x	x
Confidentiality/security	x	x				x
Accurate:						
technical information	x		x		x	
complex argument	x	x	x[4]			x
statistical data/graphs	x		x		x	
Recipient friendly	x[5]	x[6]		x[7]	x[8]	
Speed		x		x		
Personal contact		x		x		x
Misunderstanding		x	x[9]	x		x[10]
Cost		x				
Feedback		x		x[11]		x
The personal touch	x	x				
Distraction factor	x		x		x[12]	
Large target audience	x	x	x			
Language difficulties			x	x[13]	x[13]	

Notes

1 No formal record
2 If recorded
3 If not recorded
4 Usually as an aid to written and oral communication
5 Can take in information in own time
6 Depends on the person and their skills
7 Can be cold
8 Depends on the person and their skills
9 Good for simple ideas
10 No control unless supported by other means
11 Can be delayed
12 Interruptions
13 Depends on communication skills

Fig 2.2 The advantages and disadvantages of methods of communication – can you add any more?

correspondence activities and composing correspondence for personal projects and tasks. For example, the following are some of the correspondence tasks undertaken by the PA to the editor of *Prima* magazine. Some correspondence she would deal with herself and compose replies, others would require the editor's input. How would you prioritise the work and which areas would you deal with yourself?

1 Invitations to attend the launch of a new book or a new perfume.
2 Literature relating to new products such as cosmetics, holidays and garden furniture which could be featured in future editions of *Prima*.
3 Requests from readers for further information about products featured in *Prima*.
4 Offers to write articles for *Prima*.
5 Queries regarding magazine subscription rates.
6 Notices of meetings.
7 Requests from readers for help in using the sewing patterns from previous editions.
8 Memos concerning production problems, e.g. schedules for the receipt of material.
9 Notices of film screenings.

10 A letter from a reader whose photograph of her pet had gone astray in the post.

11 Letters congratulating the editor on the quality of the magazine.

Checklist for effective writing of letters and memos

- Prepare an outline plan of your message to marshal your thoughts, noting down all the points you wish to make and arranging them in logical order.
- Group the points into paragraphs, each dealing with one major area of concern or discussion. Then arrange them as follows:
    - opening paragraph: introducing your subject
    - body of the letter: further subdivided into paragraphs in logical order
    - closing paragraph: containing concluding remarks
- Use a heading whenever it will provide a quick reference to the content of the letter.
- Use the appropriate salutations and complimentary closes (see the forms of address on pages 21–23).
- If the letter is in response to another letter, a meeting or a telephone call, refer to it and quote any reference given.
- Use language that is clear and can be understood by your correspondent in simple and concise sentences, whether English mother tongue or not!
- Adopt the correct style and tone of writing with due regard to the relationship existing between correspondents.
- Check the letter carefully to ensure that no punctuation, spelling or typographical errors pass without detection and correction.
- Always aim to be courteous and as helpful as possible in your letter writing.
- Consider whether a letter is necessary. Would a telephone call be more appropriate, cheaper or quicker? This will depend on the intention of your communication and relates to the necessity of writing.
- Memos, rather than letters, are normally used for internal communication between departments, branches or regions, wherever written records are essential.
- When replying to formal invitations use the invitation text itself, and if the invitation is written in the third person reply to it in the same form. No salutation, complimentary close or signature is required. When refusing an invitation, it is courteous to give a reason.

Examples of business letters in English, French, German, Italian and Spanish are given in M Cashin and D Jones, *Professional Text Production Plus* (Pitman Publishing).

FORM DESIGN

Forms provide essential information concisely and in a logical order for ease of processing and for making quick decisions. They are an important means of communicating information, but if they are not well designed they can defeat their whole purpose and prove to be time-wasting error creators causing difficulties for the 'form fillers' as well as for those responsible for issuing them and those processing and acting on the information.

Checklist of essential requirements of a well-designed form

It must:

- have a title relating to its function (e.g. application form);
- be numbered with a distinctive number (e.g. P45, P60);
- state the name of the organisation at the top (if used externally);
- have the questions and information listed logically;
- be clear and concise;
- have sufficient space for entries to be made;
- contain clear instructions for completion of the form at the beginning (e.g. use a pen or use block capitals);
- minimise the amount of information which has to be written (e.g. use boxes with alternative answers for ticking);
- be pleasing to the eye, easy to read and uncluttered;
- highlight any important aspects;
- be colour-coded where several copies are required;
- meet the requirement for data to be entered on the form by computer or typewriter.

A well-designed form conveys information:

- accurately
- efficiently
- quickly

FORMS OF ADDRESS FOR LETTERS TO EUROPE

Country	Form of address	Salutation	Complimentary close
United Kingdom			
Men	Mr —	Dear Sir or Dear Mr —	
Married women	Mrs — or Ms —	Dear Madam Dear Mrs — Dear Ms —	Yours faithfully *or* Yours sincerely
Unmarried women	Miss — or Ms —	Dear Madam Dear Miss — Dear Ms —	
Belgium			
Use French (as for France) or Dutch (as for The Netherlands)			
Denmark			
Men	Hr —	Hr —	
Married women	Frue —	Fru —	Med venlig Hilsen
Unmarried women	Frøken —	Frøken —	

Country	Form of address	Salutation	Complimentary close
Finland			
Men	Herra —	Arvoisa vastaanottaja *or* Hyvä —	Parhain terveisin *or* Ystävällisin terveisin
Married women	Rouva —		
Unmarried women	Neiti —		
France			
Men	M —	Monsieur	Veuillez agréer (name) l'expression de mes sentiments distingués(ées) *or* Avec mes meilleurs sentiments
Married women	Mme —	Madame	
Unmarried women	Mlle —	Mademoiselle	
Germany			
Men	Herr —	Sehr geehrter Herr —	Mit freundlichen Grüssen
Women	Frau —	Sehr geehrte Frau —	

Note: When writing formally to a company, address the letter to Sehr geehrte Damen und Herren

Country	Form of address	Salutation	Complimentary close
Greece			
Men	Kyrios	Agapete Kyrie	Eilikrina dikos sas
Women	Kyria	Agapete Kyria	Eilikrina dikos sas (if the letter is signed by a man) *or* dike sas (if the letter is signed by a woman)

Note: The majority of unmarried women wish to be called 'Mrs'. There are, of course, some exceptions who wish to keep the title Despoinis, so say Despoinis X but write to Despoinida X.

Country	Form of address	Salutation	Complimentary close
Italy			
Men	Egr Signor	Egregio signor —	Cordiali saluti *or* Distinti saluti
Married women	Gent ma Signora	Gentile signora —	
Unmarried women	Gent ma Signorina	Gentile signorina —	

Note: The titles Doctor (Dottoressa) and Professor (Avvocato) are always used where relevant.

Country	Form of address	Salutation	Complimentary close
Luxembourg			
Use French (as for France) or German (as for Germany)			
The Netherlands			
Men	De heer —	Geachte heer —	*Formal:* Hoogachtend *Informal:* Met vriendelijke groeten
Women	Mevrouw —	Geachte mevrouw —	
Portugal			
Men	Exmo —	Senhor —	Com os melhores cumprimentos
Women	Exma —	Senhora —	

Country	Form of address	Salutation	Complimentary close
Spain			
Men	Señor D	Señor *or* Estimado Sr	le saluda atentamente *or* le saluda cordialmente *or* un atento saludo *or* un cordial saludo
Married women	Señora Da	Señora *or* Estimada Sra	
Unmarried women	Señorita Da	Señorita *or* Estimada Srta	

Note: Women keep their family name even if they get married. They take the name of their husband for social events or when they are named together, but the married name is never used in commercial transactions.

Switzerland

Use French (as for France), German (as for Germany) or Italian (as for Italy).

PREPARATION AND PRESENTATION OF REPORTS

There are five fundamentals to successful report writing. They are:

1 Be aware of what the readers will know about the subject already and what they will want to know.
2 Collect all relevant facts, information and ideas.
3 Organise the evidence in such a way that it is balanced and represents all shades of opinion.
4 Be concise, accurate and clear in expressing your evidence and recommendations.
5 Recommend appropriate action: be logical and realistic.

Checklist for contents of reports

- The *report heading* will normally contain:
  - recipient's name/title or distribution list;
  - writer's name and description;
  - date of report;
  - identifying number/reference of report;
  - security classification, e.g. CONFIDENTIAL;
  - subject title.
- The *opening paragraph* gives the main issues relating to the subject; this may include a statement as to the report's content, an explanation of how the subject-matter is handled, any background information which is essential to the reader.
- The *body of the report* should contain the main issues relating to the subject, which must be set out in their correct, logical sequence.
- Recommendations/conclusions must be reached.
- Further action to implement the recommendations must be made, including:
  - the names of the people who should take the action;
  - the date by which the action should be taken;
  - the date by which the situation should be reviewed again.

REPORT

To: Training Manager
             Copy to: Safety Manager

Date: 1 October 199 –

Ref: SC/T1

Subject: Day course: EUROPEAN HEALTH

As requested in your memo dated 7 September, I am reporting on the Training Institute's Course 'European Health' which I attended on 28 September.

The course was held at the Town House Hotel, Middletown, and about 50 people were present from various local companies. The speaker, Martin Pemberton, a health and safety expert on the staff of the Institute, dealt with the topic under the following headings and discussed the key issues for employers:

1 Reasons for the changes
2 General provisions for health and safety
3 Work equipment regulations
4 Workplace regulations
5 Display screen equipment regulations
6 Action for change

The new regulations have been introduced in order to implement the EC Directives on health and safety at work in all member states. The Directives form part of the European Commission's programme of action on health and safety under Article 118A added to the Treaty of Rome for this purpose. Leaflets issued by the Health and Safety Executive set out the new regulations and codes of practice.

I attach a list of the principal requirements for both employers and their employees.

Conclusions

The speaker explained that the new EC Regulations clarify and make more explicit what has been the practice under previous health and safety law. As our company has previously complied with the Health and Safety at Work Act 1974 and the Regulations linked with it, I do not envisage that we shall experience much difficulty in adapting to the new requirements.

I have arranged to discuss my report with the Safety Manager on 14 October, and copies of the approved codes of practice have been ordered for his use.

Recommendations

1 I suggest that a series of departmental meetings should be organised by the Training Department during the next four weeks to acquaint staff with the new regulations.
2 I recommend that the Safety Manager should be requested to obtain copies of the updated leaflet 'Working with VDUs' for distribution to all office supervisors within the next month.
3 The conference was enjoyable; it was well organised and certainly achieved its objectives. Based on this experience, the Training Institute's courses can be confidently recommended for future use.

SARAH HARDCASTLE
Executive Secretary

Fig 2.3 Example of a report

PERSONAL ACTION PLAN 3

▶ How would you summarise and present on paper a large amount of statistical and financial data in an interesting and eye-catching way?

▶ Experiment with the presentation of data in a variety of visual formats – graphs, charts (bar, line, pie), computer graphics (including unusual graphic representations of market share, for example). Discuss your ideas with your boss/mentor.

▶ How would an audience/readership of mixed nationality and mixed language ability influence your organisation and presentation of information?

ORAL COMMUNICATION

Oral communication is made up of three major components:

1 Visual impact and body language, i.e. what is *seen*
  – constitutes over 50 per cent of communication

How we look

2 Aural impact, i.e. what is *heard*
  – constitutes over 30 per cent of communication

How we sound

3 Subject matter impact, i.e. what is *said*
  – constitutes less than 10 per cent of communication

What we say

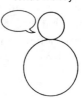

These are probably not the proportions we would expect. They highlight the importance of getting right *all* elements of the communication package:

Correct subject-matter, worded and presented in such a way that will make the subject-matter interesting, informative, persuasive and memorable.

This ancient Chinese proverb has a great deal of truth in it:

> I hear and I forget;
> I see and I remember;
> I do and I understand.

The way we present ourselves to others is signalled in our body language. Consider the following points when you are working on your positive body language. Whether you are preparing for an interview, making a presentation at a meeting or handling a difficult meeting with a client, this list is a useful *aide-mémoire*.

1 Monitor your body posture, gestures and facial expressions when talking and listening. Who wants to co-operate with a person who does not appear to be interested in them?
2 Be aware of your voice volume, tempo and timing in speech. Is it suitable for the situation in which you find yourself? Watch your diction and delivery. Be clear and audible, especially with people whose mother tongue is not your own. Let your tone of voice be professional and helpful.
3 Be prepared to listen. Information is power.
4 Show positive intent in your communication by 'backtracking' and 'confirming'.

Backtracking involves using some of the words the person with whom you are communicating has used. This is a vital part of reducing the differences that may appear to exist between individuals, especially of different nationalities. A more physical form of backtracking is also important as part of the psychology of positive body language. This can be called 'syntony' whereby in a subtle, almost subconscious way, the differences between people are reduced and a rapport is built up. Syntony may involve adopting a similar stance to that of the person with whom you are talking, or nodding when the other person nods.

Confirmation involves asking questions and ascertaining exactly what the other person wants from you. It may even extend to confirming agreements in writing, thereby securing the other person's commitment to deliver. This also helps to ensure that no misunderstandings emerge if business is conducted and agreed in a foreign language.

Even when presenting ideas verbally, it can be useful to support them in writing. Not only will this confirm agreed action but will draw your boss's attention to the fact that you are proactive and contributing. It will also make it more difficult for him or her to be unaware of or to ignore your efforts. Psychologically, the printed word has a strong reinforcement effect.

PERSONAL ACTION PLAN 4

▶ **How aware of yourself are you when communicating at work?**

▶ **What kind of impression do you give in the way you:**
  – look and react when talking;
  – actively listen?

▶ **What impression do you give in the substance of your conversation?**

▶ **What efforts do you make to backtrack, syntonise and confirm in conversation? Monitor and evaluate your progress on a monthly basis.**

▶ **Have you ever had a video made of your presentation of work in a conference or meeting scenario? If so, what did you learn? If not, how would your boss react to this as a suggestion to improve oral communication within the department?**

Styles of oral communication

There are as many styles of communication as there are people. However, there are three main styles, as shown in Fig 2.4.

Fig 2.4 Styles of communication

We may all find ourselves sliding between all three styles in a typical day. Different people may elicit different styles of behaviour from us. This 'chemistry' factor causes barriers to effective communication and can impede understanding. The foundation for rewarding communication is the middle path of assertiveness.

Assertiveness

This involves communicating wants, needs and desires in an appropriate manner, without intimidating others and affecting their ability to express their feelings to you. Assertiveness actually enhances the two-way communication process and assists personal confidence and control without eliciting the feelings of personal guilt that a 'passive' communication style might bring, such as 'I wish I'd said something to him but I didn't want to upset him', or getting what you want by aggression at the expense of someone else, such as 'I made him feel small. Now he knows who's boss!'

TELEPHONE COMMUNICATION

A good telephone technique is vital for the executive secretary/PA working with international partners. Follow the principles set out in the Checklist for effective use of the telephone.

Checklist for telephone communication

1 Know the telephone system in depth. It is a tool to be used to your advantage – not a barrier to effective communication.
   - How do I transfer calls?
   - What is the memory facility?
   - What teleconferencing facilities are available?
   - In my absence, what answering machine facilities exist?
   - Are extension numbers accessible?
   - Are time zone differences, public holidays, international codes easily accessible?

2 Plan ahead: have to hand all stationery, pads, directories, and so on, that you may need for quick reference. Does the rest of the team know where everything is, if you are not present?

3 Enjoy a telephone conversation and *smile*. The telephone magnifies accents and speech defects or habits. If you smile, your enthusiasm will transfer clearly to the listener. Telephone 'body language' does exist!

4 Try standing up to make an important or difficult call. This will let your adrenalin move around and psychologically can make you feel more forceful and in control of the conversation.

5 Be courteous and professional at all times. This provides positive PR for yourself and the company. You never know to whom you might be speaking.

6 Be audible. The humorous adage 'When in doubt, mumble' is not advisable on the telephone. This will only irritate the person to whom you are mumbling, will weaken the point you are trying to articulate and make the person highly suspicious of your intentions.

7 Make notes when necessary when receiving and making calls.

8 Clarify the reason for a call.

9 Try to avoid making calls at peak-rate times if possible and spend as little time as you can on the telephone.

10 Set priorities in making calls: plan the call and make notes, outlining the information you require or will pass on. At the end of a call, check the points you have agreed and ensure that you action them promptly.

11 Try not to lose your temper, especially when dealing with a difficult person. The person who loses their 'cool' usually loses control of the conversation. Once you have achieved a difficult goal on the telephone, confirm it and then 'get off the line'. The person may change their mind if you lose your business-like approach.

PERSONAL ACTION PLAN 5

▶ Have you heard a recording of yourself on the telephone recently? How do you come across to the listener? You may be surprised.

▶ Do you need some advanced training in telephone technique? Do you 'sell' over the telephone as part of your job? How could you improve your success rate?

▶ How could you use the telephone more effectively as a means of international communication?

▶ What challenges do you face when dealing with foreign business partners on the telephone?

CONFERENCE COMMUNICATIONS IN THE UK

1 **Videoconferencing**
A British Telecom Closed Circuit Television Service links together groups of people at different locations for meetings and conferences. Studios are located at major city centres which have conference rooms equipped with cameras and monitor screens. Slides, videos and charts can be displayed, as well as close-ups of documents, drawings or samples, using a video display station (Fig 2.5).

Fig 2.5 A videoconferencing centre in the UK

2 **Teleconferencing**
A British Telecom Telephone Service for meetings and conferences of between 3 and 60 people at different locations throughout the UK and worldwide. Organisations requiring regular teleconferences will normally acquire their own equipment, but for occasional conferences the Conference Call Service may be used to link the participants by their own telephones. An interpreter can be provided for most languages and a tape recording and play-back service avoids the need for anyone to take the minutes while the meeting is in progress.

These are cost-effective methods which reduce the expenditure and travelling time of executives and yet still retain their personal interaction with others in different parts of the country or the world.

MAKING CLEAR AND EFFECTIVE PRESENTATIONS

Once the requisite information is amassed, it must be presented either to your boss or to a group of colleagues or a client in the shape of a formal or informal presentation in a meeting or over the telephone. This will depend on the size of the task and on the format agreed at the preparation stage of the process.

Remember: the way executive secretaries present their work says much about them as people. For large and small information-gathering projects and tasks alike, marshal information and present it in a way which will:

1 *Motivate others*
   Make the audience want to make decisions or act on the results of your information exchange or presentation.
2 *Be succinct*
   Avoid losing the audience's attention through being boring or overloading them with too much information. Keep the message simple where possible.
3 *Be informative – whether the vehicle for presentation is the written or spoken word*
   Impart your knowledge clearly, avoiding waffle. Remember, the attention span is limited and may be affected by language difficulties.
4 *Be accessible to the audience in form and content*
   Consider your audience and tailor your approach and turn of phrase accordingly. This is as relevant to your fellow countrymen as to foreign nationals. Allow for eye contact, which establishes a rapport and allows for interaction.

These four rules for presenting information apply as much to simple as to complex tasks. Finding out the times of air flights to Frankfurt from Manchester on a weekday is an information-gathering task that may take five minutes. To compare amounts of money spent in 1985 in five European markets and three Latin American markets in mixed media for a leading washing powder may take considerably longer to carry out, be more problematic and require more time to prepare for formal presentation to management. However, the aims in presenting the findings are the same.

A further important rule to add to making formal presentations in front of a group or larger audience is:

5 *Provide some entertainment value*
   It is much easier to remember the message someone is trying to convey if the education process has been an enjoyable one. Too concentrated a flow of information results in loss of interest. Let your own personality shine through!

In order to mark your progress in the field of information-gathering and presentation, confirm your findings in writing, where appropriate, or provide a written 'back-up' copy of your presentation to your audience. This is a useful exercise in self-marketing and can sometimes avoid difficult situations, such as the misunderstanding of data.

Checklist for making presentations

1 Preparation

This is going to be the most important time and the most valuable investment. Being a good speaker or presenter is 90 per cent preparation and practice *before* the event, especially if you have not presented information in public before. Spend time:

- looking at the room where you will conduct your presentation. Plan the layout you want.
- trying out the visual aids you will require. Make sure you are at ease with them and know how they work and what might malfunction.
- carrying out a dress rehearsal. This is vital for judging your timing, content and familiarity with the subject-matter. Practice makes perfect.

2 Set objectives

Ask yourself fundamental questions from the outset:

- Why am I presenting this information? What is the purpose of the presentation?
- Who is the audience? How will this affect the pitch and tone of my presentation?
- How long will I take to prepare the presentation?
- For how long will I be making the presentation? Is there a time limit? Must I allow for questions and discussion time at the end or during the presentation?
- Which audiovisual aids are suitable for my subject-matter? Note cards, flip chart, projector, video?
  Remember: a picture or diagram can encapsulate an idea more succinctly than a hundred words. It may also be more eye-catching and interesting for the audience.
- What *key message* do you want the audience to take away with them?

3 During the presentation, be aware of yourself

- Be clear in your speech, vary the tone and pace.
- Keep eye contact with the audience. Slow your pace of speaking, particularly if you are nervous. Breathe deeply to slow yourself down.
- Vary your facial expressions and gestures. Display humour, seriousness, enthusiasm, and so on.
- Demonstrate positive body language. Avoid personal, nervous mannerisms.
- Allow for questions. This is an opportunity to show your knowledge and build a rapport with the audience.
- Try to read the audience reaction and modify your approach accordingly.

4 After the presentation, evaluate your performance

Consider your own performance against your objectives. Try to elicit some feedback from a colleague or your boss in order to make changes and improvements for the next time.

PERSONAL ACTION PLAN 6

▶ Have you had the opportunity to make any presentations at training sessions, contributions to meetings, votes of thanks or to run induction courses? How do you approach these projects?

▶ Volunteer to give presentations as an important element in your career development.

▶ How does the prospect of making a presentation to a group of mixed nationality and mixed language ability affect your presentation preparation and technique?

EXAMINE YOUR KNOWLEDGE

1 You are PA/secretary to Mrs Catherine Walsh (Case Study 1). Mrs Walsh is concerned about the increasing costs of telephone, fax and telex throughout the company.

    a) Prepare a memo to be sent to all staff about the economic use of these services.

    b) Explain the call-logging and call-barring systems which will be introduced at head office in August.

                (*LCCI PESD*)

2 *a)* What are the principal factors to be taken into account when designing a new form?

    b) Design a simple form for booking the boardroom and equipment/facilities for meetings.

                (*PEI ASP*)

3 You are personal assistant to Mrs Sylvia Fairbanks (Case Study 4). Reply to the following invitation:

The Brighton and Hove Chamber of Commerce

requests the pleasure of the company of

Mrs Sylvia Fairbanks

at their Annual Dinner to be held on Friday,

16th March 19.. at the Grand Hotel, Brighton

Champagne Reception at 7.30 pm.

RSVP 148 Warren Road
BRIGHTON
East Sussex
BN2 6DD

*Already committed
Please reply
formally
S.F.*

                (*PEI ASP*)

4 One of the contributory factors to effective communication is listening.

    a) Describe situations in which listening is particularly important.

    b) Identify the characteristics you would expect to be present in a good listener.

                (*PEI ASP*)

5 Advise, with reasons, on the best method of communication to use for each of the following tasks:

a) A package which must be delivered today in a town 100 kilometres away.

b) Urgent memos to be sent to the main branches of a firm in New York, Tokyo, Paris and Rome.

c) An urgent message for an executive whose location is uncertain but who is thought to be somewhere in the factory.

d) Information required by a sales representative who is on the road.

e) Inform job applicants that they were unsuccessful in their interviews.

f) A mailshot advertising a new range of products to be sent to 5000 potential customers.

g) A letter which may be required as evidence in a court of law.

h) Inform a junior assistant that an item of work is not up to standard.

i) Consult senior executives about a new scheme.

WORK TASKS

Assessment of competence for Element 1.2
Use the telephone system to the full

Performance criteria

- *Telephone calls are made, received and transferred courteously using approved organisation procedures.*
- *Incoming calls are screened in accordance with approved organisation procedures.*
- *The principal is represented effectively in both the content and style of calls made and received on his/her behalf.*
- *Messages are recorded accurately and passed promptly to the correct location.*
- *Answering machine messages are transmitted and received clearly and accurately.*
- *A proper balance is maintained between economy and the efficient use of time, in accordance with the organisation's rules and procedures.*
- *A schedule of calls is kept up to date, legible and accurate.*
- *Tasks delegated to others are accurately defined and monitored.*
- *Safe working practices are always followed and implemented.*
- *Security and confidentiality procedures are always followed and implemented.*

Range statement

Competent performance must be demonstrated across a range of:

- *Successful achievement both by oneself and through organising others.*
- *Telephone Calls:*
  internal and external (including international); incoming and outgoing; for action by self, own principal and others.
- *People:*
  at all levels within own organisation and associates; customers; suppliers; community and public bodies; press; private individuals.

- *Purpose of call:*
  receipt or giving of confidential information; urgent and emergency messages; making and dealing with enquiries and complaints; arranging meetings, appointments, travel.
- *Equipment:*
  telephones with single and multiple connections; answering machines.

Personal action plans 4 and 5 refer to this work.

Assessment of competence for Element 2.3
Organise and present information in a variety of formats

Performance criteria

- *The information content is interpreted correctly and organised logically.*
- *The presentation conforms to organisational housestyle and/or accepted conventions.*
- *Completed information is made available to the appropriate person/location within the required deadlines.*
- *Appropriate display formats, to suit the specified purpose, are always selected.*
- *Sources are acknowledged and copyright or other legal requirements are always observed.*
- *Safe working practices are always followed and implemented.*
- *Security and confidentiality procedures are always followed and implemented.*

Range statement

Competent performance must be demonstrated across a range of formats:

- *Two formal reports each combining narrative, graphic and tabular formats.*
- *Two narrative items combined with at least one other format.*
- *Two graphic items combined with at least one other format.*
- *Two tabular items combined with at least one other format.*

Personal action plan 3 relates to this work.

Assessment of competence for Element 6.1
Identify and respond to correspondence for own action

Performance criteria

- *Correspondence for own action is correctly identified and prioritised.*
- *Correspondence outside own area of responsibility is promptly passed to correct recipient.*
- *Own correspondence is promptly answered according to its priority.*
- *A proper balance is maintained between speed, mode and cost of response.*
- *The correct meaning and tone are conveyed by the language and grammar used at all times.*

- *All correspondence (prepared by self or others) is checked for accuracy and any errors or omissions are identified and corrected.*
- *Own correspondence is always signed as appropriate prior to distribution.*
- *The postage class or service required is clearly annotated.*
- *Records are kept up to date, legible and accurate.*
- *Safe working practices are always followed and implemented.*
- *Security and confidentiality procedures are always followed and implemented.*

Range statement

Competent performance must be demonstrated across a range of:

- *Correspondence received:*
  letters; memos; circulars; enquiries; quotations; invoices; statements; advertisements; notices; invitations.
- *Responses made:*
  standardised and individual replies; those requiring investigation; those calling for the refusal of a demand; placatory and explanatory items; oral and written examples; work produced (in part) by other staff.
- *Correspondents and Recipients:*
  internal and external to organisation; own principal and more senior staff; regular clients or customers; first time enquirers; occasional contacts; overseas contacts.

Personal action plan 23 relates to this work.

CHAPTER 3

International information skills and sources

The phrase 'knowledge is power' is relevant in all departments of professional and personal life. For the secretary or personal assistant, possessing knowledge is the key to carrying out tasks and projects successfully. The key lies not necessarily in possessing the knowledge itself but in knowing how to acquire and access the information for yourself and others when needed. As Dr Samuel Johnson said, 'Knowledge is of two kinds. We know a subject ourselves or we know where we can find information upon it.' There is a real skill in using domestic and international information sources to their full potential.

As an executive secretary/PA you may be asked to gather information on any number of subjects ranging from the mundane, through the obscure and exciting to the complex or mysterious. Details of hotel conference facilities in southern Spain may be a priority followed smartly by a request for general market information concerning the sales of tuna in France region by region. You may also decide, or be expected, to take the initiative either to put together a proposal or carry out some market research without direction or initial input from your boss. In these situations it is vital to have clear objectives and solid methods in order to achieve optimum success – in other words, sufficient information which can be presented and from which a balanced decision can be taken.

The good secretary/PA who is *thinking and acting like a manager at all times* will always be open and receptive to new ideas and information. These may come from business meetings at work, newspaper articles, radio or television items or conversations with friends outside the working environment. Developing skills in information-gathering can be approached from two angles, the general and the specific.

GENERAL SKILLS IN INFORMATION-GATHERING

This requires an open-minded approach and places the emphasis on a receptive attitude rather than an analytical skill. Information is being circulated all around us on a daily basis and it is easy to become inward-looking and only focus on the areas that affect our lives directly. For executive secretaries working in the international environment it is vital to be aware of events changing and shaping the foreign as well as the domestic stage. Try to have a world perspective.

By continually keeping abreast of home, foreign, political, commercial and social affairs, you will build up a rich bank of background information against which specific task-oriented data can be set. This can not only contribute to developing the total package of communication skills that makes an effective secretary, but could also make the more specific tasks less time-consuming and more interesting if seen within the broader framework and base of existing knowledge.

Useful tips
- Remain *au fait* or in touch with current affairs in your own country and the overseas markets with which you have contact in your job. Read 'quality' newspapers, particularly those with a strong European perspective, *The Economist*, trade press journals relevant to your employer's business and supplements on specific industry sectors, and watch television documentaries that are relevant to your employer's business.
- Talk with contacts in overseas markets about events that might affect business.
- Find out who the specialists are in your company. Be aware of where expertise lies in different fields at different levels. You may want to call on the advice of the office computer enthusiast one day, and that of the marketing director on another. Take time to build up a rapport with your colleagues. Apart from it being an enjoyable process, you will learn something that could be relevant and invaluable in a specific situation at a later date.

SPECIFIC SKILLS IN INFORMATION-GATHERING

The value of your general information-gathering skills often comes to fruition when the specific request or project is initiated, for this store of general knowledge will, more often than not, form the bank of information from which the specific information can be accessed directly or will suggest leads to other data sources and networks.

Specific skills in gathering information fall into the four main categories listed in Fig 3.1. Clearly, straightforward tasks will not necessarily require the detailed planning set out in the following pages.

Preparation

This is a vital time. Ensuring that this part of the process is correct can make the gathering of information more straightforward.

1 **Set and agree clear objectives**
This avoids confusion and wasted energy, saves time and focuses you and your boss and colleagues, if they are involved, on the task and what it will involve.

2 **Clarify and confirm timing**
Assess how the task can be fulfilled within your existing workload. Assess priorities. Is the deadline realistic, given the work involved? If the deadline cannot be moved then do you need extra help or can you delegate less important tasks to other colleagues or juniors?

3 **If in doubt, reclarify and reconfirm**
This will show you are serious about the job in hand, and could avoid mistakes and poor performance. This can be of value particularly if you are communicating in a foreign language and you need to feel sure that both you and the person with whom you are liaising understand fully.

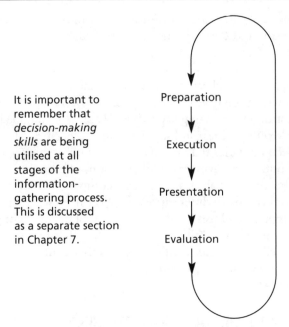

It is important to remember that *decision-making skills* are being utilised at all stages of the information-gathering process. This is discussed as a separate section in Chapter 7.

Preparation

Execution

Presentation

Evaluation

Fig 3.1 Specific information-gathering skills

4 Contacts and leads

Be sure that your boss or colleague has given you or made you aware of all existing contacts and leads. This will avoid repetition and time-wasting.

5 Plan your time

Where possible build in 'buffer' time if you are abroad and are unfamiliar with machinery or the availability of potential information providers. Try to anticipate complications. If you are liaising with contacts in countries with considerable time differences, then plan accordingly.

By planning your information-gathering task you can achieve that satisfying feeling and commercially sound concept of the minimum outlay of time and energy for the maximum effect. With this in mind, consider how you present 'work in progress' plans (Fig 3.2) to management or your boss. If you work on many information-gathering projects at one time, how concise are your progress or summary charts? Are they easily understandable and easily accessible for office circulation?

Execution

Getting down to the task of information-gathering may call on all your powers of communication, persuasion, determination and stamina. Here are some useful reminders:

1 Utilise your resources in-house before investing time and money in external resources.
   Do you have a company information centre or library with access to directories, computer database information, journals, newspapers, company reports and general market information?

WORK IN PROGRESS				
Date: 20 March 199–				
Project title and description	*Deadline*	*Status*	*Next action*	*Action by*
1 Competitive review of marketing activity for brand X shampoo incorporating data from CTC and Tear Sheets.	End April 199–	All direct mail info. collected.	Compilation of examples of TV advertising and PR activity.	Mary Smith (Project Leader)
	End April 199–	All press advertising spend/budgets compiled.	Analysis of strategies.	Joanna Day
2 NPD project Nemo.	June 199–	Market research dates confirmed (12 in UK and 4 in Europe)	Analysis of findings and strategy formulation.	John Brown
3 . . .				

Fig 3.2 Work-in-progress sheet

Which individuals in the company could you approach for advice and possible leads? Could the Personnel Department offer any direction to specialists in the company?

Remember the psychology of information-gathering: people enjoy being asked for their advice, and being considered an expert with valued opinions that carry some weight. Feel confident enough to ask members of senior management for their opinion on sources of data or on the quality of the data itself. By doing this, you are learning and becoming an authority on the subject yourself. You are marketing yourself and establishing and developing an image within the company.

2 Always keep a note of your sources of information. They could be useful to you in the future or to others who may seek your advice.

3 Be creative. Allow yourself to think laterally. Draw on all aspects of experience to find sources of information where necessary. You may be able to ask a favour of a friend who works in the kind of company that could provide some valuable data to you. Put 'networking' into practice – and in doing so, your communication skills will also develop. By thinking 'out of your square box', you could bring an original angle to the solution of a task or project.

4 Make your statistical data mean something. Researching, retrieving and interpreting statistical data are important competencies for the executive secretary. Seven key stages in this process are:
- identify appropriate sources for supplying the information;
- use correct techniques to research the information;
- abstract the relevant information;

- check your findings for accuracy;
- interpret the information, e.g. performance ratios and percentages may be used to assess the performance and profitability of a company;
- present the information in the appropriate format;
- acknowledge the sources you have used.

Graphs, charts, planboards and other visual control systems enable progress and situations to be monitored and controlled systematically and efficiently, and can indicate trends and future requirements. Skill in the use of computer packages producing spreadsheets, graphs, charts and diagrams is invaluable and can provide a route to becoming a strong member within the management team unit. Only if the executive secretary has access to this management information can she or he present it meaningfully on screen and in print-outs.

5 If you are working on a long-term project, assess progress against objectives and timescale on a regular basis. This retains focus and momentum.

6 If you work in an organisation that has an international network, ask the advice of your opposite number in the market where your research is leading you. What equivalent journals and directories do they use? What computer database information could be made accessible to you? Liaising with overseas contacts will provide you with a valuable local perspective that could influence the information on which you base your decisions or those of your boss. It is important that you are aware of them.

7 Once the internal sources are exhausted, or if they are not available at all, you may need to approach external information sources. Could any of the following be of assistance?

- External reference libraries in domestic and foreign markets;
- Chambers of Commerce at home and abroad;
- Trade bodies and associations;
- Directories;
- Industry-specific year books;
- Companies House;
- Department of Trade and Industry;
- Commercial sections of embassies both at home and abroad;
- Teletext and Viewdata services such as Ceefax, Teletext 3/4 or Prestel (Fig 3.3). Prestel is a system that lets you access and transmit information using your normal telephone line. It is an interactive system as, in addition to accessing information, users can send messages both to each other and to information providers by using response pages. Ceefax (BBC) and Teletext 3/4 (ITV) are also computer-based information retrieval systems transmitting pages of data to specially adapted television sets, but they only provide a one-way source of information.

The Information Bank at the end of this book contains further sources of information for your research projects.

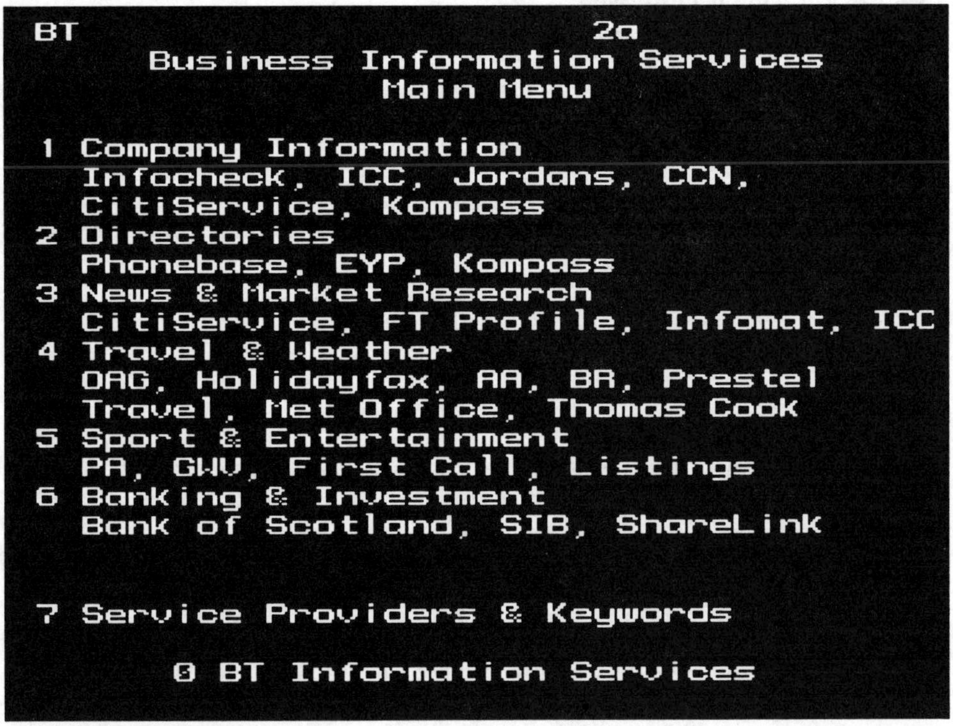

```
BT                              2a
      Business Information Services
              Main Menu

 1 Company Information
    Infocheck, ICC, Jordans, CCN,
    CitiService, Kompass
 2 Directories
    Phonebase, EYP, Kompass
 3 News & Market Research
    CitiService, FT Profile, Infomat, ICC
 4 Travel & Weather
    OAG, Holidayfax, AA, BR, Prestel
    Travel, Met Office, Thomas Cook
 5 Sport & Entertainment
    PA, GWU, First Call, Listings
 6 Banking & Investment
    Bank of Scotland, SIB, ShareLink


 7 Service Providers & Keywords

       0 BT Information Services
```

Fig 3.3 Prestel screen

Statistics: performance ratios and percentages

How many of these examples do you know or use?

Mark-up
The percentage added to the cost price to determine the selling price, i.e.

$$\frac{\text{Gross profit} \times 100}{\text{Cost of sales}}$$

Profit margin
The percentage of gross profit based on sales, i.e.

$$\frac{\text{Mark-up} \times 100}{\text{Sales}}$$

Rate of turnover
The number of times the average amount of stock is sold in a year, i.e.

$$\frac{\text{Cost of sales}}{\text{Average stock}}$$

Return on capital employed

The percentage return for the capital invested in a company, i.e.

$$\frac{\text{Net profit} \times 100}{\text{Opening capital}}$$

Acid test ratio

Indicates the ability of a company to meet its current liabilities from current assets, i.e.

$$\frac{\text{Current assets} - \text{Closing stock}}{\text{Current liabilities}}$$

Presentation

The presentation of the results of an information-gathering project is discussed in Chapter 2.

Evaluation/review

This final part of the information-gathering process is often forgotten or left out because of time constraints and the shifting of priorities to more urgent tasks.

It is a valuable experience for many reasons:

1 It summarises and reconfirms the findings of the research process and whether it has been a success or a failure. It is an opportunity to codify experience for future reference.
2 It appraises existing performance and helps improve future performance.
3 It highlights, through the review of the findings, different ways in which the same or additional useful information could have been accessed. It is a 'lessons learnt' review. If the project was a success, then evaluation provides a formula for the future. If the project was a failure or not as successful as expected, then it is vital to review and to decide how to do things differently in the future. Analysis of failure will avoid similar failure in the future or limit its consequences.
4 It provides a tool for self-marketing. Regular evaluation can be like a 'mini' performance appraisal for a single task rather than a range of abilities. It lets the boss see how hard-working the secretary is and how his/her skills are developing. Of course, it highlights any successes as well. Evaluation also alerts the boss at the earliest point to the secretary's increasing range of skills and ability to take on more responsibility. It can act as an early-warning system and prompt the boss into giving the secretary more stimulating projects to do or more training in specific areas.
5 It is a management training opportunity. If a senior secretary has delegated a task to a junior, it is vital that the senior secretary initiates the evaluation process. This gives the junior the opportunity to see how he/she has performed and gives the senior secretary experience in motivating and managing the junior.
6 It is an opportunity to develop the secretary/boss relationship. By evaluating on a regular basis, communication is steady and the prospect of honest and constructive exchange of ideas is enhanced. Team work develops. It is vital that the secretary

spends time preparing for the evaluation before discussing it with the boss. Of course, evaluation can be carried out on one's own, but solitary evalution without input from a second, more dispassionate observer is only half an evaluation. Without feedback, there can be no progress.

An example is given in Fig 3.4 on pages 44–5 of a form for evaluating a research project.

PERSONAL ACTION PLAN 7

▶ **How would you assess your general and specific abilities in information-gathering?**

▶ **Consider the sources for information-gathering that are accessible to you. How would you improve the service available?**

▶ **Give two examples of information-gathering challenges that have been satisfying to tackle. How have you evaluated with your boss the lessons learnt from the tasks and the quality of your performance?**

▶ **Find a project that you can initiate, discuss it with your boss, and take responsibility for steering it to a successful conclusion.**

USING INTERNATIONAL DIRECTORIES, FAX AND TELEX

Directories (whether computerised or manual), fax and telex are tools for speeding up and facilitating the communication process in the domestic and the international context. They can be the lifeline to a business deal, the route by which a critical piece of information arrives for a report, or the means by which mistakes in the copy of promotional material are corrected. Time should therefore be taken to understand their workings fully.

When using information-gathering tools, particularly abroad, remember the following:

1 **Understand the process fully**
   The method of operating fax and telex machines will vary from model to model and country to country. It is vital to learn by practical experience.
   Read the operating manual and experiment with a 'dummy run', or ask someone to demonstrate how the machine works. Then, try it for yourself. Even if someone offers to send all your documents by fax or telex for you, make the effort to learn the operating procedure. Emergencies will always arise, particularly when liaising with overseas markets. Expect the unexpected.

2 **Arrange for a deputy**
   Ensure that there is someone other than yourself who can operate the machines who is accessible, and can help if complications arise.

3 **Check and double check**
   Check that transmissions have been completed and the correct number of pages have been sent by fax. Check that the telex printout you send or have sent is correct.

PROJECT EVALUATION SHEET

PROJECT/TASK:
DATE OF EVALUATION:
PARTICIPANTS:

	PROJECTED	*ACTUAL*
OBJECTIVES:		
TIMING:		
COSTING:		

What would you do differently?

Why?

How?

What have you learnt from this project/task?
General:

Personal efficiency:

Planning:

Execution:

Presentation of findings/information:

General Performance Rating: Personal
(Marks out of 10)   Second Opinion:

Recommendations: Operational Training	
Any other comments	
Signed: Dated:	Signed:

Fig 3.4 Form for evaluating a research project

If necessary, use directories to check the numbers but remember that the business world is constantly changing and directory information can be out of date.

4 **Telephone *v.* fax**

Use the appropriate information–gathering/dissemination tool. There are times when a telephone conversation is more suitable than sending data by a fax machine. To take up references from Italy for a new junior secretary, for example, might involve telephone conversations and sending information by fax. Be aware of the advantages and disadvantages of both means of communication.

Telephone	*Fax*
• immediate	• immediate
• personal and confidential	• difficult to read between the lines
• good for clarification of issues/misunderstandings	• time delay in clarification
• rapport and feedback possible	• confidentiality can be a problem
• difficult to express complex data/ statistical information	• good way to transmit diagrams/ pictures/physical likeness
	• good method of confirming information passed by telephone

Figure 3.5 illustrates one of British Telecom's most advanced fax machines. It uses a laser printer to reproduce documents and photographs to the finest detail on standard copier paper. This model has a memory transmission which allows a document to be held in its 36-page memory and automatically broadcast to 50 different fax numbers. The automatic document feeder accommodates 30 sheets.

Fig 3.5 A fax machine

PERSONAL ACTION PLAN 8

▶ Are you fully conversant with the *modus operandi* of all the communication tools available in-house?

▶ If you are not, make plans to change this situation tomorrow. Today's ignorance could be tomorrow's skill.

INFORMATION SOURCES

See the Information Bank at the end of this book for specific names and addresses and sources of reference, including home and overseas companies and international organisations. Information available internally clearly depends on the resources of each company and will vary from a telephone directory to a fully equipped reference library with teletext. Always be aware of new publications and updated editions of sources of information that you use.

Examples of information sources

Information	Internal	External
Home Companies Overseas Companies	Information centre/ library; Newspaper cuttings	Dunn and Bradstreet's *Key British Enterprises*; *The Times 1000* Leading Companies in Britain and Overseas

Information	Internal	External
		Chambers of Commerce in the UK and abroad; DTI; Libraries; Companies House; Commercial Section of Foreign Embassies; Sell's *British Exporters*; Trade Centres
International organisations	Existing membership of organisation	*The Statesman's Year-book*
Economic develop- ments/Stock market prices/International current affairs	Teletext/Viewdata; Newspapers/journals	Cable Network News; Reuters; DTI
Financial affairs	Teletext/Viewdata	International Stock Exchange *Official Year Book*; *Financial Times*; Business Research Centre
Forms of Address		Black's *Titles and Forms of Address: Guide to Correct Usage*; Debrett's *Correct Form*
Industry-specific requests	Specialists in different departments	Trade bodies and associations; Industry-specific manuals/ yearbooks
Manufacturers/ Suppliers	Microfiche/computer files	Kelly's *Business Directory*; UK *Kompass Register*
Competitors	Manual files; Press cuttings	Examples of competitive advertising from Tear Sheets and CTC
Europe		*Doing Business in Europe*; *1992 Strategies for the Single Market*; *Doing business in the European Community*; *The European Year Book*; *The European Business Directory*
Languages	Staff with language abilities; Multilingual dictionaries	Translation agencies; Recruitment consultancies

Information	Internal	External
Statistics	Computer/spreadsheets	*Statistical Yearbook* (UN); *Eurostat: Europe in Figures*
International associations	Existing membership	*Directory of European Associations*, Parts 1 and 2
Travel and hotels	In-house agency Teletext/Viewdata	Agencies

EXAMINE YOUR KNOWLEDGE

1 Suggest two reference books or other sources of information that would be useful for each of the executives (and their secretaries) in Case Studies 1 and 2. Give your reasons for selecting them.

2 As a secretary you may be required to keep a record of information on proposed projects or those currently in progress (e.g. toll motorways) with which Comlon International plc is involved.

   a) Explain how you would go about collecting such information from the media. How would you store the material?

   b) Suggest how you would present this type of material for use by management.

   (*LCCI PESD*)

3 You are personal assistant to Mrs Sylvia Fairbanks (Case Study 4). DZ Ltd is considering opening a factory and offices in Belgium, where they already do a substantial amount of business. A conference is to be held next week to discuss some basic considerations. The Marketing Manager's Secretary is off sick and you are asked to assist in supplying the following information which will be required at the conference:

   a) The current rate of exchange of Belgium francs against the other European currencies.

   b) The total population of Belgium.

   c) The population, position and industries of the town of Charleroi in Belgium, where the development is planned to take place.

   d) The address and telephone number of the Belgian Embassy in London and in your own country.

   e) The name, address and telephone number of the government department in the UK which may be able to assist in this project and any government publications which may be helpful.

   f) The name and address of the member of the European Parliament for Brighton who may be consulted on the proposed project.

   g) Sources which might be contacted to engage an interpreter.

   h) Any other information which you consider may be useful.

4 *a*) What are the advantages of recording statistical data in graphic form (manual or computerised)?

   b) Plot the share offer prices of three well-known national or international companies during a three-month period and display the information in graphic form.

   c) Comment on the performance of each of the shares.

5 Over the next few weeks, compile an annotated folder of press/magazine cuttings and other media reports relevant or useful to your organisation. Your folder could contain articles on such items as:

   a) matters relating to the organisation, its products or services, its interests or competitors;
   b) new technology applicable to the organisation;
   c) EC developments which affect the organisation;
   d) changes in legislation relating to the organisation;
   e) general business matters, e.g. interest rate, government economic policy, etc.;
   f) reviews of relevant books, conferences, broadcasts, etc.

WORK TASKS

Assessment of competence for Element 1.3
Transmit and receive information using electronic equipment

Performance criteria

- *The most appropriate transmission system (in relation to urgency, cost and security) is selected.*
- *The equipment selected is correctly used as laid down in operating instructions.*
- *Written and typescript material is prepared accurately and correctly for transmission.*
- *Information is transmitted to correct location within required deadlines.*
- *Incoming information is promptly delivered to correct location.*
- *The clarity and completeness of outgoing and incoming transmissions are monitored and maintained.*
- *Any faults are promptly rectified or reported.*
- *Records are kept up to date, legible and accurate.*
- *Tasks delegated to others are accurately defined and monitored.*
- *Safe working practices are always followed and implemented.*
- *Security and confidentiality procedures are always followed and implemented.*

Range statement

Competent performance must be demonstrated across a range of:

- *Successful achievement both by oneself and through organising others.*
- *Equipment:*
  Facsimile (Fax); Telex; Electronic Mail; Electronic Paging.
- *Contingencies:*
  faulty equipment; urgent and critical material; poor quality originals and copies.

- *Destinations:*
  in-house; local; national; international.
- *Confidential as well as routine material.*

Personal action plan 8 relates to this work.

Assessment of competence for Element 2.2
Locate and abstract information from unspecified sources

Performance criteria

- *The correct sources are identified for specific information requests.*
- *Specified information needs are promptly researched.*
- *The relevant elements of information are abstracted correctly.*
- *Where potential or available sources are exhausted without success this is reported to the principal.*
- *All information content is checked for accuracy and relevance.*
- *Safe working practices are always followed and implemented.*
- *Security and confidentiality procedures are always followed and implemented.*

Range statement

Competent performance must be demonstrated across a range of:

- *Information:*
  statistics; narrative; graphics; tables; photographs.
- *Unspecified Sources:*
  internal and external to organisation; public documents including statistics; timetables; manual and computer files; books; listings; viewdata; microfiche; trade manuals.

Personal action plan 7 relates to this work.

CHAPTER 4

Administrative support services

'Administration' is a somewhat nebulous term that means 'management of business, estate or public affairs'. It can refer to any responsibility in the office other than typing and shorthand. With experience and responsibility, the percentage of administrative tasks delegated to an executive secretary increases. One of the most important areas of administrative support lies in information and records management.

Administrative services, whether computerised or manual, are essential for the successful operation of any type of organisation, as illustrated in Fig 4.1. This chart shows the five stages in the functions of an office, together with the principal administrative and secretarial services which are needed to carry them out. Adding an international dimension to business, and the extra information and data that such involvement inevitably brings, requires systems which can adapt and cope efficiently with new sources of data which can be cross-referred with existing sources. This international aspect makes the management of information and records more complex

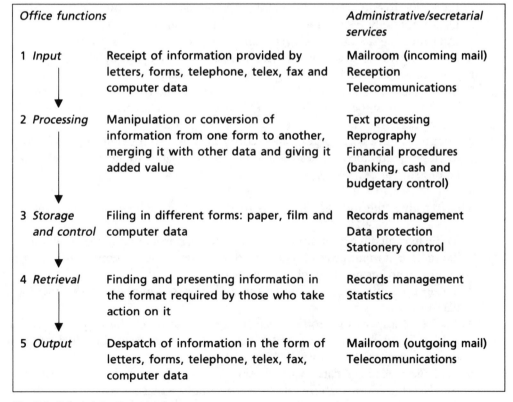

Office functions		Administrative/secretarial services
1 Input	Receipt of information provided by letters, forms, telephone, telex, fax and computer data	Mailroom (incoming mail) Reception Telecommunications
2 Processing	Manipulation or conversion of information from one form to another, merging it with other data and giving it added value	Text processing Reprography Financial procedures (banking, cash and budgetary control)
3 Storage and control	Filing in different forms: paper, film and computer data	Records management Data protection Stationery control
4 Retrieval	Finding and presenting information in the format required by those who take action on it	Records management Statistics
5 Output	Despatch of information in the form of letters, forms, telephone, telex, fax, computer data	Mailroom (outgoing mail) Telecommunications

Fig 4.1 Administrative services

and problematic. The systems, therefore, need to be well thought out and planned to provide efficient support services.

DATA PROTECTION ACT 1984

Before looking at information records and management in depth, it is important to mention the Data Protection Act 1984, as developments in electronic data storage have revolutionised not only the speed of retrieval but also allowed greater and easier access to vast quantities of records. The Data Protection Act protects individuals from misuse of personal information held about them on computer files and lays down codes of practice for those who use or process data relating to personnel.

The Data Protection Act 1984 establishes rights for individuals to have access to their own personal data held on computer files. The following principles govern the processing of personal data:

1 Data must be obtained fairly and lawfully. People must not be misled as to the use to which the information they supply about themselves will be put.
2 Data must only be held for registered and lawful purposes. Data users are required to register the personal data they hold with the Data Protection Registrar. Failure to register can incur substantial fines of up to £5000. To receive details regarding registration, guidelines, exemptions and application forms, contact: The Data Protection Registrar, Springfield House, Water Lane, Wilmslow, Cheshire, SK9 5AX.
3 Data must only be used and disclosed for the purposes registered.
4 Data must be adequate, relevant, and not excessive for its purpose.
5 Data must be accurate and, where necessary, kept up to date.
6 Data must be held for no longer than is necessary.
7 Individuals must be allowed access to data about themselves at reasonable intervals and they must be provided with a copy of it in an intelligible form. Where appropriate, the data must be erased or corrected.
8 Data users must take appropriate security measures to prevent unauthorised access, disclosure, alteration or destruction of personal data and against its accidental loss or destruction.

The Act gives the individual, that is to say, the data subject, certain rights:

1 To be informed whether or not a data user has personal information about him or her.
2 To receive at minimal cost, within 40 days of the request, a copy of this information expressed in terms intelligible to him or her.
3 To seek a court order to enforce the data user to comply with this request if the data user refuses to do so.
4 To seek compensation for any damage or distress he or she may incur if the data held by the data user is inaccurate, misleading, lost, destroyed or disclosed without the data subject's authority.
5 To have inaccurate data rectified, erased or supplemented by a statement of the true facts if a court is satisfied that it is inaccurate or that the data subject has suffered damage by reason of the disclosure of the information.

INFORMATION AND RECORDS MANAGEMENT

Any information storage and retrieval system must fulfil five main functions. They must be:

1 quick and simple to operate;
2 easily accessible;
3 appropriate for the requirements;
4 capable of expansion if or when necessary;
5 capable of safeguarding documents and confidential information.

Data is stored in three main ways:
– paper
– film
– computer

Contrary to many predictions, hard copy storage is still a critical factor in the running of a successful business. The 'paperless office' has not become a reality and it seems that it is unlikely to materialise for some time yet. Consider the facts: as much as 90 per cent of business information is output as hard copy and, in Europe alone, 3500 million sheets of paper are generated each day. Considerable developments are taking place, however, which will eliminate much of the need for hard copy, especially in large operations.

Electronically managed systems and document image processing which transfer data electronically render paper and filmed documents such as orders, invoices and statements obsolete. These systems are, however, only economically viable in large companies handling vast quantities of fast-moving lines, and these companies now have less need for traditional paper filing methods.

In the UK, over 90 per cent of companies are classified as 'small', and are therefore unlikely to have the volume of trade or budgets to justify expenditure on sophisticated electronic systems. They will continue to rely on hard copy storage for their records, and because of this the executive secretary should be capable of handling traditional paper or film as well as computerised systems.

The following factors should be considered when analysing the suitability and efficiency of a filing system:

● Speed of access	Is a delay caused by: unsuitable classification; unsuitable equipment; location of equipment; misfiling of papers; missing papers or files; bulky files?
● Security	What provision is made to safeguard documents?
● Access to information	Are the records retained for as long as is necessary?
● Use of office space	Does the system make the most efficient use of space?
● Handling of materials	Can the filed materials be handled with ease?
● Cost of maintaining equipment and materials	Is there a cheaper system which will produce the required results?

Checklist for setting up/reorganising a filing system

Is the proposed system capable of handling:

- the quantity of records;
- the frequency of reference required;
- the speed of access required?

The system must:

- take account of the length of time documents must be retained in the office (*see* File retention policy on page 56);
- control and accurately record file movements;
- take into account the number and location of staff requiring access to the records and the location of the filing equipment, microfilm viewers or computer terminals;
- provide adequate protection against fire, theft and unauthorised reference, involving security procedures such as locking devices, codes and passwords; precautions which should be taken to safeguard computerised data against loss or corruption include:

  a back-up duplicate copies of disks kept in a secure (fireproof) place (this ensures your work is not lost if working disks are corrupted or destroyed);
  b personal passwords used by the staff who are authorised to have access to computer files, the passwords being changed at regular intervals;
  c codes used for document files, known only to users;
  d write-protect tags used on system disks to prevent data from being altered or added;
  e controlled entry to the offices where computers are housed by issuing pass cards or other security devices.

- take into account the nature and size of the records and the requirements for working on them, e.g. the desirability of using paper, filmed or computerised records.

Computerised filing system

Why should your organisation have a computerised system of information and records management?

Advantages

- Speed of retrieval.
- Saving in office space.
- Reduced paperwork as storage of data is transferred to disks, tapes, etc. (as illustrated in Fig 4.2).
- Interaction with other data, e.g. mainframe computer or shared resource link-up and international access to data sources in branch offices.
- Ease of access to central records through networking.
- Security/confidentiality.
- Files are not removed when accessed. The possibility of losing or misplacing data is then reduced. This is good for international access where time differences may apply.

Fig 4.2 Data storage

- Possibility of rationalising information systems on an international scale. Paper-based systems may vary from one country to another. With one computer-based format, less retraining costs and time are spent in training personnel moved from one office to another around the world.
- Cross-referral of data on an international scale is facilitated, e.g. the advertising budget data per office in four European branches can be recorded and presented in a standardised form.

Disadvantages

- Initial cost of acquiring equipment and servicing contracts.
- Time and cost of training staff to use equipment.
- Time and cost of printing data when necessary.
- Time and cost of inputting data.
- Human error – erasing data.
- Power cuts or system breakdowns/bugs.
- Security must be constantly monitored, codes changed.

When considering changing, updating or improving an information/retrieval system, whether on paper or computerised, five key areas must be addressed:

1 Research/investigate the needs of the information system, on an international scale if applicable.
2 File retention policy.
3 Access limitation.
4 Evaluation of system.
5 Cost.

File retention policy

The length of time files should be retained for reference purposes is governed by the following:

- any legal requirements for the records to be retained;
- any audit requirements;
- the need for documents to be produced as evidence in a court of law;
- whether the organisation would be at a disadvantage if the records could not be produced on a future date;
- whether the records are duplicated elsewhere – in this case, both copies may not need to be retained;
- whether the records are working papers which need not be kept once the matter has been completed satisfactorily;
- whether foreign subsidiaries or new offices abroad would find reference to past data on file useful material.

The following are examples of suggested retention periods for a selection of different classes of business documents.

Retention period

Originals to be kept permanently
Board meeting minutes
Memorandum and articles of association
Register of directors and secretaries
Register of members
Major agreements of historical significance
Patent and trade mark records
Taxation returns and records
Labour agreements
Public liability insurance policies

Originals to be kept for 12 years
Paid dividend and interest warrants
Property lease documents (after lease has terminated)
Payrolls
Accident books
Deeds of covenant (after final payment)

Originals to be kept for seven years
Staff personal records (after employment ceases)
Employee expense accounts

Originals to be kept for six years
Contracts with customers, suppliers and agents (after expiry)
Rental and hire-purchase agreements (after expiry)
Agreements with architects and builders (after completion of contract)
Accounting records complying with the Companies Act (three years if a private company)

Cheques, bills of exchange, etc.
Bank statements
Shipping documents (after shipment completed)

Originals to be kept for five years
Wage records
Customs and Excise returns
Drivers' log books (after completion)

Originals to be kept for three years
Insurance claims, correspondence and accident reports (after settlement)

Originals to be kept for two years
Time cards and piece-work records
Vehicle mileage and maintenance records
MOT test records

PERSONAL ACTION PLAN 9

▶ **Assess the efficacy of your current manual and/or computerised filing system and share your findings and recommendations with your boss or departmental head. Against which criteria would you assess the systems and why? In what ways could your system be developed or improved?**

▶ **How would you set out your findings and recommendations?**

CONTROL OF OFFICE SUPPLIES AND EQUIPMENT

Effective systems for controlling stationery and equipment are important. Office efficiency depends on the availability of suitable materials in suitable numbers as and when required. Wastage of supplies adds to the running costs of a business.

- Do you think and act like a manager at all times?
- How can you ensure economies in the areas of stationery, general office costs and even telephone bills?
- If you ran the office with your own money as your own business, would you take a closer look at the cost of items such as office supplies?

Checklists

1 The control and reordering of office supplies

- Anticipate demand for supplies and general office requirements based on the previous year's activities and needs.
- Set a budget for the year. Is there any seasonality in your business that might affect demand throughout the year?
- Keep a constant check and review your needs. Talk to staff about their requirements. Ask for suggestions or improvements.

- Have one person in charge of supplies, where possible.
- Keep all supplies in one place. Allocate a central storeroom for housing and controlling stocks of all office supplies.
- Have specific times for the issue and ordering of supplies.
- Store items clearly labelled so that stocks can be seen and checked at a glance.
- Heavy items must be accessible.
- Dangerous goods must be kept in a safe place and sealed.
- Avoid deterioration – first in is first out (FIFO system).
- Check authorisation to avoid pilfering.
- Keep stock control cards to record receipts and issues.
- If staff from branches abroad come to the office, keep a separate note of 'international usage' for needs ranging from stationery to ordering a computer to office space.
- Compare notes with other offices within your organisation, to exchange ideas, achieve economies of scale, etc.
- Use requisition forms to authorise and provide documentary evidence of the release of stock.

2 Storage and handling of stock

Store and handle stock safely by:

- placing heavy items on the lower shelves and arranging the items used frequently in the most accessible places;
- storing any highly inflammable materials in sealed containers and preferably in a metal cupboard or cabinet;
- prohibiting smoking in the storeroom;
- complying with the organisation's health and safety regulations (see Chapter 9);
- when receiving goods into stock, ensure that they are supplied in accordance with the order and that the seller has complied with the conditions laid down in the Sale of Goods Act 1979 (for example, that the goods are of 'merchantable quality', that they are fit for the purpose intended and that they correspond with their description).

3 Equipment

- Follow carefully the operating instructions relating to the safe use and regular maintenance of equipment.
- Operators should not smoke, drink or eat when using equipment.
- If equipment has to be moved, disconnect it from the electrical supply.
- Keep a log record of any intermittent faults which occur and the dates and times when maintenance engineers call to maintain or repair equipment.
- Before calling in a mechanic for a repair or breakdown, check the following points:

    - the power supply is on;
    - the fuse in the equipment is working; if not, the reason for its failure should be investigated by an electrician;
    - there are no faults in the connecting cable and plug;
    - the 'trouble shooting' section of the operating manual has been consulted for any useful tips on tracing the fault.

    If, after taking this action, there is still a fault, the services of a maintenance engineer should be requested and the maintenance contract located.

▶ **Could the responsibility for office supplies be a project to initiate or delegate?**

▶ **How could you make better use of the systems you already have in place and the materials you use?**

MAIL PROCEDURES

Mail handling covers three areas:

- incoming
- outgoing
- internal

Incoming and outgoing mail

Where international business is concerned, using the appropriate means of mail can mean the difference between success and failure. At the heart of the effective and cost-efficient handling of mail is access to the services available (*see* services listed on page 288). An appropriate decision can then be taken, especially where time, money and distance are of the essence.

Pointers to efficiency

Incoming mail
- Check for damage and always ensure that you have the correct package before signing documents.
- Only open mail you are authorised to open.
- Stamp all mail with the date of receipt.
- Distribute mail as soon as possible to the right persons.
- Translate anything required. If your skills are good, do it yourself. If not, find the appropriate translation source. Remember timing.

Outgoing mail
- Check that all enclosures and signatures are present.
- Are the addresses correct and legible?
- Check that the postage amount and method are appropriate.
- Retain receipts where necessary.
- Have at hand details of all postal services and other delivery services with costs, such as:

Domestic	Datapost, Parcelforce
International	Europe – letter rates
	Outside Europe – letter rates
	– Swiftair
	Customs declaration requirements/compensation

Parcels	Parcelforce International
	Parcelforce Datapost
Mailsort contracts	Letters posted in bulk
	British Rail services
	Private delivery services

Internal mail
- Prioritise. Deal with urgent mail first.
- Make sure that the distribution channels are efficient, using circulation slips for distributing single copies.
- Decide on the number of copies to be made and send to the relevant departments.
- Remember to provide for file copies.

PERSONAL ACTION PLAN 11

▶ **How well do you know the advantages and disadvantages of the services used for items commonly despatched in your business?**

▶ **Do you have your own booklet of useful services/addresses and information? Is this an area where you can become an expert?**

REPROGRAPHICS AND COPYRIGHT LAW

Reprography (document and image creation and making copies and duplicates for circulation) is a key area of expertise for the executive secretary. At the heart of this service is the development of desktop publishing systems (*see* Fig 4.3) which provide high-quality printed documents and slides from computer tape and WP disks.

The diagram in Fig 4.4 shows the different items of software and hardware involved in producing camera-ready copy from a desktop publishing system. Desktop publishing

Fig 4.3 Desktop publishing equipment

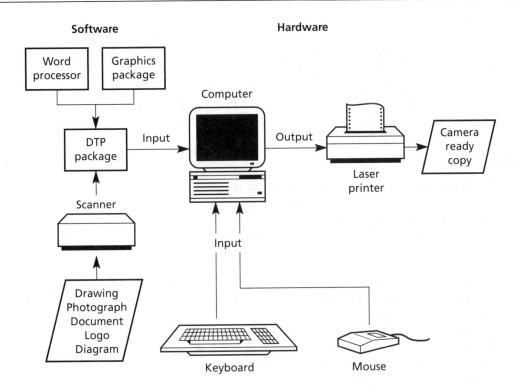

Fig 4.4 Desktop publishing diagram

has emerged as yet another important skill for the executive secretary who is expected to produce high-quality professional 'printing' of all paperwork.

Desktop publishing is a multi-functional process integrating the use of:

- a scanner (optional)
- a computer (with a hard disk)
- a laser printer
- software combining text creation, editing and graphics

Copiers, word processors and desktop publishing equipment provide the bulk of reprographic machinery, although duplicators and carbon paper are still used. Paper-handling equipment such as binders, bursters, collators and laminators also contribute to the end product within a reprographics department.

The following NVQ performance criteria for the competence 'Organise and arrange the copying, collating and binding of documents' are a useful guide for the supervisor when assessing staff performance:

- Reprographic equipment and materials are selected and used correctly and cost effectively, for specified purposes.
- Documents for reproduction are prepared correctly.
- Copies of appropriate quality are produced from original documents.
- Copies and originals are collated, fastened and distributed correctly.
- Reported equipment faults are dealt with promptly.

- Material wastage is kept to a minimum.
- Precise requirements are conveyed to colleagues and confirmed where appropriate.
- Tasks delegated to others are accurately defined and progress monitored.
- Work progress is planned and monitored to meet all deadlines.
- Records are kept up to date, legible and accurate.
- Safe working practices are always followed and implemented.
- Security and confidentiality procedures are always followed and implemented.

Checklist

What operators should know about their copiers
1 The warm-up procedure at the beginning of the day.
2 How to insert the copy paper.
3 How to prepare originals for reproduction.
4 How to insert originals and set up the machine for copying.
5 How to top-up toner.
6 Techniques of image editing.
7 Essential standards of quality for copies produced.
8 Copyright restrictions (see page 63).
9 Methods used for sorting, collating and binding copies.
10 How to prepare overhead projector transparencies.
11 The method used to control the use of the copier.
12 Ways of ensuring economic use of the copier.
13 Safety, security and confidentiality procedures.
14 How to plan and monitor work schedules to meet the deadlines set.
15 The procedure for clearing paper jammed in the machine.
16 The procedure for reporting faults and arranging for a mechanic to attend.
17 The closing-down procedure at the end of the day.
18 Day-to-day maintenance in accordance with the operating manual.

Factors to consider when selecting a new copier
1 Price and method of purchase.
2 Size.
3 Speed of copying.
4 Type of document feed.
5 Type of paper feed.
6 Paper sizes accommodated.
7 Image-editing facilities.
8 Reduction and enlargement facilities.
9 Memory capability.
10 Finishing functions such as collating, stapling and binding.
11 Colour or black-and-white copying.
12 Method of controlling use.

Copyright law

Under the 'fair dealing' provisions of the Copyright, Designs and Patents Act 1988 you are permitted to make one copy of an agreed maximum amount of any published material for the purposes of research, private study, criticism, or review, but you are not permitted to copy a substantial part of the work. In addition, for the purposes of review, sufficient acknowledgement must be made. In order to copy a substantial part of a work, i.e. more than a single chapter or article of a publication, or to copy for any purpose outside the 'fair dealing' provision, it is necessary that you first obtain the permission of the copyright holder (usually the publisher or author) or you must have taken all reasonable steps to find out the name and address of the copyright holder and have been unsuccessful. You must make at least three attempts at regular (say monthly) intervals before you can be regarded as having made 'all reasonable attempts' to contact the copyright holder. If you do not succeed, you must indicate this in your publication or review in the form of an acknowledgement along the following lines:

> Unfortunately, I have been unable to trace the copyright holder(s) of the following material (*list material*) and would welcome any information which would enable me to do so.

The main provisions of the Act and Regulations should be brought to the notice of staff using copying facilities.

PERSONAL ACTION PLAN 12

▶ **Outline the planning process for the implementation of a reprography project. Do you keep to your deadlines?**

▶ **When you delegate copying, collating and binding tasks to a junior, does he or she meet with your expectations as regards quality and performance? If not, how do you set about enhancing his or her performance?**

▶ **Is your boss aware of the logistics involved in copying, collating and binding documents for large projects? How could you improve your existing systems? How can you anticipate and accommodate 'last minute' rush jobs more efficiently?**

Controlling and monitoring the use of the copier

Various methods are available for controlling and monitoring the number of copies made by individual departments and/or members of staff. These include:

- A written record kept by the supervisor and completed by staff whenever they use the machine, stating their name, date, number of copies taken, size, single or double sided, etc.
- Requisition forms completed by users and authorised by heads of department.
- Plastic 'credit' cards or keys used by each member of staff which, when inserted, automatically register the use made by each card- or key-holder. Print-outs then show an analysis of usage.

- Code numbers can be allocated to each user and, when keyed in, operate and record the number of copies. Print-outs can also show usage.

In-house reprographics and external printing agencies

As offices become more 'hi–tech' and deadlines tighten, executive secretaries are faced with the challenge of deciding whether to create or expand reprographic facilities to meet the demand internally, or recommend the use of external printing agencies.

The volume and nature of the material to be copied, as well as the cost of printing, influence the decision whether to use an external printer or to acquire the necessary equipment and staff for the material to be copied in-house. Desktop publishing has now replaced many of the applications previously undertaken by external agencies but this depends on the following factors:

- availability of staff within the organisation with the necessary skills and ability;
- cost of acquiring the equipment for preparing the artwork and binding the copies;
- volume and frequency of copying required to justify the staff and equipment;
- nature of the work involved;
- quality of reproduction required.

Advantages

In-house reprographic department
- Saves time, in the case of tight deadlines and emergencies/unscheduled needs.
- Investment in the latest technology/ machinery.
- Easy access after office hours for last-minute presentations.
- Easy access at short notice.
- Can tailor machinery to needs and choose systems versatile enough to meet the organisation's needs and accommodate future growth.
- Staff training/motivation in learning new skills.
- Develops professionalism in new skills.
- Allows for flexibility. The more staff that can use the system, the greater the increase in efficiency.
- Long term this can be cost-effective as training and other costs are reduced.
- Good storage of information with desktop publishing. Good for reuse.
- Smaller stocks of forms, letterheads and brochures are needed, as these can be reproduced when required.

External printing agencies
- No wastage/abuse of machinery.
- Quality advice from professionals.
- No interruptions, allowing you to do other work while the agency completes the copying.
- No need for training of staff.

Disadvantages

In-house reprographic department
- Initial cost of investing in equipment.
- Teething problems at set-up.
- Training and ability of staff dictate quality of work.
- Need to control use to avoid abuse.
- Must issue codes/cards.
- Must devote time to department and rejuggle priorities.
- Need back-up available for support/ breakdown.
- Overload. Must have adequate systems for the use of different departments.

External printing agencies
- Cost of service on a regular basis.
- Time – restricted to office hours or increased costs for late or last-minute changes.
- Less control over changes.
- Need to plan further in advance; less flexible to change of any kind.
- Security risk with confidential data.
- Slower feedback for any change in style or format.
- Risk attached in booking in work at short notice.

Many companies find that they have to use both internal and external facilities in order to take advantage of the most flexible and economic services of both.

EXAMINE YOUR KNOWLEDGE

1 A newly-appointed junior secretary says that she has not been required to operate a franking machine in her previous appointments and has no knowledge of it. As she will be expected periodically to assist the mailroom staff, you are asked to plan and devise appropriate training for her on the use of the franking machine.

2 Memorandum

    To: Company Secretary
    From: Managing Director via Personal Secretary

I am disturbed at the state of affairs existing in relation to our stationery stocks. I find that no one person is responsible for ordering and dispensing stationery; instead, when any item cannot immediately be found, any of the senior staff telephone further orders. Tables, shelves and floor in the stockroom are piled high with mixed stationery; many packets have their wrappers torn open, allowing contents to be soiled and creased. I would recommend that we institute a control system right away and I submit the following ideas for your consideration:

Complete this memorandum.   *(LCCI PESD)*

3 You are PA/secretary to Mrs Catherine Walsh (Case Study 1). As the chief buyer is moving into new premises in October there is an opportunity to set up a new filing system. Recommend the best system to allow the following type of record to be kept together with the information required.

(a) Using a paper-based system

    (i) Records of current stock levels of gems, pearls and diamonds as well as the usual office stock items. This should be kept in such a way as to be used as an inventory.

    (ii) Full details of existing and potential suppliers.

(b) What are the advantages of setting up a computerised system?   *(LCCI PESD)*

4 Your company is considering setting up its own centralised in-house reprographics provision rather than relying on departmental copiers and the services of outside bureaux. State the advantages and disadvantages of such a change.   *(PEI ASP)*

5 A new, more sophisticated copier has been installed in your department and it is your responsibility to ensure that all staff are trained to use it correctly. Explain how you would plan and organise such training and list the major items you would expect to cover.

WORK TASKS

Assessment of competence for Element 1.1
Organise allocation and despatch of mail

Performance criteria

- *Mail is correctly processed and promptly distributed to correct locations.*
- *Mail is correctly prepared for despatch and, where applicable, correct postal rates are applied.*
- *Delivery services are identified and selected to suit the specific requirements.*
- *Work progress of others is monitored to ensure that instructions are precisely followed.*
- *Records are kept up to date, legible and accurate.*
- *Tasks delegated to others are accurately defined and monitored.*
- *Safe working practices are always followed and implemented.*
- *Security and confidentiality procedures are always followed and implemented.*

Range statement

Competent performance must be demonstrated across a range of:

- *Successful achievement both by oneself and through organising others.*
- *Types of mail:*
  internal and external; letters, packages and parcels; differing cost and urgency; suspect items.
- *Destinations:*
  in-house, local, national, overseas
- *Types of service:*
  at least three different agencies of which one is international.

- *Confidentiality:*
  confidential within own organisation; personal to employees or members; private to external clients; commercially confidential.

Personal action plans 11 and 24 relate to this work.

Assessment of competence for Element 2.1
Use and develop manual and computerised filing systems

Performance criteria

- *Established filing systems are operated correctly.*
- *Changing information requirements are identified and agreed with users.*
- *Recommendations for filing system improvements and developments are made to meet the identified requirements.*
- *Once approved, new and/or improved systems are implemented and monitored for correct operation.*
- *All users of existing and modified systems are consulted and informed during system development.*
- *Information is always retained or deleted in accordance with organisational policy and/or legal requirements.*
- *Tasks delegated to others are accurately defined and monitored.*
- *Safe working practices are always followed and implemented.*
- *Security and confidentiality procedures are always followed and implemented.*

Range statement

Competent performance must be demonstrated across a range of:

- *Successful achievement both by oneself and through organising others.*
- *Filing Systems:*
  manual and computerised; dedicated and shared; microfiche.
- *Filing Classifications:*
  at least three of the following: alphabetical; numerical; alphanumerical; subject; geographical; cross-referencing.
- *Information:*
  text; financial; technical; confidential.
- *Changing requirements:*
  new legislation; reorganisation; new business or products; efficiency and storage pressures.

Personal action plan 9 relates to this work.

Assessment of competence for Element 5.3
Organise and arrange the copying, collating and binding of documents

The performance criteria for these tasks is given on pages 61–2.

Range statement

Competent performance must be demonstrated across a range of:

- *Successful achievement through organising others (support staff or colleagues) to produce the completed documents.*
- *Equipment:*
  enlarging and reducing functions; collating and binding options.
- *Documents:*
  at least three paper sizes (A3, A4, A5); master copies combining two or more originals.

Personal action plan 12 relates to this work.

Assessment of competence for Element 9.1
Maintain office supplies

Performance criteria

- *Office supplies are maintained at operational levels.*
- *Variations in stock usage are identified and ordering procedures adjusted accordingly.*
- *Reported or witnessed equipment faults and storage problems are dealt with promptly.*
- *Stock is stored and handled safely.*
- *Stock and issue records are kept up to date, legible and accurate.*
- *Tasks delegated to others are accurately defined and progress monitored.*
- *Safe working practices are always followed and implemented.*
- *Security and confidentiality procedures are always followed and implemented.*

Range statement

Competent performance must be demonstrated across a range of:

- *Successful achievement both by oneself and through organising others.*
- *Approval procedures:*
  written or oral from principal; requisitioned from other authority.
- *Reordering procedures:*
  automatic; discretionary (own authority); discretionary (delegated to others).
- *Storage and handling requirements:*
  small consumables; paper and stationery; electronic and computerised items; secure and confidential items; dangerous and valuable items.
- *Levels of demand:*
  both static and fluctuating; requiring forward planning.

Personal action plan 10 relates to this work.

CHAPTER 5

Financial aspects of management

The executive secretary at a senior level will often find that the nature of her or his involvement with financial procedures is supervisory in nature. Accurate financial records are vital, especially if foreign currencies and exchange rates are involved. If monetary matters are agreed or negotiated with individuals whose mother tongue is not English, then be sure to check, check and double check.

CONTROL OF BANKING TRANSACTIONS

As an executive secretary you are likely to be responsible for ensuring that authorised banking procedures are used and that banking documents are checked and monitored for any errors which can be rectified. This entails:

- processing all banking transactions accurately;
- identifying all errors and discrepancies, and dealing with them promptly;
- ensuring that all paying-in and withdrawal documents, including cheques and card transactions, are correctly completed;
- reconciling bank statements correctly;
- checking that all calculations are correct;
- adhering to laid-down security and confidentiality procedures;
- ensuring that records are kept up to date, legible and accurate.

Three checklists follow as an *aide-mémoire* for carrying out and supervising such routine tasks as receiving cheques, paying money into the bank and making out cheques.

Checklist for receiving cheques

Check the following:

- the current date has been used;
- amounts in words and figures are the same;
- cheques have been signed;
- the payee's name (your organisation) is correct;
- any alterations on the cheque are clear and are signed.

When accepting cheques with a cheque card, check the following:

- the card has the same account name and number and bank sort code number;
- the signature on the card is the same as the one on the cheque;
- the date on the card has not expired;

- the cheque has been fully and correctly completed with:

  current date;
  correct name of payee;
  correct amount in both words and figures;
  drawer's signature.

Enter the card number and expiry date on the reverse of the cheque.

Checklist for paying money into the bank

Check on the paying-in slip:

- the current date has been used;
- bank, branch and codes are correct;
- the payee's name and account number for your organisation are correct;
- total cash (front) and total cheques (reverse) are calculated accurately;
- the number of cheques agrees with the number of items entered on the reverse of the form.

Checklist for making out a cheque

- always use a pen;
- write the payee's name exactly as described on the invoice or notice to pay;
- write the amount of pounds or foreign currency in words as well as figures, starting as far to the left as possible;
- do not leave spaces where other words or figures could be added;
- the date must contain the day, month and year;
- the drawer should sign the cheque with his or her normal signature as supplied to the bank;
- write the words 'A/c Payee' in the crossing if this has not been pre-printed;
- keep a record of the date, payee's name and amount on the counterfoil;
- if an alteration has been made, the drawer must sign alongside it;
- the cheque book should be kept in a safe place and the cheque guarantee card kept separate from it for security reasons.

BANK STATEMENT RECONCILIATION

Periodically, usually at the end of the month, the bank supplies a statement which records all the transactions that have taken place between the customer and the bank involving the receipt and payment of monies. The statement shows:

- the balance of the account at the end of the previous statement (credit for cash held; debit for overdrawn);
- credits for money paid into the account;
- debits for money paid out by cheques and other means;
- debits for bank charges;
- balance of the account at the end of the statement (credit for cash held; debit for overdrawn).

The bank statement balance may not agree with the customer's bank account balance for the following reasons:

- cheques and cash paid into the bank may not have arrived in time to be credited;
- unpresented cheques will not be shown, i.e. those cheques that have been posted or handed to payees but have not yet been processed through the bank's clearing house system, such as cheques to foreign suppliers;
- bank charges;
- credit transfers;
- standing orders and direct debits.

A bank reconciliation statement is drawn up to check the accuracy of the bank statement with the customer's bank account after taking account of these items, as shown in Fig 5.1. This way cash flow and outgoings can be monitored and controlled.

Bank reconciliation statement at 31 December 199 –

	£	£
Balance as per bank statement		4352.60 Cr
Add: Money paid in but not credited	450.50	
Credit transfers	120.00	
		570.50
		4923.10
Deduct: Unpresented cheques	2000.00	
Direct debits	50.90	
Standing orders	120.00	
Bank charges	20.00	
		2190.90
Balance as per bank account		£2732.20 Cr

Fig 5.1 Bank reconciliation statement

PERSONAL ACTION PLAN 13

▶ How would you train a junior in basic banking procedures? Which areas would you cover and why?

▶ Are the tasks which you delegate clearly and accurately defined, and do you monitor the work progress and priorities of your juniors so that all deadlines are met?

▶ Suggest systems for financial record-keeping in a small office start-up situation. What stationery and equipment is necessary?

▶ Assess the procedures involved in accepting and banking foreign currency cheques.

▶ **Suggest ways in which you might persuade a reluctant boss to delegate financial responsibilities to you. What would be the benefits for the boss and for yourself in assuming such responsibility?**

BUDGETING AND BUDGETARY CONTROL

Budgets are estimates of costs to be incurred, a provision for the costs in a particular area. Accurate budgeting and control of a budget are responsible tasks involving time, effort, forward planning, regular revision and honesty.

Preparing a budget is the first step in controlling expenditure. Mechanisms such as regular budget reviews (often monthly) help to control budgets. These reviews indicate where departments are over or under spending, where deviations and discrepancies occur and why.

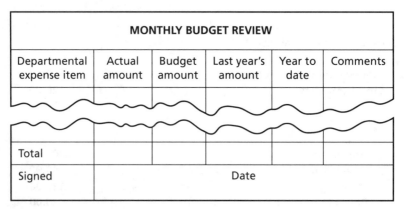

Fig 5.2 **Example of a budget review form**

Types of budget

Recruitment budget

Annual recruitment budgets allocate money to be spent on recruiting staff. The money may be spent in paying recruitment consultancy fees for permanent staff or rates for temporary staff. A large part of the budget could also be directed towards placing direct advertising for particular positions.

Remember, when advertising, to confirm rates before the advertisement appears. When liaising with employment agencies, always negotiate the fee, the terms of payment and the guarantee period to your advantage. Always keep a record of any recruitment advertising carried out for referral. Mark the number of responses and calculate the cost per response. This is also vital for monitoring which advertisements attract high-calibre or high-number responses or, ideally, both.

If you have to pay any invoices in a foreign currency, you should confirm the rate of exchange, and take account of any extra fees or reductions for prompt payment which might affect your budget calculations.

Training budget

In-house trainers, external, residential, half-day, full-day and WP cross-training are all training areas that may come under your control. You may prepare weekly summary sheets for training activity and for the staff involved. *See* the section on training, page 171.

Advertising and public relations budget

This is usually an annual budget figure broken down by quarter and by month. You may be involved in the advertising of your company's services or products. Always keep examples of your own advertisements (and those of the competition), with cost per insertion if print media is used. Keep an eye on the production costs as they can mount up surprisingly quickly. Be sure to negotiate reductions if errors are made, and discounts for block bookings. Keep all records consistent – for example, all figures either exclude or include VAT, but not a mixture of the two. Allow for some contingency emergency money for foreign currency transactions or for problems.

Entertainment budget

This may be a very busy budget area and a highly sensitive one! Always keep receipts and monitor very closely the return on investment. How does it benefit you to entertain clients? Quantify the results in more than just goodwill terms. Has business been increased?

Office budget

You may have responsibility for the income and expenditure of a fee-based office. You may be involved in obtaining all office supplies, printing, stationery, furniture, computing and photocopying, for example. This will involve deciding priorities, and preparing and reviewing cash flow charts and analyses. A cash flow analysis is a projection, i.e. a realistic forecast, of what money is coming in and when, and of what money is going out and when. This is vital when running a company and may dictate the type of new business you take on. Small clients may be preferable, to keep a steady flow of some money coming into the office, rather than having one big client that only pays two or three times a year. An example of an office budget is shown in Figs 5.3–5.7.

Cash flow budget

Summary sheet for twelve-month period

	£
Income	144 864
Expenditure	99 739
Cash surplus	£45 125

A 10% contingency sum has not been included in this example.

ADMINISTRATION FOR THE YEAR 199 –
All figures are inclusive of VAT (where applicable).

	This year £	Previous year £
Rent and service charge	15 000	
Rates	5 000	
Electricity	6 000	
Insurance	500	
Repairs	400	
Office cleaning	500	
Computer (including support fee)	8 000	
Salaries (including NI contributions and pensions)	44 000	
Advertising	7 000	
PR	2 000	
Promotion	2 000	
Stationery	3 000	
Printing	2 500	
Subscriptions (publications and organisations)	250	
Travel expenses	250	
Furniture	1 000	
Fax and telephone	5 000	
Postage	1 500	
Legal fees	5 000	
Accountant's fees	5 000	
Bank charges and interest	5 000	
Sundries (including newspapers)	500	
	£119 400	
10% contingency	11 940	
TOTAL	£131 340	

Date: Prepared by:

Fig 5.3 Example of an office budget

CASH FLOW BUDGET

	January £	February £	March £
*Income	2 012	12 072	10 060
Expenditure			
Computer	2 500	227	227
Office cleaning	42	42	42
Salaries (including NI and pensions)	2 200	2 200	2 200
Commission	121	724	604
Travel	17	17	17
Advertising	417	417	417
Telephone and fax	500	45	45
Postage	125	125	125
Bank charges	416	416	416
Rent and service	2 750	–	–
Rates	750	–	–
Electricity	2 500	–	–
Insurance	200	–	–
Repairs	250	–	–
Furniture	1 000	–	–
Subscriptions	150	–	–
Accountant's fees	2 000	–	–
Legal fees	3 000	–	–
PR	–	500	500
Stationery and printing	–	2 500	–
Sundries	42	42	42
	18 980	7 255	4 635
Cash surplus/(deficit)	(16 968)	4 817	5 425

* Assumption of payment of invoices by customers/clients on the following basis:

	1 January	6 February	5 March

Such fluctuations in the income level reflect some seasonality and time lapse in the receipt of the payment of invoices issued.

Fig 5.4 Example of a cash flow budget for January to March in the first twelve-month period of a small start-up situation office

CASH FLOW BUDGET

	April £	May £	June £
*Income	<u>10 060</u>	<u>10 060</u>	<u>14 084</u>
Expenditure			
Computer	227	227	227
Office cleaning	42	42	42
Salaries (including NI and pensions)	2 200	2 200	2 200
Commission	604	604	845
Travel	17	17	17
Advertising	417	417	681
Telephone and fax	45	45	45
Postage	125	125	125
Bank charges	416	416	416
Rent and service	2 750	–	–
Rates	750	–	–
Electricity	2 500	–	–
Insurance	–	–	–
Repairs	–	–	–
Furniture	1 000	–	–
Subscriptions	–	–	–
Accountant's fees	–	–	–
Legal fees	–	–	–
PR	500	500	–
Stationery and printing	–	–	–
Sundries	42	42	42
	11 635	4 635	4 640
Cash surplus/(deficit)	(1 575)	5 425	9 444

* Assumption of payment of invoices by customers/clients on the following basis:

	5 April	5 May	7 June

Fig 5.5 Example of a cash flow budget for April to June in the first twelve-month period of a small start-up situation office

CASH FLOW BUDGET

	July £	August £	September £
*Income	<u>10 060</u>	<u>20 120</u>	<u>20 120</u>
Expenditure			
Computer	227	227	227
Office cleaning	42	42	42
Salaries (including NI and pensions)	2 200	2 200	2 200
Commission	604	1 207	1 207
Travel	17	17	17
Advertising	600	600	417
Telephone and fax	45	45	45
Postage	125	125	125
Bank charges	416	416	416
Rent and service	2 750	–	–
Rates	750	–	–
Electricity	2 500	–	–
Insurance	–	–	–
Repairs	250	–	–
Furniture	–	–	–
Subscriptions	100	–	–
Accountant's fees	1 000	–	–
Legal fees	2 000	–	–
PR	500	500	–
Stationery and printing	–	2 500	–
Sundries	42	42	42
	14 168	7 921	4 738
Cash surplus/(deficit)	(4 108)	12 199	15 382

* Assumption of payment of invoices by customers/clients on the following basis:

	5 July	10 August	10 September

Fig 5.6 Example of a cash flow budget for July to September in the first twelve-month period of a small start-up situation office

CASH FLOW BUDGET

	October £	November £	December £
*Income	20 120	8 048	8 048
Expenditure			
Computer	227	227	227
Office cleaning	42	42	42
Salaries (including NI and pensions)	2 200	2 200	2 200
Commission	1 207	483	483
Travel	17	17	17
Advertising	417	200	–
Telephone and fax	45	45	45
Postage	125	125	125
Bank charges	416	416	416
Rent and service	2 750	–	–
Rates	750	–	–
Electricity	2 500	–	–
Insurance	–	–	–
Repairs	–	–	–
Furniture	–	–	–
Subscriptions	–	–	–
Accountant's fees	–	–	2 000
Legal fees	–	–	–
PR	500	500	–
Stationery and printing	–	–	–
Sundries	42	42	42
	11 238	4 297	5 597
Cash surplus/(deficit)	8 882	3 751	2 451

* Assumption of payment of invoices by customers/clients on the following basis:

10 October	4 November	4 December

Fig 5.7 Example of a cash flow budget for October to December in the first twelve-month period of a small start-up situation office

Advantages of operating a budgetary control system

- You can plan business activity based on a budget. You know your financial position. A budget gives form and direction. Some months you may need to spend more than others, and your expenditure will take a pattern.
- It imposes regulation on extravagances and impulse financial outlay. It draws attention to over-expenditure, and reasons must be provided for this.
- You can control activity and set priorities.
- You can anticipate needs and be a prudent financial manager, e.g. building in 10 per cent contingency figures for unexpected items.
- It is a management tool for growth and expansion or rationalisation where necessary.
- It helps in your personal development. Managing a budget is a responsible task. If you are supervising a junior's work in budgetary control, this provides management training for you and the start of responsibility for the junior. Budgets require close examination, the working out of particular departmental activities and full understanding of the business. Emphasis should be on setting practical goals. The responsibility for budget control provides an incentive to perform well and keep to the budget.
- By constantly reviewing cash flow and budgets you are aware of the needs of the business and how the market-place is affecting your business.
- If your budget responsibility involves monitoring income and expenditure, you can take decisions. For example, cut down on cash transfers by delaying payments or staggering buying decisions.
- You can save money if you plan activity, buy in bulk and secure discounts.
- By planning and budgeting you promote flexibility and avoid putting financial strains on the business.

A word should be said concerning the potential negative effects of controlling a budget which should be borne in mind:

- A budget is an aid to monitoring costs, it is not a regulator of costs. Any additional funds that might be required must be argued for and not immediately seen to be impossible.
- Tight budgetary control can impose a blinkered approach. For example, where budgets are separately prepared for typing requirements and photocopying needs, surplus from one budget is often not passed over to the other, which may be in deficit. Nothing is gained by holding back surplus funds in one small department which could help another.

How to prepare a budget

Past   Look at previous data on activities and budgets. How does this match up against future plans, i.e. current v future needs?

Present   What are the current needs and objectives?

Future   Consider plans for the next year. Build in a percentage growth/inflation factor. Show figures in an accessible format by month, quarter and year.

Unexpected factor   Include buffer money for any contingency – perhaps 10 per cent.

▶ **How much of your current job involves budget and cash responsibilities?**

▶ **How much is it computerised?**

▶ **What argument would you use to change the systems?**

▶ **Can you produce accurate financial data quickly when required?**

▶ **If not, take immediate steps to improve the control you have over financial matters.**

CONTROL OF PETTY CASH

The executive secretary is expected to maintain or supervise a petty cash system for the office cash transactions. The following NVQ performance criteria are a useful check on the standards required for this task:

- expenditure heads are identified and approval obtained;
- approved funds are obtained in accordance with organisational procedures;
- receipts and other financial records meet auditing requirements;
- need for adjustment to the imprest is identified and authority sought;
- cash handling security and confidentiality procedures are always followed and implemented;
- cash is issued in accordance with organisational procedures;
- all errors or discrepancies are identified and dealt with promptly.

A petty cash account is used to record small items of business expenditure or the private expenses of executives. Incidental cash payments are made from this type of fund. It is usually a monthly reconciliation procedure, referred to as an imprest system, where the amount spent is refunded.

In an imprest system of petty cash an agreed sum of money (the imprest) is allocated by the cashier out of which cash payments are made. At the end of the month or other monitoring period the amount spent is refunded, thus restoring the imprest to the original amount allocated.

Whenever cash is paid out, vouchers or receipts are obtained so that at all times the total of cash plus the current period's vouchers equals the 'float' or imprest. Vouchers are numbered and filed in numerical order. The petty cash account is an extension of the cash account, relieving the cash account of the many small items of cash expenditure that are so important in the day-to-day running of an office. In a supervisory role, the executive secretary may need to adjust petty cash floats, dependent on the needs and previously recorded levels of business, or identify and correct errors.

Guidelines for the security of petty cash

- Check sums of money carefully before handing them over.
- Lock the cash in a cash box and keep it in a safe place.
- Do not leave the office unattended with the cash box unlocked.
- Ensure that every payment of cash is supported by an authorised petty cash voucher.

- Make regular checks of the petty cash account and cash to ensure that the petty cash vouchers and cash held in the box equal the imprest.

Checklist for Petty Cash Book entries

Check that:

- Every item of expenditure has been entered twice on the expenditure side, that is, in the total column and in the appropriate analysis column.
- Where VAT has been paid it equals 17½ per cent (or current rate) of the total paid. Clarify which items incur VAT and which do not.
- Each analysis column entry plus the VAT (where applicable) equals the total paid out.
- The additions of each of the following are correct:

  total paid column;
  analysis columns;
  total of analysis = total paid column.

- Balance c/f (carried forward) plus the cash paid equals the imprest.
- Balance b/f (brought forward) plus the cash received equals the imprest.

PERSONAL ACTION PLAN 15

▶ **In dealing with petty cash, how can you ensure that:**

  (a) **your records meet auditing requirements;**
  (b) **cash handling, security and confidentiality procedures are always followed and implemented;**
  (c) **cash is issued in accordance with organisational procedures;**
  (d) **any errors or discrepancies are identified and dealt with promptly?**

EXAMINE YOUR KNOWLEDGE

1 (a) Draw up a cash flow budget for January to follow on from the 'start-up' situation office budget on page 78, with the following estimated figures:

Expenditure	£
Rent and service charge	2 800
Rates	800
Electricity	2 500
Insurance	220
Repairs	260
Computer	227
Office cleaning	50
Salaries (including NI and pensions)	2 310
Commission	1 000
Advertising	420
Subscriptions	120
Travel	20

PETTY CASH ACCOUNT

Received	Date	Fo	Details	V No	Total paid out	Stationery	Postage	Travel	Cleaning	Office Sundries
23 45	Jan 1	b/f	Balance							
76 55	1	c4	Cash received							
	1		Postage stamps	21	12 00					12 00
	2		Cleaning materials	22	15 65				15 65	
	4		Bond paper	23	21 60	21 60				
	8		Coffee and sugar	24	4 20					4 20
	9		Flowers for foyer	25	8 00	8 00				
	11		Taxi fare	26	6 50			6 50		
	15		Postal order	27	8 10		8 10			
	18		Parking fee	28	1 50			1 50		
	22		Magazines for reception	29	3 75					3 75
	25		Paper clips	30	1 24	1 24				
					82 54	22 84	8 10	8 00	15 56	19 95
	31	c/f	Balance		82 54					
100 00					165 08					
82 54	Feb 1	b/f	Balance							
17 46	1	c5	Cash received							

Fig 5.8 Petty cash account

Expenditure	£
Fax and telephone	52
Postage	130
Bank charges	430
Accountant's fees	2 200
Sundries	60

Income

assuming payment of invoices on 1 January	12 000

(*b*) Compare the surplus/deficit in your calculation with the same month last year (page 75) and comment on your findings.

2 You are secretary to Mr Michael Vivoir (Case Study 3) and are required to check the petty cash account (*see* Fig 5.8). (*PEI ASP*)

3 Once a month you receive your organisation's bank statement and it is your responsibility to use it to bring the bank account up to date with the bank statement and, after doing this, to draw up a bank reconciliation statement to check the accuracy of the bank statement and your account records. You are required to complete this work for January 199– using the documents shown in Figs 5.9–5.10.

BARCLOYMID BANK PLC
Godalming Branch

A Customer
21 High Street
Guildford
Surrey

STATEMENT OF ACCOUNT

Sheet 14   Account No: 30126894

199 –			Dr £	Cr £	Balance £	
Jan	1	BALANCE B/F			1156.52	CR
	2	101387	52.00		1104.52	CR
	2	101386	6.50		1098.02	CR
	3	SUNDRIES		249.62	1347.64	CR
	4	PRB JOURNALS – DD	23.00		1324.64	CR
	5	101390	114.82		1209.82	CR
	8	SURREY CC – DD	49.10		1160.72	CR
	9	R JONES – CT		100.00	1260.72	CR
	9	101389	10.50		1250.22	CR
	10	101388	105.15		1145.07	CR
	11	SUNDRIES		305.00	1450.07	CR
	12	101390	22.31		1427.76	CR

15	DUPLEX LTD – DD	156.00		1271.76	CR
16	101392	24.60		1247.16	CR
17	101391	104.00		1143.16	CR
18	T BROWN – CT		186.50	1329.66	CR
22	101394	141.00		1188.66	CR
24	101393	8.90		1179.76	CR
31	NET INTEREST		1.05	1180.81	CR

CT = Credit transfer DD = Direct debit

Fig 5.9

BANK ACCOUNT OF A CUSTOMER

199 –		Dr £	Cr £	Balance £	
Jan 1	Balance b/f			1098.02	Dr
1	Sundries	249.62		1347.64	Dr
1	P White		114.82	1232.82	Dr
5	LTA Products		10.50	1222.32	Dr
6	R Cox		105.15	1117.17	Dr
10	Sundries	305.00		1422.17	Dr
9	Surrey CC		22.31	1399.86	Dr
13	XYZ Ltd		24.60	1375.26	Dr
14	Carter & Sons		104.00	1271.26	Dr
18	P Parker		141.00	1130.26	Dr
20	Cornwell Ltd		8.90	1121.36	Dr
29	Hard Metals Ltd		100.00	1021.36	Dr
30	L Mark		180.00	841.36	Dr
31	Sundries	102.30		943.66	Dr

Fig 5.10

4 (a) Briefly explain how budgets are prepared, indicating the types of budget you would expect to operate in an office.

(b) Indicate the advantages to be gained from introducing budgetary control systems.

(*PEI ASP*)

WORK TASKS

Assessment of competence for Element 9.2
Maintain a petty cash system

Performance criteria

- *Expenditure heads are identified and approval obtained.*
- *Approved funds are obtained in accordance with organisational procedures.*
- *Receipts and other financial records meet auditing requirements.*
- *Need for adjustment to the imprest (float) is identified and authority sought.*
- *Cash handling security and confidentiality procedures are always followed and implemented.*
- *Cash is issued in accordance with organisational procedures.*
- *All errors or discrepancies are identified and dealt with promptly.*
- *Safe working practices are always followed and implemented.*

Range statement

Competent performance must be demonstrated across a range of:

- *Requests for cash:*
  routine; emergency; acceptable; unacceptable; exceeding funds immediately available.

Personal action plans 14 and 15 relate to this work.

Assessment of competence for Element 9.3
Ensure the use of authorised banking procedures

Performance criteria

- *All transactions are processed accurately.*
- *Bank statements are reconciled correctly.*
- *All errors and discrepancies are identified and dealt with promptly.*
- *Records are kept up to date, legible and accurate.*
- *Work progress and priorities are monitored to ensure that all deadlines are met.*
- *Tasks delegated to others are accurately defined and progress monitored.*
- *Safe working practices are always followed and implemented.*
- *Security and confidentiality procedures are always followed and implemented.*

Range statement

Competent performance must be demonstrated across a range of:

- *Successful achievement both by oneself and through organising others.*
- *Documents processed:*
  paying-in slips; standing orders and direct debits; bank drafts; cheques; statements.
- *Services and transactions:*
  payments for goods and services; cash analysis; foreign currency and traveller's cheques.

Personal action plan 13 relates to this work.

CHAPTER 6

Secretarial support services

Secretarial support services can range from organising complex itineraries to recommending staff for WP training, or from organising a conference abroad for a hundred people, to taking the minutes of a meeting. This chapter is divided into four sections covering the following:

- appointments;
- text processing;
- travel and accommodation;
- meetings, conferences and exhibitions.

Careful planning of work schedules in general is an art, especially when there is an international dimension to complicate procedures with time differences and language barriers. Planning ensures that workloads are controlled and spread evenly, and that priorities are set and goals achieved on time. Remember:

- Use lists to keep a record of tasks to be done, with deadlines and final deadline.
- Forward plan: estimate the time involved to complete elements of tasks.
- Plan each day and assess priorities:
  - urgent
  - important
  - not urgent.
- Make use of planning aids such as diaries, card racks, etc.

An illustration of a visual planning system for scheduling tasks is given in Fig 6.1.

APPOINTMENTS

If appointment planning aids such as diaries, electronic diaries, year planners and follow-up files are to be effective, the four 'W' questions should always be asked:

- *What* is the meeting and what shall I record?
- *Where* is the meeting and where shall I record it?
- *When* is the meeting and when shall I record it?
- *Why* is the meeting happening, i.e. purpose?

Checklist for making appointments

- *Basic details*
  Obtain names, addresses, telephone numbers, venues, times, durations and subject to be discussed.

Fig 6.1 A visual planning system

- *Confirmation*
  This may involve oral and written confirmation to those involved, especially if abroad.

- *Routine*
  Avoid blocking out time when your boss deals with routine matters, e.g. first thing on a Monday morning when there is usually a departmental morning meeting to assess targets for the coming week.

- *If in doubt . . .*
  Make provisional appointments and confirm when definite.

- *The absence factor*
  Avoid appointments immediately on return of boss or participants from business trips or holiday.

- *Cancellation*
  If appointments have to be cancelled for unforeseen reasons, let the participants know as soon as possible, apologise and rearrange.

- *Buffer time*
  Do not overload the diary. Take into account travel to and from appointments and allow for meetings to overrun.

- *Electronic diary*
  Always confirm entries made in electronic diaries with participants. This is a good *aide-mémoire* for brought-forward work, follow-up correspondence and preparing an agenda for a meeting. It can save time when planning meetings if you can 'plug' into the availability of three or four people at once.

- *Conflict of appointments*
  Assess priorities and suggest alternatives if conflicts arise.

- *Refusing appointments*
  Always be polite but firm. State alternatives, agree options and confirm.

- *Keep records*
  They can be useful and may need to be transferred to files for reference or other diaries. This includes dates, addresses, holidays and days when out of the office.

PERSONAL ACTION PLAN 16

▶ How regularly do you confirm diary activities with your boss?

▶ How do you deal with:
  a) double bookings;
  b) meetings running late and delaying other activities;
  c) insistent callers for appointments;
  d) persistent postponers?

▶ What administrative procedure do you follow when managing appointments? Is it computerised? How could you improve it?

TEXT PROCESSING

Text processing is an important element of the secretarial support service. It may involve any of the following office skills:

- typing;
- audio–typing;
- shorthand;
- word processing;
- desktop publishing.

An illustration of a text processing workstation with an IBM word processor is given in Fig 6.2.

The principal aims of a text processing service should be to prepare and produce documents which:

Fig 6.2 A text processing workstation

- are well presented at the time required;
- conform to the organisation's house style;
- are error-free, that is to say, that the documents are free of both typographical and factual errors and that any corrections are unobtrusive.

PERSONAL ACTION PLAN 17

▶ How can you develop your computer skills? Is this an area in which to specialise? Is your boss aware of your range of IT skills? How could your skills in IT lead to more management and senior-level responsibility?

▶ If your system breaks down what procedure do you follow?

▶ How do you assess your needs for updated software packages?

▶ Suggest three ways in which further IT training would enhance the business in which you work.

The text-processing supervisor

The secretary working in the capacity of a text-processing supervisor has the following responsibilities:

1 For controlling the quality and quantity of output:
 (a) setting standards;
 (b) monitoring and recording performance;
 (c) diagnosing causes of failure and taking preventive action for the future;
 (d) arranging work schedules to accommodate changing priorities.

2 For controlling and supporting staff:
 (a) counselling;
 (b) training and induction;
 (c) dealing with grievances;
 (d) taking appropriate action to reduce lateness and absenteeism and dealing with human relations problems;
 (e) advising management on:
 - job evaluation;
 - job design;
 - foreign language requirements;
 - performance appraisal;
 - remuneration;
 - promotion;
 - recruitment and selection of new staff;
 - redundancies;
 (f) following and implementing security and confidentiality procedures by backing up files, i.e. making copies of system disks and application program disks and restricting access to the hardware (locking doors) and to the software (using passwords).

3 For controlling the workplace environment:
 (a) layout of workstations;
 (b) tidiness and orderliness;
 (c) good housekeeping;
 (d) physical conditions, i.e. lighting, heating, ventilation.

4 For controlling the equipment and materials:
 (a) disk/tape management;
 (b) maintenance and servicing of equipment;
 (c) dealing with equipment faults;
 (d) following and implementing safe working practices;
 (e) requisitioning materials, using them economically and monitoring supplies regularly to ensure adequate stock levels.

The training cycle

A large part of the supervisory role in text processing will involve planning and implementation of further training, anticipating needs and fulfilling them cost-effectively

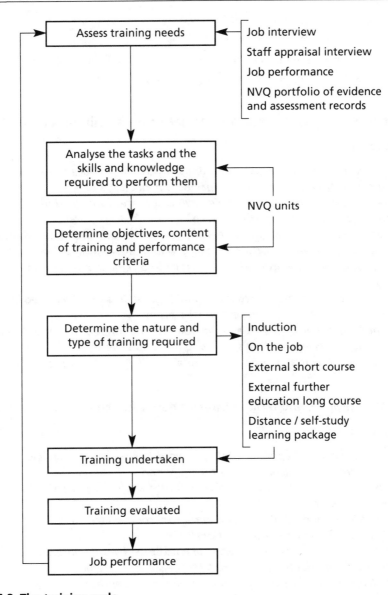

Fig 6.3 The training cycle

and in a way which is of benefit both to the company in commercial terms and to the individual in personal development terms.

What are the pointers signalling the need for training?

- slow and inaccurate text production;
- poor spelling, punctuation and layout;
- lack of initiative;
- failure to plan and organise work within deadlines;
- inability to adapt to new methods, equipment and systems;
- unsatisfactory keyboarding techniques;

- unsystematic management of disks;
- lack of familiarity with new software package.

The *NVQ Level 3 Administration Secretarial Standards* booklet gives the following performance criteria for preparing and producing documents.

Produce text from oral and written material using an alphanumeric keyboard

Performance criteria

- *Error-free documents of approximately 1500 words are produced in a 2½ hour working period from screen, manuscript and amended typescript.*
- *Error-free documents of approximately 1200 words are transcribed in a 2½ hour working period from pre-recorded speech.*
- *Error-free documents of approximately 300 words are composed and produced from brief notes and spoken instructions within a one hour working period.*
- *Any uncertainty in the source text is identified and remedied so that the intended meaning is conveyed.*
- *The presentation conforms to organisational housestyle and/or accepted conventions.*
- *Equipment faults are dealt with or reported promptly.*
- *Work schedules are arranged to accommodate changing priorities and deadlines.*
- *Safe working practices are always followed and implemented.*
- *Security and confidentiality procedures are always followed and implemented.*

Present narrative, graphic and tabular information using an alphanumeric keyboard

Performance criteria

- *Error-free documents of approximately 300 words are compiled from a variety of sources and produced in a one hour working period.*
- *Any uncertainty in the source material is identified and remedied so that the intended meaning is conveyed.*
- *Narrative, graphic and tabular styles and formats conform to organisational house style and/or accepted presentation conventions.*
- *All deadlines are met or delays reported and accepted by the principal.*
- *The information produced correctly reflects the source material.*
- *Safe working practices are always followed and implemented.*
- *Security and confidentiality procedures are always followed and implemented.*

These are nationally-recognised standards which may be used as a basis for setting objectives and performance measures.

Professional Text Production Plus by Margaret Cashin and Diana Jones (Pitman Publishing, 1994) contains text production material for use in the languages of several European countries.

PERSONAL ACTION PLAN 18

▶ How effective are you as a text processing supervisor? Against what criteria do you judge your performance? Are you still thinking and acting like a manager at all times?

How does your work as a supervisor set a good example to your juniors?

▶ Consider your counselling skills:
  Do juniors ask you for help and advice?
  Are you approachable?
  Are you a good listener?
  How do you deal with grievances from colleagues/juniors?

▶ How could you improve your supervisory skills? Can you identify someone who could assist you in developing this important management skill?

TRAVEL AND ACCOMMODATION

Systems and procedures

The key to successful travel and accommodation arrangements is planning and access to up-to-date information. Checklists here are vital to the PA's efficiency, as are reference books and sources of information.

The following is a detailed checklist for arranging travel abroad. The same list can be reduced or adapted for inland road and rail travel.

Checklist for travel abroad

Initial steps

- Agree dates for visit and enter in diary. Do the dates coincide with public holidays in foreign countries? Will some businesses be closed?
- Book airline tickets. Take passenger reference numbers where possible to speed up the process of changing plans/flights.
- Arrange insurance (if applicable).
- Book hotels. Negotiate a rate. Select a hotel based on previous use or recommendation. Confirm any special room requirements, hotel amenities, distance from meeting venue.
- Arrange medical preparations, if necessary, such as vaccinations, first aid kit.
- Check that the passport is current.
- Arrange meetings/appointments abroad. Take care not to overbook. Allow for travel time, jet lag, time differences and allow for any entertainment time.
- Visiting cards. Check if any foreign language printing is needed.
- Obtain any market information required.
- Arrange for executive to be met or for car hire.
- Check international driving licence permit is valid if required.
- Provide useful basic language phrases for executive to learn to greet and bid farewell if his or her language skills are limited. Will a translation service be required there? If so, have some examples and try to make contact with one to brief them in advance.
- Liaise with sister office in market of proposed trip, if there is one, for valuable market information or cultural differences/nuances to be aware of.

One week before visit

- Check receipt of:
  - tickets

  - insurance
  - visa (if necessary)
  - driving permit, if required.
- Confirm hotel booking.
- Order traveller's cheques and currency. Agree executive's requirements concerning traveller's cheques, currency and credit cards.
- Prepare itinerary.
- Organise transport to airport outward bound.

One to two days before departure

- Collect traveller's cheques and currency.
- Give executive or confirm that he or she has:
  - tickets
  - insurance
  - vaccination certificate
  - passport and visa
  - traveller's cheques
  - currency
  - itinerary
  - hotel information
  - confirmation of booking
  - hotel voucher
  - driving permit
  - confirmation of transport arrangements
  - files, documentation/presentations for meetings and appointments
  - stationery where applicable, business cards, company credit/charge cards, gifts.
- Discuss any outstanding work to be handled in executive's absence.

On return

- Follow up on the quality of:
  - hotel
  - flight
  - entertainment/venues.
- Follow up action points from meetings.
- Make sure that reports are written, and that people are contacted.
- File useful points of cultural interest for future reference.
- Check exchange rate and preparation of expenses.
- File trip information and itinerary for reference.
- Discuss any changes for future trips.

Checklist for preparing an itinerary

The itinerary for a trip can be complex or simple, dependent on the trip itself and the detail the executive likes to see.

- Use paper that is of a size that the executive can refer to easily.
- Make a note of special data/reservations, such as non-smoking or special meal requirements which have been made.
- Allow for transfer time between airports/hotels/railway stations.

- Allow for changes in timetables, time differences between countries.
- Always record:
  - name of traveller
  - individual dates
  - departure and arrival times of plane/train/car, including check-in times and flight numbers
  - hotel names, addresses, telephone numbers, fax and telex numbers and contact names if known
  - business/company names, addresses, telephone and fax numbers and name of contact
  - to avoid confusion, use 24-hour clock.
- Keep more than one copy of the itinerary and distribute it to colleagues who need to know the movements of your boss.

Tips for arranging trips

- Hotels, service bureaux and travel agencies: maintain a good relationship with them. Develop a rapport. Keep records of agreements and brochures.
- Organising entertainment: tailor this to the client's needs/interests. Use local knowledge where possible.
- If making plans in a foreign language, check, check and double check.

PERSONAL ACTION PLAN 19

▶ **What challenges/pitfalls do you encounter when arranging travel abroad?**

▶ **Examine your own travel and accommodation systems. How efficient are they? Could they be picked up and used easily in your absence?**

▶ **Do you discuss with your boss his/her specific travel and accommodation needs sufficiently? How could you improve your communication in this area?**

▶ **Do you use any computerised services in organising travel and accommodation? Would you benefit from more use of them? Why?**

MEETINGS, CONFERENCES AND EXHIBITIONS

'Meeting' simply means an encounter, by chance or arranged. At its more complex level it is a formal gathering of individuals with specific information/skills to decide on particular matters by means of procedures and interaction, in other words, teamwork.

A survey of the activities of senior managers in manufacturing industry revealed that as much as 50 per cent of their time is spent in meetings and discussions. It is reasonable to assume that their secretaries will also be involved in meetings for a considerable amount of this time. Meetings are very expensive in terms of time and resources, and every effort should be made to reduce the number of meetings held and the amount of time devoted to them. Meetings do, however, serve a number of useful purposes, for example:

- to inform;
- to arrive at decisions to be implemented;
- to consult others on proposed strategies and policies;

ITINERARY FOR MR P JONES
14–17 October 199 –

Tuesday, 14 October

Check-in:	London Heathrow Terminal 2	1000
Depart:	Heathrow (Flight AF811)	1135
Arrive:	Paris Charles de Gaulle	1340

Hotel: Penta Hotel
               10 rue Baudin, Pl Charras,
               F-92400 Courbevoie, Paris
               Tel: 4788 5051
               Telex: 610 470   Fax: 4768 8332

Appointment with Mr M Petrescou at hotel   1600

Wednesday, 15 October

Marketing Conference   0930–
at Chambre de Commerce et d'Industrie   1700
2 Rue de Viarmes, 75001 Paris
Tel: 4508 3685   Fax: 4508 3580

Dinner at hotel with Mr E Delbaere   1930

Thursday, 16 October

Check-in:	Charles de Gaulle Airport	0915
Depart:	Paris (Flight LH 1745)	1045
Arrive:	Frankfurt	1205

Hotel: Sheraton
               Flughafen, Frankfurt
               Tel: 069 6977-0
               Telex: 841 418924
               Fax: 069 69772209

International Book Fair   1400–
Reineckstrasse 3, Frankfurt   1800

Friday, 17 October

Check-in:	Frankfurt Airport	0950
Depart:	Frankfurt (Flight BA903)	1120
Arrive:	Heathrow (Terminal 1)	1200

Fig 6.4 An example of an itinerary

- to pool and exchange ideas and opinions; determine and agree solutions;
- to plan and monitor tasks/workloads;
- to train personnel;
- to negotiate agreements in pay and conditions of service, for example with unions, staff associations, etc.;
- to investigate occurrences – for example, the cause of an accident;
- to comply with statutory requirements as laid down, for example, in the Companies Act 1985 to hold an annual general meeting of shareholders.

Types of meeting

There are many types of meeting and these fall into two categories, 'formal' or 'informal'.

Formal meetings are those which are prescribed by law, standing orders or constitution and include:

- annual general meetings of shareholders;
- extraordinary general meetings;
- board meetings;
- standing committees, etc.

They are conducted in a formal manner, with decision-making by resolutions in accordance with a prescribed agenda and held on specified dates.

Informal meetings do not require the formalities and procedures involved in formal meetings. Word of mouth may prevail in organising and discussing an agenda. Written material may only be used at the end, when action necessary is agreed or dissemination of agreed information is conveyed to all involved in the meeting. Executive meetings, staff meetings, advisory committees and working party meetings will normally be informal to allow participants to contribute freely without having to adhere to a rigid procedure.

Official roles at formal meetings

Chairperson/chairman/chair

Appointed by the meeting or a superior body to control the conduct of the meeting. The appointment of a chairperson is set out in the meeting constitution or articles.

Responsibilities

- To prepare for the meeting:
  - authorise agenda for distribution to members;
  - be familiar with procedures.
- To open the meeting and manage its proceedings and keep order. The chairperson must be punctual and insist on punctuality in others. If the chairperson is five minutes late for a meeting attended by twenty people, you waste one hundred minutes of people's time!
- To keep the discussion within prescribed limits and allow all points of view to be aired.
- To welcome and state the purpose of the meeting. To provide apologies for absence and approval of minutes of the last meeting.
- To deal with points of order.

- To follow the agenda within time constraints.
- To state the issues clearly, insist that all contributors stick to the point under discussion, and to sum up at the end of each discussion topic.
- To guide discussions, ensure agreements and to make decisions by passing resolutions or amendments.
- To take a vote or poll and declare a result.
- To adjourn meetings.
- To sign the minutes.
- To close or postpone meetings and to give dates for future meetings.

The role of a chairperson requires considerable abilities to lead and control a meeting. Rules and procedures govern the actions of the chairperson, who is not always free to respond to situations in the way he or she would like. Formal procedures may constrain such responses. The chairperson is normally appointed before the meeting takes place and has the opportunity to prepare for it.

Vice-chair

A vice-chair may be appointed but has no particular official role unless the chairperson is absent, when he or she will take the chair.

Convenor

The person authorised to call a meeting.

Ex officio member

A person who is a member of a committee by virtue of office.

Proxy

A person appointed to attend a meeting and vote on behalf of a member who is unable to attend.

Secretary

This is a very important role since the secretary carries out all the administration and communication functions associated with the meeting by handling documents and records. The secretary is responsible for practical arrangements for organising a meeting. The secretary must have administrative and organisational skills, as well as good listening skills and the ability to summarise information effectively. A departmental secretary is seen in Fig 6.5 taking the minutes of a meeting.

Responsibilities

Before the meeting

1 Prepare notice of the meeting and the agenda in consultation with the chairperson. Distribute agenda to members.

Fig 6.5 A departmental secretary taking the minutes of a meeting

2 Prepare chairperson's agenda.
3 Book meeting room and any visual aids/flip charts required.
4 Obtain statements and documents from members who will not be present but who have a strong view to be discussed.
5 Collect items for the meeting:
stationery, paper, shorthand notebook
spare copies of the agenda
minutes of the previous meeting
all relevant papers/files required during meeting
attendance register and letters of apology
any books of reference, standing orders.

During the meeting

1 Prepare the meeting room and any direction signs required.
2 Prepare seating arrangements.
3 Supply stationery and notepads.
4 Check that members sign the attendance register.
5 Read the minutes of the last meeting, letters of apology and any other correspondence.
6 Supply information from files as required.
7 Record details of decisions made, details of motions proposed and seconded and the results of the voting.

8 Prompt the chairperson as to whether the meeting is being conducted in accordance with the constitution or meeting procedure.

9 As observer/recorder of the meeting, the secretary does not take a direct part in the discussions.

After the meeting

1 Return all documents to the office.

2 Prepare the draft minutes for approval by the chairperson.

3 When approved, type the minutes in final form and distribute to members.

4 Type any correspondence resulting from the meeting.

5 File papers from the meeting.

6 Confirm the date of the next meeting with the chairperson and other members.

Teller

Person who counts the votes at a meeting ballot.

Treasurer

The treasurer is involved when a meeting is responsible for the receipt and payment of money. Duties include:

- preparation and presentation of financial reports;
- advice and information to the meeting on financial matters;
- submission of audited accounts.

Checklist for making meetings meaningful with minimum cost

- Organise meetings systematically to ensure that nothing is overlooked – a meeting control sheet, as illustrated in Fig 6.8, provides a useful checklist of action to be taken.
- Never bring people together for a meeting if a series of telephone calls or teleconferencing (*see* page 29) will serve the purpose. Consider alternative means of communication; for example, if the communication is one way and there is no need for discussion, a simple memo may be adequate and certainly much cheaper.
- Call meetings only when business justifies it. If the chairperson has the authority to take action on behalf of the meeting, this can be helpful in reducing the number of meetings held.
- The preparation of comprehensive meeting papers with proposals can reduce meeting time.
- Setting up smaller meetings with fewer participants, for example subcommittees or working parties to investigate and report on areas of concern, is often a more efficient and cheaper method.
- Make sure that the agenda is clear and that the items of business will not be misunderstood. Unnecessary time can be taken up when there is confusion and lack of clarity over agenda items.
- See that the agenda reaches the participants in sufficient time for it to be read and considered before the meeting takes place.
- Ensure that your oral contributions to meetings are effective, for example:
  - organise your thoughts before you speak – if necessary, prepare brief notes covering the main points of your contribution;

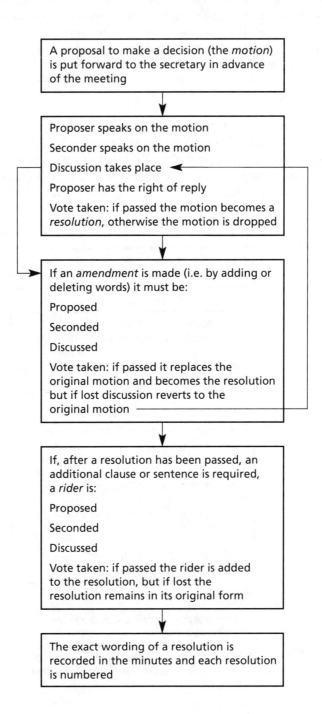

Fig 6.6 Procedures for making decisions at formal meetings

- present your ideas logically and clearly;
- keep to the point, avoid unnecessarily long explanations and conclude your remarks with a recapitulation of the main points of your argument and contribution;
- be courteous, polite and respect other people's points of view and arguments;
- be a patient listener, do not interrupt before a speaker has finished and wait for the chairperson to invite you to make your contribution.

If the secretary can make meetings more efficient, they will certainly be more enjoyable and productive. You will have released staff from unproductive meetings so that their time and yours is used more profitably. You will also have succeeded in increasing the rate of decision-making in your organisation and, as a result, improved staff health and morale as well as efficiency.

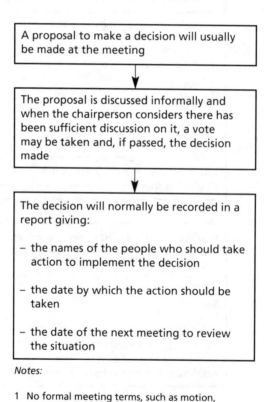

A proposal to make a decision will usually be made at the meeting

The proposal is discussed informally and when the chairperson considers there has been sufficient discussion on it, a vote may be taken and, if passed, the decision made

The decision will normally be recorded in a report giving:

- the names of the people who should take action to implement the decision

- the date by which the action should be taken

- the date of the next meeting to review the situation

Notes:

1 No formal meeting terms, such as motion, resolution, are used.

2 There are no formal procedures for making the decision involving proposers, seconders, right of reply, etc.

Fig 6.7 Procedures for making decisions at informal meetings

MEETING CONTROL SHEET

Subject _____   Starting time _____

Date _____   Duration approx. _____

People to contact

Ext/Tel No	Name	Proposed dates/times	Comment/notes

Refreshments

Coffee: _____

Tea: _____

Lunch: _____

Notified:

_____

Paperwork/action

Agenda completed: _____

Sent out: _____

Minutes completed: _____

Sent out: _____

Other items: _____

Rooms

Own office: _____

Boardroom: _____

Lecture room.: _____

Other: _____

Outside: _____

Name of contact/number: _____

Booked: _____

Confirmed: _____

Special requirements: _____

Equipment: _____

Refreshments: _____

Parking: _____

Any follow-up action

_____

Action after meeting:

_____

Reception/switchboard informed:

_____

Fig 6.8 Meeting control sheet

Agenda

An example of an agenda for a committee meeting is given in Fig 6.9.

SYLVAN LIMITED

SAFETY COMMITTEE MEETING

A meeting of the Safety Committee will be held in the Boardroom on Friday, 6 October 199 – , at 1030.

AGENDA

1 Apologies for absence.
2 Minutes of the last meeting.
3 Matters arising from the minutes.
4 Safety Officer's Progress Report.   Paper attached
5 New European Regulations and Codes of Practice for health and safety.
6 Eyesight tests for VDU operators.
7 First-aid courses.
8 Layout and design of workstations in new office extension.
9 Any other business.
10 Date of next meeting.

LAWRENCE REYNOLDS
Safety Officer

Fig 6.9 An example of a committee meeting agenda

Checklist for compiling an agenda

- The notice convening the meeting must contain the date, time and venue.
- List the agenda items in the order in which they are to be taken at the meeting.
- Discuss and agree the agenda items with the chairperson, taking account of:
  - recurring items from the previous agenda, such as apologies for absence, minutes of the last meeting, matters arising from the minutes, any other business, date of next meeting, etc.;

- continuing items from the previous minutes;
- constitutional items, for example to approve accounts;
- requests for items from the chairperson and members.
- Send the agenda to the participants by the prescribed date to give them adequate notice, as laid down in the constitution.
- Prepare the chairperson's agenda with more information than is given to the ordinary agenda and with spaces for note-taking. The additional information assists the chairperson in conducting the meeting efficiently – for example, names of members who have sent apologies for absence, any matters arising from the minutes and any information which has to be considered when reaching decisions.

Minutes

An example of minutes for a committee meeting is given in Fig 6.10.

MINUTES OF MEETING

A meeting of the Safety Committee was held in the Boardroom on Friday, 6 October 199 – , at 1030.

Present:
Mrs C T Clarke	– Chairperson
Miss H Aziz	– Accounts
Mr W Davignon	– Research
Mr P H Donaldson	– Marketing
Mr C Evans	– Production
Mrs G R Hubert	– Purchasing
Ms R K McGreggor	– Personnel
Mr P T Warner	– Training
Mr L Reynolds	– Safety Officer

ACTION

1 Apologies

An apology was received on behalf of Miss J R Kent (Secretarial Services) who was unwell.

2 Minutes

The minutes of the last meeting held on 4 September 199 – were taken as read and approved and were signed by the Chairperson.

3 Matters arising

The Safety Officer reported that the new 'no parking' signs had been erected in the road leading to the main staff car park.

4 Safety Officer's Progress Report

The Safety Officer's Progress Report was received and noted. Miss Aziz said that it would be useful if the inspections and follow-up action could be given publicity in the company's House Magazine. After discussion, it was agreed that the Safety Officer should pass this information on to the Editor of the House Magazine for publication.

Safety Officer

---

5 New European Regulations and Codes of Practice for health and safety	The Chairperson outlined the new regulations and codes of practice which come into operation on 1 January 199 – . In view of the importance of the changes, it was agreed to recommend a series of departmental meetings to disseminate the information to all staff. The Safety Officer was asked to agree dates with the Heads of Department during the next month.	Safety Officer
6 Eyesight tests for VDU operators	Mrs Hubert pointed out that, under the new regulations, employees could ask their employers to provide and pay for eyesight tests at regular intervals and also to provide spectacles if special ones were needed. It was agreed that this was a service which should be offered to the staff concerned and the Safety Officer was asked to make provision for this in next year's budget, and the Chairperson agreed to discuss the matter with the Personnel Manager.	Safety Officer Chairperson
9 Any other business	Mr Evans reported that he had received a complaint about the unsatisfactory cleaning of the Stores. He was asked to monitor the situation over the next 4 weeks and to report on the outcome to the Safety Officer.	Mr Evans Safety Officer
10 Date of next meeting	It was decided to hold the next meeting of the Committee on Friday, 3 November 199 – , at 1030.	

Chairperson

3 November 199 –

Fig 6.10 Extract from minutes of meeting (excluding items 7 and 8), *see* **Fig 6.9.**

Notes:
These are narrative minutes which record the decisions and the reasons leading to them. However, company formal meetings, such as annual general meetings, would normally use resolution minutes in which decisions are recorded by *resolutions*. For example, the following resolution recorded the decision reached at an annual general meeting of a building society:

Mr X proposed, Mrs Y seconded and it was resolved:
That the following amendments be made to the Memorandum of the Society:
'The Society may make advances secured on land in any member state outside the United Kingdom'.

Checklist for writing minutes

- If a formal meeting, record the exact wording of resolutions passed with the names of the proposers and seconders and the result of the voting. If an informal meeting, note the exact wording of decisions reached.
- Note the main arguments for and against the decisions, together with action required, when and by whom.

- During the meeting ask about any points which you do not understand or ask participants to repeat information which you have not heard clearly.
- Write the minutes as soon as possible after the meeting while the discussions are fresh in your mind.
- Write minutes wholly in the third person and in the past tense.
- Be brief without being ambiguous – a summary is required, not a verbatim record.
- Arrange the items in the same order as on the agenda.
- Prepare a draft for approval by the chairperson before printing the final copy.
- On approval, distribute the minutes to members, including those absent from the meeting.
- File the minutes in chronological order.

PERSONAL ACTION PLAN 20

▶ How efficient are the meetings that you organise? Rate them on a 1–10 scale. Explain your score and how you reached it. How could your meetings be made more 'time effective'?

▶ Consider your agenda and minutes. Do they require amendment? How often and why? How could you improve your skills in this area? How could the chairperson help you? Monitor your progress on a monthly basis.

▶ Would a colleague who had not been present at the meeting be fully conversant with what went on by reading your minutes? If not, you need guidance in extracting the key points, issues raised and agreements made at the meeting. Practise by writing a précis of an article written in the business section of a quality newspaper.

Conferences and exhibitions

The successful organisation of conferences and exhibitions depends on five factors:

1 Feasibility.
2 Planning – to free you to cope with 'the unexpected'.
3 Costing.
4 Follow-up.
5 Attention to detail. This is essential for success, and you should pay attention to the 'small print' from the start: choice of venue; timetabling; getting to know people and deciding on accountability all ensure success.

Checklist for organising a conference

- *Timing*
  Put together a critical path development plan for the conference outlining deadlines for the different elements of the event (*see* Fig 6.11). This technique determines the critical elements in a project so that the total project can be completed on time. Activities and timing for each step are plotted in order to calculate the total completion time of the whole project. These critical path development plans, which may be computerised, can be highly complex

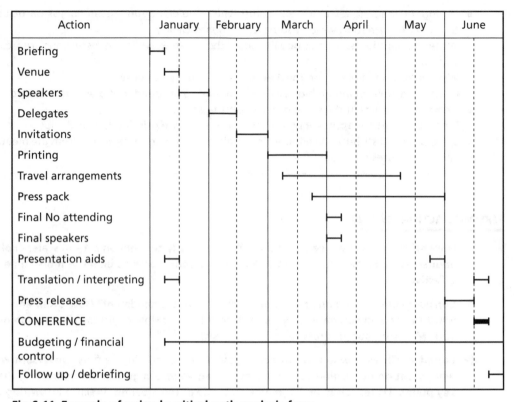

Action	January	February	March	April	May	June
Briefing						
Venue						
Speakers						
Delegates						
Invitations						
Printing						
Travel arrangements						
Press pack						
Final No attending						
Final speakers						
Presentation aids						
Translation / interpreting						
Press releases						
CONFERENCE						
Budgeting / financial control						
Follow up / debriefing						

Fig 6.11 Example of a simple critical path analysis form

and take into account the shortest, normal and longest possible timings. Critical path analysis tends to assume accurate predictions of time involved for each activity.

- *Costing*
  Prepare an estimate or budget to cover all conceivable expenses.
- *Programme*
  Agree the title and content of the programme.
  Provide drafts and obtain approval.
  Organise printing and proofreading.
  Distribute to potential participants.
  Organise publicity both internally and externally.
- *Venue*
  Select and book the venue according to requirements and within the budget figures. Consider the 'internal' versus 'external' argument. This will depend on the number of delegates, costs, aims in having an external venue (e.g. to avoid interruptions from the office, PR exercise), presentation aids available, availability of outside speakers.
  When planning conferences abroad, where possible, try to plan a reconnaissance trip to the venue to discuss plans face to face, make contact and avoid any unfortunate surprises at the conference itself.
  Make arrangements for:
  – catering: coffee, sherry, lunch, tea, etc.
  – cloakroom facilities
  – room decoration, flowers, etc.

- direction signs.
  Confirm final numbers.
- *Speakers*
  Confirm invitations and subject matter.
  Send programme and agree timing and presentation requirements.
  Discuss travel arrangements.
  Arrange hotel accommodation, if required.
  Letter of thanks and fee.
- *Financial matters*
  Calculate conference fee based on estimated costs.
  Determine minimum number of delegates required for break-even and for profit.
  Check booking levels regularly.
  Record bank receipts.
  Record expenses and file documentary evidence.
- *Presentation aids*
  Order lectern, microphones, projectors, video recorders, etc.
  Set up equipment and check that it works.
  Return equipment to suppliers.
- *Delegates*
  Compile delegates list with their names, companies and positions.
  Prepare and present delegate pack: folders and badges.
  Hosting arrangements and any entertaining.
- *Literature and merchandise*
  Book stands.
  Order forms and invoices.
- *Press*
  Invitations.
  Press packs/releases.
  Press desk.
- *Staff*
  Briefing.
  Accountability.
  Presentation.
  Debriefing.
- *Foreign-language requirements*
  Translation services.
  Interpreters.
- *Review of conference*
  Lessons learnt.
  Prepare statement to show estimated costs versus actual.
  Returns: profit/loss.

The two developments in meeting technology, teleconferencing and videoconferencing facilities (referred to on page 29), should be considered as options when the secretary is planning a conference or meeting.

ORGANISING SOCIAL FUNCTIONS

Whether you are involved in organising a dinner, an opening ceremony or retirement celebration, a social function is another good opportunity for you to display your organisational skills and provide positive PR for yourself and your company. The same rules and attention to detail apply as for organising a conference.

The key to success lies in organising an event that is appropriate to the person/product involved – in other words, 'match the mood to the crowd'!

Checklist for organising a social event

- Set and agree:
  - the budget
  - the date
  - the venue.
- Prepare invitation cards.
- Select the guests.
- Determine the menu and any special requirements, e.g. vegetarians.
- Arrange for entertainment, dancing, etc.
- Order gifts, cards.
- Record expenses.
- Arrange for speeches.
- Consider a charity element.
- Arrange for flowers/decorations.
- Follow-up/feedback on venue, meal, etc. – keep for future reference.
- Costs: compare actual against estimated.

EXAMINE YOUR KNOWLEDGE

1 You are PA/secretary to Mrs Catherine Walsh (Case Study 1).

a) Explain the advantages and disadvantages of a computerised diary system.

b) How would you avoid the problems of Mrs Walsh putting appointments in her personal diary and not telling you about them?   (*LCCI PESD*)

2 You are secretary to Mr Patrick Moreland (Case Study 2). A new satellite linking London and Malaysia is to be launched on 5 October. You have been requested to arrange a celebratory buffet luncheon at the London Headquarters. It is suggested that an *ad hoc* committee be set up to assist you, and a representative from each section will attend the first meeting.

a) Explain the purposes of an *ad hoc* committee. List the preparations you will make for the first meeting and draft an agenda.

b) Draft a suitable formal invitation to the celebratory luncheon and list 3 reference books you might use to assist you in preparing the invitation list. Give details of why you would choose each book.

c) List the records which should be kept when organising such a function.

d) Describe the preparations you will make to arrange a video conference linking up offices in this country, and why would this method of a meeting be preferable to holding a meeting at Head Office?

e) As you will be absent for the video conference, prepare a checklist for your assistant on how to take and write the minutes.   *(LCCI PESD)*

3 You are personal assistant to Mrs Sylvia Fairbanks (Case Study 4). Draft the minutes from the notes supplied in Figs 6.12–6.14.   *(PEI ASP)*

4 You are secretary to Mr Patrick Moreland (Case Study 2). You have been asked to accompany Mr Moreland on a visit overseas. He has been invited to help organise a new office and attend several business and social events. He will be expected to return the hospitality shown to him.

a) What travel arrangements will you make for the visit?

b) How can you help Mr Moreland in promoting the company?   *(LCCI PESD)*

5 For a 1000 appointment 2 visitors arrive but the name of only 1 person is recorded in your diary.

a) Explain how you would cope with this situation.

b) How would you avoid this occurring in the future?   *(LCCI PESD)*

6 Mr Davies and Mr Dempsey will complete 25 years' service with Comlon in November this year. You have been asked to organise a dinner to recognise this achievement. It is intended that both these directors will receive a gift from the Company and these will be presented during the social event.
Explain the procedures you will adopt before and after the event.   *(LCCI PESD)*

7 Meetings can be very time-consuming. How can chairmen ensure that meetings in Comlon are cost-effective?   *(LCCI PESD)*

8 Mr Landers is interested in using videoconferencing for regular meetings of Comlon International plc. Write a memo to Mr Landers describing videoconferencing and listing the advantages and disadvantages of using such a system.   *(LCCI PESD)*

9 Mr R C Maidment, the managing director, has arranged a trip to the United States offices in one week's time but is suddenly taken ill. Mrs Forster is asked to undertake the trip instead. What arrangements will you make for Mrs Forster?   *(LCCI PESD)*

10 The secretary you have appointed to undertake your assistant's work during her absence on maternity leave has no experience of using the WordPerfect word processing software package, although she is familiar with Word. Devise and plan appropriate training sessions for her to learn the new software package.

These are the notes from last week's Safety Committee Mtg. which I attended when you were off sick

I hadn't done this sort of thing before and I don't take shorthand. As you can see I'm not much of a Typist either but I have had a go on the Word processor!! These seemed to be the main points discussed. Mrs F. also gave me her agenda and I'm attaching it also. Please excuse poor typing and you'd better check my spelling!!

Martina Smith

Notes from safety committee

The attached list tells you who attended. A sheet was passed round the table during the meething. I hope I have managed to make our their signatures!

Someone also gave apologies for Jane Robertson from Catering (I can't remember who − does it matter?)

They were talking about the shortfall in signing up departmental Safety Reps. I think it was on the agenda for the last meeting, but it appears that all departments now have a rep.

They talked about accident statistics and there was a 30% improvement as compared with the same time last year. It seems that we are now better than national figures for the industry but Bob Charles was going on about the fact that they would have to be better still if we wanted to be in the running to receive a commendation for good practise.

Re the Blood donor Unit TUES and wed seemed best and Mrs F was going to confirm this. Its First Aid course time again and programme outlines were passed round − safety reps to bring to notice of their depts. and let Bob C know names of volunteers.

No other business was discussed and the next meeting is to be on22 May.

Hope this makes sense to you.

Fig 6.12

SAFETY COMMITTEE MEETING

Attendance Register

Name	Department
F Mason	Electrical
M Hamid	Stores
J Bosch	Computing
M James	Production
A Murphy	Sales
C Carr	Production
S Fairbanks	Personnel
A France	Production
B Charles	Safety Officer

Fig 6.13

NOTICE OF MEETING

There will be a meeting of the Safety Committee in the Main Committee Room on Tuesday, 7 February 19.. at 1400 hours.

S. Fairbanks
Chairman

AGENDA

1. Apologies for absence
   + P Jackson (Accounts)
) D Khan (Transport)
)

2. Minutes of the previous meeting
   + S Colby (Sales) omitted from
) last minutes and she attended
)

3. Matters arising from the Minutes
   + All depts now have an
) elected safety representative
)
)

4. Accident Report
   (Annex 1)
   + Ask Bob Charles to comment
)
)
) 1st week in March for 2 days
)

5. Mobile Blood Donor Unit
   + Do we have a preference for
) particular days?
)

6. First Aid Courses
   (Paper to be tabled)
)
)
)

7. Any Other Business
)
)
)

8. Date of next meeting
   + later in May rather than
   earlier?

Fig 6.14

WORK TASKS

Assessment of competence for Element 4.1
Arrange travel and accommodation

Performance criteria

- *Travel, accommodation, entertainment and personal requirements are identified.*
- *A clear and accurate itinerary, containing all the arrangements made, is compiled well before the date of departure.*
- *A proper balance is maintained between economy and the efficient use of time, in accordance with the organisation's rules and procedures.*
- *Selected bookings are correctly made and confirmed.*
- *Travel documents are obtained and checked, and any discrepancies identified and rectified.*
- *Credit transfers, currency and traveller's cheques are arranged correctly.*
- *Medical packs are arranged for overseas emergency and high risk areas.*
- *Safety practices are always followed and implemented.*
- *Security and confidentiality procedures are always followed and implemented.*

Range statement

Competent performance must be demonstrated across a range of:

- *Numbers and types of traveller:*
  individual; small group; large party; own principal; more senior staff; clients or customers.
- *Modes of travel:*
  road (including hire cars); rail; sea; air.
- *Destinations:*
  UK; European; intercontinental.
- *Accommodation types and requirements:*
  hotels; residential centres; overnight; meals only.
- *Health and Insurance requirements:*
  pre-travel vaccinations and medicines during travel; personal accident, baggage and car insurance.
- *Travel documents:*
  passport; visa; international driving licence.
- *Monetary requirements:*
  foreign currency; traveller's cheques; letters of credit; valid credit and charge cards.

Personal action plan 19 relates to these tasks.

Assessment of competence for Element 4.2
Plan and organise business visits

Performance criteria

- *Requirements for meetings with own and other organisations are established.*
- *All essential information is obtained and individual contacts are identified.*

- *Special arrangements for social or informal contacts are included in schedule.*
- *Visits are planned to operate within the prescribed time schedule.*
- *Unspecified events are allowed for in the programme.*
- *Arrangements for meetings are made and confirmed.*
- *A travel programme including the purpose and agenda for the visits is prepared and distributed in advance.*
- *Detailed meeting briefs for the principal are accurately prepared as directed.*
- *Safe working practices are always followed and implemented.*
- *Security and confidentiality procedures are always followed and implemented.*

Range statement

Competent performance must be demonstrated across a range of:

- *Destinations:*
  local; national; international.
- *Contacts:*
  internal and external to own organisation; informal activities as well as formal business meetings.
- *Travellers:*
  own principal; own principal together with colleagues from own organisation; own principal together with colleagues from associated organisations; visitors to own organisation.

Personal action plan 19 relates to these tasks.

Assessment of competence for Element 5.1
Produce text from oral and written material using an alphanumeric keyboard

The performance criteria for these tasks is given on page 92.

Range statement

Competent performance must be demonstrated across a range of:

- *Documents:*
  letters; memos; forms; envelopes; labels; display material; appropriate copies.
- *Language:*
  familiar and unfamiliar vocabulary; simple and complex grammatical structures.
- *Equipment:*
  manual, electric or electronic typewriters; word processors.
- *Contingencies:*
  the production times specified in the Performance Criteria include the usual pressures and interruptions, conflicts of demand and changes of priority experienced in a normal working environment.

Assessment of competence for Element 5.2
Present narrative, graphic and tabular information using an alphanumeric keyboard

The performance criteria for these tasks is given on page 92.

Range statement

Competent performance must be demonstrated across a range of:

- *Source materials:*
  some must include ambiguities and errors requiring investigation and correction.
- *Documents:*
  combining narrative text, graphics and tables.
- *Equipment:*
  manual, electric or electronic typewriters; word processors (including desktop publishing systems).

Personal action plans 17 and 18 relate to these tasks.

Assessment of competence for Element 7.1
Manage appointments

Performance criteria

- *Appointments are negotiated and agreed within given time constraints.*
- *Appointments are always confirmed.*
- *Essential information is entered in all relevant scheduling aids.*
- *Action notes are entered in all scheduling aids and progress monitored.*
- *Non-routine and emergency demands are dealt with promptly and effectively.*
- *Entries are kept up to date, legible and accurate.*
- *Safe working practices are always followed and implemented.*
- *Security and confidentiality procedures are always followed and implemented.*

Range statement

Competent performance must be demonstrated across a range of:

- *Scheduling aids:*
  pocket and desk diaries; personal organisers and visual planners; in manual or computerised form.
- *Degrees of initiative:*
  arranging appointments both on request and on one's own initiative; using scheduling aids to which one has open access and those controlled by others.
- *Contingencies:*
  the simultaneous management of the office and portable scheduling aids of two principals; conflicting demands including an urgent meeting to be arranged within twenty-four hours; dealing with a double booking; rescheduling a previously arranged

meeting involving at least three people; refusing a requested appointment.

- *Appointments:*
  internal and external meetings; involving at least five participants; some hosted and others attended by the principal.

Personal action plan 16 relates to this work.

Assessment of competence for Element 8.1
Organise and prepare for meetings

Performance criteria

- *All planning and booking procedures are carried out correctly and confirmed.*
- *Agenda items are agreed with the principal (or chair of the meeting).*
- *All papers are checked for relevance and accuracy; any errors are identified and corrected.*
- *Papers are despatched to participants in advance as directed.*
- *The principal (or chair of the meeting) is fully briefed prior to the meeting.*
- *Meeting rooms are fully prepared in advance.*
- *Audio-visual requirements are identified and the necessary equipment is provided in working order.*
- *Refreshments are ordered as directed.*
- *Safe working practices are always followed and implemented.*
- *Security and confidentiality procedures are always followed and implemented.*

Range statement

Competent performance must be demonstrated across a range of:

- *Types of meeting:*
  both formal and informal in style; chaired or hosted by at least two different individuals.
- *Participants:*
  involving both internal and external participants; at least once a minimum of ten participants.
- *Venues:*
  both on the organisation's own premises and at external venues.
- *Requirements:*
  including provision for participants with special physical or environmental needs; provision at short notice of materials and equipment.

Assessment of competence for Element 8.2
Administer and take notes of meetings

Performance criteria

- *All previously planned and booked arrangements are checked before the meeting.*
- *Remedial action is taken to meet changed or unforeseen requirements.*
- *Additional or spare papers are provided at the meeting as directed.*

- *The identity and designation of attenders and non-attenders are accurately recorded.*
- *Notes are taken which enable a sufficient and accurate record of the meeting.*
- *A formal record is transcribed which reflects the outcomes of the meeting.*
- *The formal record is checked for accuracy and approved by the principal (or chair of the meeting).*
- *Copies of the formal record are despatched to participants within the required timescales.*
- *Tasks delegated to others are accurately defined and monitored.*
- *Safe working practices are always followed and implemented.*
- *Security and confidentiality procedures are always followed and implemented.*

Range statement

Competent performance must be demonstrated across a range of:

- *Types of meeting:*
  both formal and informal in style; chaired or hosted by at least two different individuals.
- *Participants:*
  involving both internal and external participants; at least once a minimum of ten participants.
- *Venues:*
  both on the organisation's own premises and at external venues.
- *Requirements:*
  including provision for participants with special physical or environmental needs; provision at short notice of materials and equipment.
- *Contingencies:*
  emergency interruptions (e.g. illness, evacuation); urgent messages for participants; rescheduling start times/agenda/meals; extra copies of papers required at short notice; subsequent information requested by participants.

Personal action plan 20 relates to these tasks.

CHAPTER 7

Aspects of supervision

This chapter deals with supervision and particularly the supervisory role of the executive secretary. To supervise means 'to keep an authoritative watch over, to direct the work of another'. In other words, to manage.

Little has been written about the management role which the executive secretary currently plays in the office. This chapter outlines the key management areas and shows how the executive secretary can develop and utilise these skills. The four key ingredients to the management cocktail are:

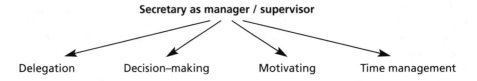

Fig 7.1 Essentials of management

In the international environment of business today, an executive secretary has an important responsibility to communicate effectively in English, and increasingly in other languages, both within the organisation and as a representative to clients. The secretary is both carrying out secretarial tasks successfully and acting as an unrecognised manager. Much time is spent in organising and motivating colleagues, bosses or juniors to carry out their tasks successfully. The management potential of the executive secretary still needs to be recognised by senior management. Secretaries must therefore 'market' themselves to bosses in order to gain this recognition.

PERSONAL ACTION PLAN 22

▶ **Do you think and act like a manager at all times – in the way you present yourself, carry out tasks, delegate responsibility and relate to work colleagues?**

▶ **What kind of image do you project in the workplace?**

▶ **Assess the personal contribution you make to the way in which your office services and operations are managed, and discuss your findings and recommendations with your boss or departmental head. Consider the following aspects:**
  • **quality, quantity, cost and resource requirements;**
  • **organisational policy, practices and procedures;**
  • **health and safety legislation;**
  • **employment and other legal requirements;**
  • **customer requirements and expectations;**

- **objectives and performance measures;**
- **environmental constraints.**

A positive self-image and appropriate self-projection are keys to successful supervisory management. If an executive secretary presents a sloppy personal image, this could (and often does) extend to the calibre and quality of work and lack of respect from others. Even if work is good but presentation is sloppy, it is more likely that a secretary will be noted for unkempt looks than for good work. Work may be perceived to be sloppy due to a powerful message being communicated by a careless personal appearance – a sad yet all too often true reflection of reality. The smart, professionally presented secretary gives out completely different signals, and will be perceived and treated differently. Minimal efforts to improve image can reap great professional rewards. So get smart! Use 'psychology in the workplace' to your advantage and instil it in your juniors. Their success will reflect on you too.

THE SUPERVISOR'S ROLE

The executive secretary will normally expect to have the supervisory responsibilities of planning, organising, monitoring and controlling the work of junior secretaries and other office employees. For example, in *Secretarial Case Studies* by John Harrison and Marion Leishman (Pitman Publishing), the Southern Area Administrator and Secretary to the Area Manager of the Industrial Society has the following supervisory responsibilities in her job description:

- to recruit, train and maintain the morale of the department's team of secretaries/course administrators;
- to be responsible for monitoring and organising the secretaries' workload;
- to be responsible for the secretaries'/course administrators' performance in supporting their advisers.

Standards of performance are acceptable when:

- An induction/training plan for new secretaries is planned prior to their arrival and fully briefed on day one in accordance with procedure notes.
- All course administration and other secretarial tasks are allocated fairly among the team.
- All secretaries have a job description and up-to-date targets which include a personal development target. Targets are to be discussed at least every four months.
- All appraisals are carried out by the due date, and appraisal forms are completed and passed to the appropriate advisers for completion within 48 hours of appraisal.
- Team meetings are held monthly.
- One-to-one interviews with secretaries are held at least monthly.
- Course and conference routines, including associated paperwork, are followed up, due dates are met and programmes printed accurately and on time.
- Disciplinary and complaint procedures are dealt with fairly and in accordance with procedure notes.

P W Betts, in his book *Supervisory Management* (Pitman Publishing), suggests that 'supervisors', managers and any others who are responsible for the work of people, at any level and in any type of organisation, should regard themselves as managers. Executive secretaries have such responsibilities and should regard themselves as managers, for they play an important role in the management structure of any organisation.

The secretary's role as supervisor will normally involve:

- Liaison with the personnel department on employment matters:
  - recruitment
  - engagement
  - training
  - appraisal/monitoring
  - promotion
  - redundancy
  - dismissal.

See Chapters 8 and 9 for further information.

- Staff relationships:
  - counselling
  - discipline
  - reprimands
  - grievances.
- Work production: controlling the quality and quantity of work output.
- Physical conditions: controlling the workplace environment.
- Equipment and materials:
  - controlling maintenance
  - controlling supplies and servicing
  - safe work practices.

See also the role of the text processing supervisor in Chapter 6.

DELEGATION

All office supervisors, indeed all secretaries/PAs, face a fundamental challenge in their work – they need to produce results beyond their individual capabilities. Success requires teamworking, motivating and delegating skills. They are tools for achieving results. Of the three communication skills mentioned, the ability to delegate is the most important, as it is a skill that defines a manager and a manager is someone who gets results, in other words, gets things done through people. As a secretary/PA, work is delegated to you, and work is therefore entrusted to your powers. You delegate when you ask an office junior to draft a reply to routine enquiries or when you ask your assistant to handle your duties when you are on holiday or sick.

Delegation is not just assigning work. It is assigning responsibility, autonomy and accountability. The secretary who has been delegated a task must exercise his or her judgement based on the circumstances. Delegation can produce better-quality and better-timed decisions, simply because if the secretary/PA delegates a task dealing with a specific situation, she or he will have a better 'feel' for the situation.

Objections to delegation

- 'My junior does not know what to do.'
- 'It would be quicker to do it myself.'
- 'The client expects me to be there and to do the work.'
- 'What if my assistant gets it wrong? I shall get the blame.'
- 'I am indispensable. The meeting could not go ahead without me.'
- 'I do not want her to have any responsibility. She might steal the limelight.'

Why delegate?

1 To improve business effectiveness and move decision-making responsibility to a different and often more appropriate level. Decisions can become out of date. By the time the background and basic facts concerning a situation pass through the channels, a situation can change. Time is wasted commentating on the changing situation rather than making a decision and acting on it.

2 To motivate others and create job satisfaction. By apportioning responsibility, a project or one area where a secretary/office junior can develop a niche or show a skill, a job becomes more satisfying and enjoyable. You open up other people's potential. This leads to creativity, new ideas and a positive working environment.

3 To improve management skills. Delegation is an interpersonal process. Delegation rather than ordering requires good communication skills and the ability to listen, and conveys trust, confidence and loyalty in other people. The challenge is made all the more complex if you are communicating in a foreign language. Determine tasks that are suitable for delegation, from the overall work responsibility point of view and from the point of view of the organisational benefit.

4 To develop decision-making skills. Delegation develops decision-making skills in the delegator and the individual delegated a task. The practical experience of making independent decisions about a 'live' situation has no substitute. The delegator must decide on which tasks to delegate, whether the candidate has the skills and potential to carry out the assignment, how to delegate a task and how much information to pass on. Becoming a good delegator is a learning process in itself. It is not easy to pass on responsibility but still be responsible should things go wrong. Select carefully to whom authority is delegated, with special regard to personal qualities and competence.

   The person with the task to fulfil must manage the situation and steer it to the right conclusion. She or he will need to gather information, consider its implications and make timely choices from available options – in other words, use their judgement. There may be a deadline involved. The secretary must estimate the work involved, pace energies and be motivated to fulfil the task, aided by the delegator.

5 To establish accountability for actions. As a delegator, the secretary must establish the accountability for the task. This will make it clear that the responsibility to accomplish the job lies with the delegatee. As a result the delegator must allow the secretary free rein to make necessary decisions. As part of the delegation process the smart executive secretary should also confirm that the credit for a successfully

completed task lies with the delegatee. This is positive motivation. If it is passed over it can create resentment and poor teamworking atmosphere, and thus affect results.

6 To improve time management. Delegation is the best way to free time for the more important duties. What routine tasks can be passed on to juniors or even delegated up? By delegating, you can concentrate on your key tasks, eliminate trivia, and plan, direct and organise your workload effectively.

PERSONAL ACTION PLAN 23

▶ For how many 'special projects' are you responsible? Suggest two areas for which you can have special responsibility where your own skills in receiving and sending correspondence will be developed. How can these be used as personal PR opportunities? Does your boss delegate to you the writing of correspondence? If not, why not?

▶ Suggest review times to assess your writing skills and to earmark projects/tasks where they can be utilised. How would this benefit you and your boss?

DECISION-MAKING

A typical business day is littered with instances of decision-making based on the needs, wants and desires of the secretary and boss concerned and the demands of the situation. The flow chart in Fig 7.2 sets out the principal stages and options in the process of making decisions. Choices are made from available options. Where good delegation technique is at the heart of the good manager, the ability to make the right decision to meet specific deadlines assists the process enormously.

Good decisions are based on:

- planning, setting objectives and retaining long-term goals in sight;
- knowledge and recognition of the options;
- assessment and evaluation of options set against objectives, and the withdrawal of obsolete options;
- experience;
- sound judgement;
- application of logic to a situation;
- balancing priorities;
- the element of 'gut feeling' for a situation.

Bad decisions are based on:

- lack of planning;
- short-term goal-setting;
- gut feeling alone;
- failure to investigate all the options;
- failure to recognise priorities;
- poor time management;
- the panic factor.

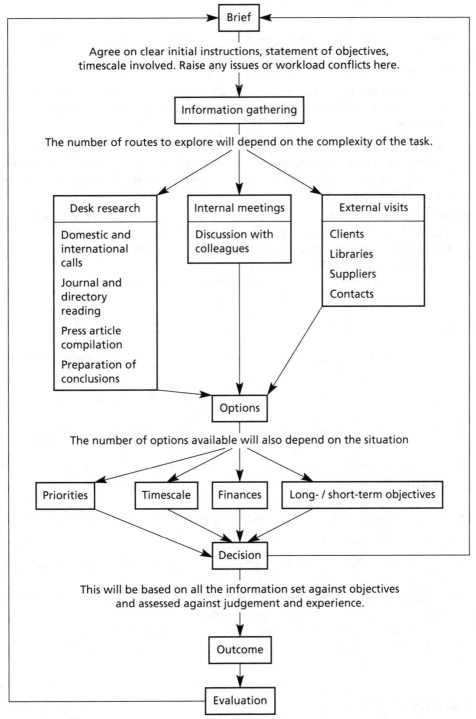

Fig 7.2 Flow chart of the decision-making process

▶ Good decision-making skills are developed by 'doing' and coping with real situations. Textbook learning cannot take the place of real life, although it can speed up the preparation for 'doing'.

▶ Consider the breakdown of your typical day. How many projects or tasks are you involved in which develop your decision-making ability, both as delegator and delegatee?

▶ Consider your boss. Does your boss plot the course of your working day to such a degree that you are gaining no new experience in your skills? If so, discuss this with him or her. Does your boss find it hard to delegate? Suggest specific projects you are capable of handling.

▶ When you delegate to a junior, does his or her performance meet with your expectations, exceed or fall below them? Why? What are the reasons for this? How could you enhance their performance, thereby improving your own management and communication skills?

TRAINING

Many of the problems in offices can be attributed to lack of training or inadequate instruction, such as:

- unsatisfactory communication by letters, memos, fax and the telephone;
- inaccurate data;
- delays in business transactions as a result of poor operating techniques in using computers, word processors, fax, telex, etc.;
- accidents caused by faulty machine operation or lack of knowledge about safety regulations;
- poor quality of work affecting the company's image and public relations;
- untidy and disorganised offices resulting in mislaid data and inefficiency.

Training has the following benefits:

- improved standards of work, resulting in greater accuracy, quality and speed of output;
- managers are able to delegate more of their administrative work to their trained staff;
- morale is improved and labour turnover reduced;
- staff are motivated and developed for work of a higher level;
- safety standards meet legal requirements;
- public relations are improved.

The secretary as trainer

Pointers to effective instruction in the training of office staff:

- *Define objectives clearly*
  Both instructor and trainee should know at the outset what they are aiming to

achieve. They should have a clear understanding of what they should know and be able to do at the end of each training session, as well as at the conclusion of the course of training.

- *Preparation*
Thorough preparation is essential. Devise a training plan, using the essential content of each training session. The material should be graded from the known to the unknown and arranged logically in short progressive steps in a sequence that takes account of the trainees' previous knowledge, abilities and individual needs.

- *Presentation*
Present the training material in a way that interests the trainees so that they are motivated to do well. Interest is generally stimulated by relating the training to the needs of the office and the individual's personal development, as well as varying the training methods used.

- *Pacing*
It is important to use correct pacing. If the instruction is too slow the trainees will tend to become bored and will not gain a sense of achievement. If it is too fast the trainees will fail to learn and will feel inadequate to the task. Allow the trainees to master each new learning experience before they proceed to the next. In order to master a unit of work the trainees require time to assimilate it, personal involvement in the learning process and reinforcement of learning with recapitulation at appropriate intervals.

- *Demonstration*
An effective demonstration is an essential preliminary to the operation of equipment, but it should be remembered that the only way for trainees to learn to use equipment is by 'doing', which should take place as soon as possible after the demonstration.

- *Assimilation*
Involve the trainees in the training session. This is essential if knowledge is to be acquired, retained, assimilated and applied. Encourage trainees to ask questions. Remember the Chinese proverb: 'I do and I understand'.

- *Environment*
Comfortable furniture and satisfactory physical surroundings are important factors in creating the right conditions for learning. If the trainees are conscious of being too hot or too cold, or they are in a noisy room, their attention will be impaired, causing the learning process to suffer.

- *Feedback*
Feedback should be conveyed to the trainees at regular intervals throughout the course of training as this provides an incentive, a stimulus to success and a confirmation/check-point marking progress.

- *Follow-up*
As soon as possible after training, the trainees should use their newly acquired skills 'in the field'. Practical implementation or 'on the job application' is vital to reinforce the fruits of training. As well as practical follow-up immediately after training, a more formal follow-up or appraisal of training results is vital. This renews motivation

and incentive and provides a boost to performance. It also allows trainers to assess the longer-term benefits of training and receive valuable feedback from trainees whose skills have been consolidated through on-the-job experience. Performance appraisals are discussed on page 176.

MOTIVATION

Our level of motivation influences every thought and action in both our professional and our private life. Adopting a positive approach to self-motivation can have a considerable knock-on effect on the successful motivation of others. Consider the reasons that stir you to get up in the morning and go to work.

What motivates you most? Is it:

- challenge
- involvement
- money
- responsibility
- achievement
- security
- status
- people contact
- use of skills, intelligence
- job satisfaction
- degree of fear
- routine
- ambition
- pleasant working environment, as illustrated in Fig 7.3

or a mixture of all these?

If you see your motivation in the list, it is likely that other people will find their motivation there too. For the executive secretary working in the international environment to have the chance of a fulfilling and happy career, it is vital to understand the theory of motivation and how it can be developed for personal and professional success.

Theory of motivation

There are many levels of motivation. Five key stages can be seen in Fig 7.4, based on levels of needs and desires as identified by A H Maslow in his 'hierarchy of basic needs' theory.

The content of this section is concerned with developing the fifth rung on the motivational ladder. This has an effect on all five levels of motivation.

Motivation is strongly linked to how we perceive ourselves, our self-image and our confidence. The level of self-motivation is also strongly linked to our ability to motivate others, and enable others to accomplish tasks and develop their own motivation. Fig 7.5 illustrates this.

Fig 7.3 A well-designed office

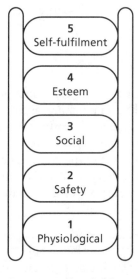

5 Need to make a positive contribution and thereby develop self-esteem; have power and show creativity. Ambition is the key here. Most usually, No 5 occurs when the other four needs have been satisfied. Equally, not everyone aspires to No 5.

4 Need to be important, to achieve, and to be respected.

3 Need to be appreciated in a social context, that is, within society.

2 Need to satisfy future needs, protection and security in order to meet the requirements of No 3.

1 Basic need to survive, to eat, sleep, be safe and have shelter.

Fig 7.4 Maslow's hierarchy of basic needs

Fig 7.5 The motivation matrix

There is a clear link between motivation and acquiring skills. At its most basic, it revolves around the desire to learn.

Motivation and skills learning

A desire to learn induces an individual to acquire knowledge. Knowledge, once acquired, can be put into practice. The repetition and practical application of knowledge will lead to the development of a skill and increased confidence. Confidence inspires the individual to want to learn again and thus develop new skills, and so the system perpetuates itself. This is how good teams are built. Good managers have teams that enjoy their work and feel they are making a contribution and learning something.

Motivation and personal confidence

Successfully developing a new skill brings a growth in personal confidence, which is at the root of the effective communicator. Outlined in Fig 7.6 is a visual reminder of how self-confidence and motivation are inextricably linked, self-perpetuating and fundamental to career and personal development.

Motivation of others and self-presentation

You are in possession of a great skill if you can motivate others positively. Some people are born with the ability, but for others it is and always will be an unnatural and difficult task to perform. Motivational skills can, however, be developed. Common sense and awareness of the other person's situation make an appreciable difference.

How you 'come across', or your presentation, is an integral part of the communication process. The process requires an element of control, both self-control and control of the other person's reactions. To control a situation for the purpose of motivating and persuading, for example when delegating a task, three skills are vital:

1 Basic knowledge of the objective or task in hand, deadline and work involved.
2 Credibility within your own area of expertise or skill. Without being able to carry out tasks well yourself, it is difficult to project a credible self-image to inspire respect from others or the desire to follow your example or emulate you.

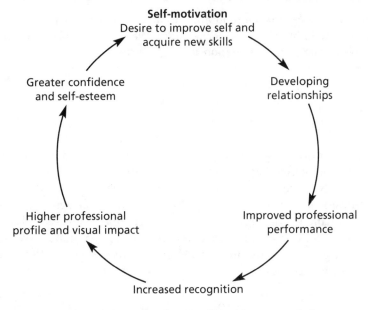

Fig 7.6 The personal confidence/professional development circle

3 Enthusiasm to communicate your message. Enthusiasm is knowledge brought to life. It requires a dynamic positive approach. Delegate tasks *you* would enjoy carrying out.

PERSONAL ACTION PLAN 25

▶ 'The messenger is the message.' How do your image and whole professional approach affect your success in motivating others?

Listed below is a ten-point reference checklist against which to evaluate your motivational skills:

Checklist for motivation techniques

- Ask questions instead of ordering.
- Show appreciation and praise for a job well done.
- Talk about your own errors before criticising others. This will help to avoid barriers being set up and show that making mistakes may be part of the learning process.
- Where appropriate, draw attention to mistakes indirectly in order to avoid confrontation.
- Allow the other person to 'save face'. What is the point of making an enemy out of a potential ally or team member?
- Praise improvements, large and small. We are all human.
- Make the person you are motivating happy to do what you request. The way you word your suggestion is vital here.
- Give encouragement and be enthusiastic. Make faults seem easy to correct. Avoid moaning. It is contagious!

- Set an example. Give others a reputation to admire and aspire to.
- Show confidence in other people's capabilities. Where appropriate, delegate the whole job. It is more satisfying to 'see a job through to the end'.

SELF-IMAGE

Personal presentation plays a large part in communication. This we already know. Clothes, accessories, behaviour and the way we fashion our environment, consciously and unconsciously, reveal elements of our personality.

Within a business context everything that your boss, colleagues and clients see can play a role in enhancing your reputation and image. First impressions last and negative ones seldom change. For you, the executive secretary, appearance has to be a balance between the image you want to project and the identity you have. Positive impressions encourage positive responses.

MANAGING STRESS

The phrase 'striking a balance' underpins much of the challenge an executive secretary takes on in working in an international environment. There are so many tasks, priorities, deadlines and personalities with which to contend. Keeping a measured pace is a self-management skill in itself. An imbalance can lead to negative pressure and too high a level of stress. This can result in personal demotivation and failure to motivate others to take positive action. See Chapter 9 for further information on stress in the workplace.

Pressure and stress in themselves are not injurious to health. They provide motivation and ensure that potential is fulfilled. Too low a stress level encourages lethargy and under-achievement: too high a stress level causes exhaustion, affects judgement, quality of work and the way we communicate with those around us. Communication stress for secretaries is considerable. The secretary is at the nerve centre of a battle to keep everyone happy and, at the same time, a 'buffer' between a boss and the outside world.

PERSONAL ACTION PLAN 26

▶ **How do you react under pressure?**

▶ **Does communicating in a foreign language add or detract pressure? How?**

▶ **Consider three ways in which your job could be made less stressful and implement them tomorrow. Remember to monitor your progress.**

Managing stress to maintain balance

For those secretaries who suffer from the negative effects of stress, listed below are some ideas for managing stress to your advantage. You may also use the ideas to help others and thereby enhance your own communication skills.

Checklist for managing stress

- Identify sources of stress and develop a personal strategy for controlling it. By helping yourself you can then help others.
- Anticipate stressful periods and prepare for them.
- Remove yourself from a stressful situation if you can. Try deep breathing to regain your equilibrium.
- Learn to be flexible and adaptable.
- Acknowledge your feelings and share them. Suppressing or 'bottling up' feelings harms your health and presents a conflicting image to others. Give feedback to others.
- Allow the logical and rational side of your personality to develop. Avoid dwelling on unimportant matters.
- Take control of your stress and yourself. Think positively and avoid words like 'cannot'.
- Be assertive. Learn to say 'no'.
- Never blame others for situations or failures.
- Be realistic in your goal-setting. Unrealistic personal deadlines are a waste of energy.
- Acknowledge a problem if it appears. If you need help, ask for it. If help is forthcoming, be positive.
- Be forward-looking. Avoid dwelling on the past.
- Enjoy your free time.
- Plan your day. Look for variety in tasks and pace. This will avoid stagnation and encourage creativity.
- Look after your body and your mind. Exercise, have a balanced diet and relax. Avoid excesses and aim for moderation.
- Set your own standards for success. Avoid judging yourself against other people or their perceptions of success.

If you are happy and fulfilling your potential, then you are a success and you can motivate others positively.

TIME MANAGEMENT

Effective time management is a sensitive issue for managers at all levels – secretaries, PAs, marketing executives, directors and chief executives. It is an area where little formal training is given, yet it is fundamental to being a good manager of others and of oneself. For secretaries, one of their major professional frustrations is lack of time with their boss. As a result, bosses do not make the best use of their secretaries. They miss a golden opportunity to free up their own time for thinking and planning and an opportunity to delegate responsibility to assistants who have potential waiting to be fulfilled.

You will undoubtedly have your own time management system. Self–help books are available on this subject alone. Use the following checklist against which to evaluate your own time management systems:

Checklist for time management

- *Plan*
  This is the key to effective time management. Set goals and priorities, consider time allowed or time necessary for tasks. Think ahead. Ask questions: 'Why do you need me at that meeting?' 'What is the purpose of the meeting?' By planning, you avoid wasting time by having to repeat tasks or elements of tasks.

- *Time*
  Plan short-term daily goals. Do you prepare a daily 'To do list' and tick off completed tasks? Plan long-term goals, such as restructuring systems, investing in a new WP, and the research involved in putting forward a recommendation to your boss/office manager.

- *Prioritise*
  Divide your tasks as follows:
  'I must do . . .' – immediate action
  'I should do . . .' – priority action
  'I want to do . . .' – non-priority action
  What percentage of time in a working day do you devote to these three categories?

- *Work to your strengths*
  Are you a 'morning person'? If so, do you tackle the more complex and difficult tasks when you are at your freshest, that is, first thing in the morning?

- *Monitor and review*
  Do you review progress according to changing demand and situations? At the end of the day, do you look at your 'To do list'? If you have tasks still unfinished, do you ask yourself why? Have you ever spent a day or a week keeping a diary record of tasks carried out and how long they took? You would be surprised. Do you write your 'To do list' for the next day before you go home at night? If not, why not?

- *Be assertive*
  Do you say 'no' to some requests? Do you articulate your requirements at the start of a project?

- *See the job through*
  Do you let telephone calls or unscheduled interruptions stop you from finishing a task? Do you go to a different room if you need peace and quiet for an hour?

- *Delegate*
  Do you delegate appropriately and sufficiently? How do you decide which tasks you can delegate? How accessible are you to your junior staff or colleagues? Do you keep in regular contact to discuss important issues with them?

- *Relationship with your boss*
  Do you request time with your boss or is it always the boss that summons you? Set aside time to discuss the future strategy of the department, planning, staff or any area that affects you significantly or takes up the bulk of your boss's time. You cannot influence

your boss or assist him or her effectively unless you have a full grasp of what is going on. Keep your personal relationship good. Raise the issues that need to be discussed. Anticipate, do not wait to be called. This way you are managing your time and that of your boss most effectively.

● *Rationalise time management systems*
Do you work from your diary, brought forward file, notepad, 'Post-it' notes littered here and there or a mixture of all of these? Should you consider rationalising your systems? If you find time management a problem, experiment and then ask for help.

PERSONAL ACTION PLAN 27

▶ **There are three dimensions to time management:**

You manage: yourself
your boss
your staff

Which do you do best and why?

Yourself: **How could you improve your existing systems and routines to achieve more in a day? If you were sick tomorrow, could your junior or boss pick up your systems and work efficiently without any input from you?**

Your boss: **How much time last week did you spend talking to your boss about non-work related issues?**

Your staff: **Does your junior assistant object to being delegated tasks? Why? What tasks do you concentrate on when you have delegated responsibility to your assistant?**

EXAMINE YOUR KNOWLEDGE

1 An important element of a secretary's work is time management. Describe three methods that you might use to ensure that work is dealt with when it is required. Which method, in your opinion, is the most effective?   *(LCCI PESD)*

2 Successful management of any office depends to a great extent on delegation.

  (*a*) Briefly explain what you understand by the term delegation and give two reasons for its importance.
  (*b*) Suggest reasons why an office supervisor might be reluctant to delegate.
  (*c*) What factors would an office supervisor take into account when delegating?
  (PEI ASP)

3 Your office is subject to considerable variation of workload on different days of the week and different weeks of the year. Suggest ways in which the problem could be overcome without the necessity of employing more full-time staff.   *(PEI ASP)*

4 Joan Marples, the managing director's secretary, is responsible for the work of two secretarial assistants. As Joan was checking through some documents processed by Marie Chambers (one of the secretarial assistants) she found she had entered the wrong date on all of them. She did not think the error was serious enough to mention to her assistant and corrected the documents herself. Would *you* have done this? Discuss the action taken by Joan in this situation.

5 You are secretary to Mr Michael Vivoir (Case Study 3). Deal with the letter (Fig 7.7) which is in your in-tray.

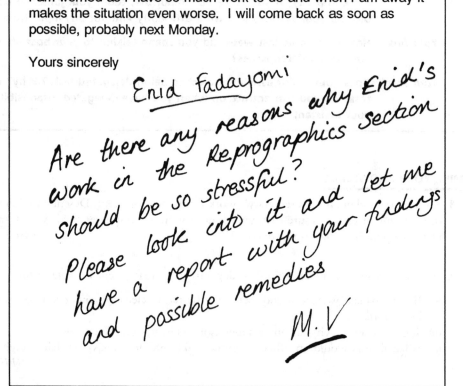

Dear Mr Vivoir

I am sorry to say that I am ill and cannot come to work this week. The Doctor says that I am in a nervous state and suffering from excessive stress. He has advised me to take the rest of the week off.

I am worried as I have so much work to do and when I am away it makes the situation even worse. I will come back as soon as possible, probably next Monday.

Yours sincerely

Enid Fadayomi

Are there any reasons why Enid's work in the Reprographics section should be so stressful? Please look into it and let me have a report with your findings and possible remedies

M.V

Fig 7.7

(PEI ASP)

WORK TASKS

Assessment of competence for Element 7.2
Organise own work schedule

Performance criteria

- *Regular and ad hoc tasks are identified and prioritised.*
- *Time and effort are allocated to complete identified tasks in order of priority.*
- *Unexpected events are catered for within a flexible plan.*
- *Changes in priorities are recognised and work schedule adapted accordingly.*
- *Relevant assistance is identified, obtained and co-ordinated to meet specific demands and deadlines.*
- *Tasks delegated to others are accurately defined and progress monitored.*
- *Effective performance is assisted by the use, adaptation and development of planning and scheduling aids.*
- *Safe working practices are always followed and implemented.*
- *Security and confidentiality procedures are always followed and implemented.*

Range statement

Competent performance must be demonstrated across a range of:

- *Relevant work:*
  secretarial and administrative functions as described in the remaining BA(S)S Units and Elements of Competence.
- *Planning periods:*
  both short and longer-term
- *Contingencies:*
  flexible adjustment of the plan is required by the unexpected absence of (i) the principal (ii) the jobholder and by the unexpected presence of the principal for a major part of the day;
  the deadline for a major piece of work, scheduled for completion the following week, is brought forward;
  there is a delay in the availability of materials required for the day's scheduled work.

Personal action plans 22 and 24 relate to this work.

CHAPTER 8

Recruitment practices

Recruitment and employment practices (*see* Chapter 9) and issues arising from them fall within the personnel function. In large organisations there is usually a personnel department headed by a personnel manager, with responsibilities for the many matters concerning employees: their welfare, their conditions of work and their career development. The personnel manager and personnel officer can be answerable directly to the chief executive and responsible for developing and implementing a company's personnel policy. The scope of the personnel department can be enormous and must be clearly defined for it to be effective and proactive.

In small organisations, the managing director or a senior secretary or both may take on the responsibility for personnel matters. For many international organisations, the personnel function is becoming an even more complex and vital department, requiring great flexibility and the ability to plan policy based on international trends. With the implementation of the concept of international staff mobility within multinational companies, personnel and human resources staff must be skilled in areas such as international employment legislation, comparative remuneration packages, conditions of employment, and equivalent educational standards and qualifications in different European markets.

For the executive secretary/PA it is vital to have a grasp of recruitment and employment practices for two reasons:

1 From the employer's point of view, you may become or are already involved in recruiting and interviewing staff for yourself or for your department. You must have a clear strategy concerning personnel requirements and how to fulfil them effectively. The ability to recruit and keep the right staff is a valuable skill.

2 From the employee's point of view, you may find yourself looking for a new job or planning for a career change. It is vital that you understand how to market yourself and achieve your professional goals. Obtaining recruitment and employment skills will help you to understand the process of selection from the two standpoints of employer and employee, and will provide a range of further skills to add to your repertoire as a manager/executive assistant.

METHODS OF RECRUITMENT

Staff can be recruited from a number of sources, using various methods. At the heart of the successful recruitment procedure is the use of the appropriate resources and methods to meet the recruitment requirement.

Source	Method
● Internal promotion	● Word of mouth/internal advertising of position
● Colleges of further education and schools	● College leaver presentations and recruitment open days
● Recruitment consultancies/ employment agencies specialising in niche market skills, e.g. languages/temps	● Consultancies and agencies
	● General advertising of services or specific advertising of a vacancy
● The general recruitment market	● Company advertising a vacancy directly in the press at local, national or international level
● Specialist staff	● Advertisements in specialist journals, professional body and trade literature
● Unsolicited applications	

JOB SPECIFICATIONS

The key to recruiting and retaining effective staff lies in correct selection. Selection of the appropriate candidate for a job depends upon a full understanding of the requirements of a job and the requirements of a candidate. The starting-point for the recruiter of staff is the preparation of the job specification. The job specification outlines the personal qualities and professional skills needed for a post. It should also include some 'cultural' background, such as a description of the office environment, the boss for whom the secretary will be working, and the corporate culture – in other words, a 'slice of life' description of the job. The more comprehensive a job specification is, the more likelihood there is of finding the right person for the job. An inaccurate or incomplete job specification will without fail produce the wrong candidate.

College leavers to senior PAs

The job descriptions that follow cover five traditional levels within the secretarial hierarchy and show different kinds of responsibility offered and experience required for each role. The examples also show how different levels of language ability are required within international environments.

The inclusion of these job descriptions is designed to show the variety that exists in the secretarial/language market, and to show the qualities that employers seek in potential employees and the level of information necessary to present a clear picture of a job. It is the employer's responsibility to provide such detail. As a candidate, it is your right to expect this amount of detail, and it is your responsibility to obtain it during the interview process. The specifications reflect the seriousness with which many employers approach the task of recruiting secretaries with international experience and language ability.

Start as you mean to go on

Many employers approach the area of recruitment of secretaries at all levels with caution. As with all levels of recruitment a company is making a capital investment in recruiting direct or utilising the services of a recruitment consultancy to find the right combination of skills, experience and personality. The strong PR role a secretary fulfils and the first point of contact responsibility they have makes secretarial recruitment a complex task. Good secretaries are difficult to find. The field of appropriate candidates is often narrowed considerably by the requirement of a particular language ability at a particular level. This is before the exigencies of other skills and personality are taken into account. Equally, the secretary with fluent French who is being sought may bring a unique skill to the company and be the only point of contact with French customers or partners, and therefore the task the boss or personnel officer has in recruiting the right person has more risk attached.

The key point to remember is that secretaries have a special combination of skills to offer, and the road to recruitment and finding the right environment in which to use that combination of skills is a two-way process. The secretary-linguist as a candidate has as much right to 'interview' and evaluate a potential employer as the employer does the candidate. Care should always be taken to start as you mean to go on, from the job interview stage to the business of day-to-day communication.

Clarify and confirm the nature of every prospective job within a company. Never accept job titles, responsibilities and levels of language content at face value without feeling confident in your right to question and probe and inform yourself of the job description in its entirety. As an employer/interviewer, look for the enquiring mind and the candidate who asks searching questions. Only then can a secretary make an informed and balanced decision based on accurate information. This is the first step towards establishing sound communication patterns.

The secretarial hierarchy

The titles that follow are used to describe different levels of secretarial role and responsibility. They are not written in stone. One boss's executive secretary is another boss's senior secretary. Some secretaries call themselves personal assistants when they are junior secretaries or even typists. These titles are intended as a guide and reference point.

1 Junior secretary: most often a 'first jobber'
2 Team secretary or management secretary: usually a 'second jobber' with an average of 12–18 months' experience and consolidated skills
3 Senior secretary
4 Executive secretary/director's secretary
5 Personal assistant

1 Junior secretary

The work has a certain amount of routine responsibility. However, in this example, due to the nature of the advertising business with its last-minute deadlines and periods of extreme activity followed by some quieter interludes, there is considerable challenge in the position and scope for initiative. Other junior secretarial roles may be more limited in their scope and reflect a need for an accurate, efficient and reliable secretarial service only.

Job description

Title	Secretary within account management team.
Company	A and B Advertising Ltd.
Salary	£11 000 per annum (all salaries quoted in the examples reflect London weighting).
Size	Two hundred staff.
Background	Company established 50 years ago. Now one of the top ten agencies in the UK. Head office in New York with 20 offices around the world.
Benefits	Four weeks' holiday plus an extra day at Christmas. Private health care after one year. Interest-free season ticket loan after one year. Free sandwich lunch. Discretionary bonus based on performance.
Hours	0930–1800. Flexibility required plus occasional weekend work for new business pitches.
Staff turnover	Low on secretarial side; average 3¼ years.
Atmosphere	Informal yet businesslike. Fast pace and very sociable. Average age 24.
Educational requirements	Five GCSEs (A–C) plus NVQ Level 2 Administration with secretarial skills or equivalent. Good English/spelling.
Language requirements	Good working knowledge of French for contact both on the telephone and written with clients. New French client. 20 per cent language content.
Secretarial skills	50 words per minute typing. 80 words per minute English shorthand. WP – WordPerfect 5.1, will cross-train.
Start date	Immediate. Temporary considered for a 'temp to perm' position.
Reason for vacancy	New business and the loss of previous French-speaking secretary to job abroad. Last secretary stayed for 3 years.
Working with	Account management team. 50% of time: Account director, woman, 30 years old; 30% of time: Account manager, man, 25 years old; 20% of time: Account executive, woman, 22 years old. All are highly ambitious, career-minded, outgoing personalities.
Responsibilities	A 60%/40% split in terms of secretarial and administrative responsibilities. The work is mainly task-oriented and will include: opening the post, extensive telephone liaison (both internal and with clients),

organising meetings and travel arrangements, typing reports, correspondence and minutes of meetings, filing, routine office administration, co-ordinating videotape transfers, organising client lunches and compiling newspaper cuttings. There will be involvement across four or five accounts and 'peaks and troughs' in terms of workload.

Most important quality sought	Reliability under pressure.
Age	Flexible, preferably a college leaver with 6 months' temporary experience who is willing to be trained. Early 20s.
Personality	Bright, a good team worker with initiative and an interest in advertisements. Flexible and outgoing and strong under pressure. Stamina and a sense of humour.
Prospects	Depends on the individual. It is a meritocracy – bright secretaries have been promoted to the account management trainee programme after 18 months.

2 Team secretary

This is often a solid secretarial position requiring a minimum of two years' experience where secretarial and general office skills have been perfected. There may typically be two bosses.

Job description

Title	Secretary to two banking analysts.
Company	F and G International Bank.
Salary	£14 000 per annum. Negotiable for an outstanding candidate.
Size	Over 500 staff.
Background	Company established for 30 years and recently involved in takeover of well known stockbroking firm. Blue chip British name.
Benefits	Four weeks' holiday. Interest-free season ticket loan on start, along with private health care. Subsidised membership of health club. Subsidised mortgage after 6 months. Luncheon vouchers £25 per month. Annual bonus. In-house foreign-language tuition.
Hours	0900–1730. Some overtime paid at time and a half.
Staff turnover	Low at all levels. Secretaries stay on average six years.
Atmosphere	Smart and highly professional. Corporate dress code. Formal setting.

Educational requirements	Preferably A-Level plus NVQ Level 3 with secretarial skills or equivalent. Secretarial skills are tested on interview.
Language requirements	Fluent German for day-to-day use. A high language content to the job, about 50 per cent used for client liaison, translations, drafting of correspondence in English and German and spoken use with clients and the two analysts.
Secretarial skills	60 words per minute typing, plus ability to take shorthand in English and German at approximately 80 words per minute. Audio in both languages. WP – Microsoft Word.
Start date	As soon as possible in order to have a crossover training period with current secretary.
Reason for vacancy	Internal promotion of secretary to trader's assistant.
Working with	Two analysts specialising in German banks. Both men are in their early 30s, and are bilingual in German/English. One is German and the other is from Yorkshire.
Responsibilities	Basic office administration and extensive screening of calls and client liaison. There is much 'fort holding' as the two analysts travel regularly in Europe, and travel arrangements have to be co-ordinated constantly. Particular research assignments will also feature as part of the work load. This type of job will require more of an understanding of the nature of the boss's work and responsibilities in order to deal with sensitive, confidential situations and information-passing.
Most important quality sought	Common sense and the ability to prioritise in analysts' absence.
Age	Flexible, although mid- to late 20s preferred.
Personality	Efficient, professional and a good eye for detail. A good sense of humour and motivation to work to tight deadlines.
Prospects	Good within the secretarial stream. Internal promotion always preferred to external recruitment. Occasional opportunity to move out of secretarial work into trading floor administration.

3 Senior secretary

This can often be a demanding role, usually working for one boss and at most two. This type of role could require three to five years' experience and will develop the responsibilities of secretarial levels 1 and 2.

Job description

Title	Partner's secretary.
Company	S & R Solicitors.
Salary	£16 000 per annum with guaranteed annual review.
Size	Eighty staff in total, of which 15 are secretaries.
Background	The company has been in existence in one shape or another since the turn of the century and is now most well known for its litigation work. This particular requirement is working alongside the partner responsible for property deals in Spanish-speaking countries, concentrating on southern Spain.
Benefits	Four weeks' holiday. Interest-free season ticket loan. Use of a company flat in Spain. Discretionary loan. Luncheon vouchers of £10 a week.
Hours	0900–1730, although overtime is usual.
Staff turnover	Average. Secretaries stay on average 2 years.
Atmosphere	Smart yet comfortable. Average age is 37.
Educational requirements	Solid secretarial skills (to PEI Level 3 standard) and excellent written and spoken English.
Language requirements	Bilingual Spanish for constant use with partner, clients and suppliers. Some knowledge of Portuguese useful although it is not essential. The partner needs a secretary who has lived and worked in Spain or has Spanish to mother tongue standard.
Secretarial skills	70 words per minute. Audio in both languages. WP: WordPerfect for Windows. Cross-training is possible.
Start date	Within the next six to eight weeks.
Reason for vacancy	Secretary leaving to start a family.
Working with	The partner specialising in Spanish property law. He is English and in his early 50s. He travels 50 per cent of the time and really relies on his secretary to organise him. He is unmarried, ambitious and with high standards. Firm and fair in the way he treats people.
Responsibilities	A high proportion of the work involves personally dealing with the partner's mail, correspondence, diary management and extensive travel itineraries. There is much organisation of internal meetings and a conference to co-ordinate every six months in London. Serious involvement in report and document presentation, and some

supervision of an office junior will be necessary. Apart from the high volume of routine legal audio work, the job requires the ability to understand the partner's style of work and priorities. Frequent contact with senior management both in house and externally is integral to the job.

Most important quality sought	Attention to detail and the ability to organise the partner.
Age	Preferably late 30s/early 40s, but flexible.
Personality	Solid and reliable. Calm in tense situations and positive in attitude towards the challenge of constantly changing plans. Happy with the role of senior secretary.
Prospects	Limited scope.

4 Executive secretary/director's secretary

This type of role requires considerable initiative and judgement based on sound experience. Such a position would need a thorough grasp of company procedures, senior personnel and the boss's needs.

Job description

Title	Secretary to the marketing director.
Company	M and N Cosmetics.
Salary	£18 000 per annum.
Size	One thousand staff in the UK at 3 locations, made up of headquarters, production, and research and development. This is a British firm with plans to relaunch its brand of cosmetics against strong competition from the USA. This is the European HQ with 150 staff.
Background	A respected cosmetics house that has been trading since the early 1940s but has suffered a dramatic decline in market share and is keen to reposition itself as a modern, environmentally aware cosmetics house.
Benefits	Four weeks' holiday. Private health care. Annual bonus. Discount on all products.
Hours	0900–1700, and a flexible approach to hours is expected. Time off in lieu of overtime is offered.
Staff turnover	High in the last three years. Average length of stay has been 12–18 months.
Atmosphere	Smart, corporate image very important. Recently refurbished offices with light open-plan work stations.

Educational requirements	GCE A-Level or BTec National, and preferably a qualification in maths and English alongside solid secretarial skills to LCCI Private and Executive Secretary's Diploma standard.
Language requirements	Any European language useful for telephone and translation work.
Secretarial skills	60 plus words per minute typing. 100 words per minute shorthand. WP – Wang; must have experience.
Start date	As soon as possible.
Reason for vacancy	Previous secretary had difficulties coping with the workload and was not keen to learn a foreign language or become more involved in the international side of the business.
Working with	Marketing director. A 45-year-old Englishman with no foreign-language skills. He is highly professional and wants to reorganise his systems. He is currently learning French and feels he would have an added incentive if his secretary had linguistic skills. He has been with the company for 8 years.
Responsibilities	This position offers a high level of administration content, at about 70 per cent. Secretarial content is small yet still vital. Main tasks fall into the following areas: screening the telephone for all personal and professional calls, giving out information without previous approval, correspondence on behalf of the director, interviewing for permanent and temporary secretarial staff, organising the director's agenda, maintaining confidential management and personnel files, dealing with expenses and some budget management.
Most important quality sought	Professionalism and initiative.
Age	Totally dependent on the calibre of the candidate and her or his ability to be credible when dealing with senior management.
Personality	Hardworking and able to anticipate the director's needs and act accordingly. Is capable and as comfortable working in a team situation as on own. A good sense of humour.
Prospects	Difficult to evaluate given the challenge at hand and plans for more European exposure. Certainly the personnel department is keen to encourage staff mobility between offices internationally but there is no guarantee as yet.

5 Personal assistant

This is a considerable role at the most senior level. Secretarial content is minimal and the management responsibility is not to be underestimated. Key judgemental ability is vital, as is a strong, confident personality to function effectively at the centre of power in an organisation.

Job description

Title	Personal assistant to chief executive officer.
Company	OBM Satellite Television Company.
Salary	£22 000–£25 000 per annum plus a company car.
Size	Team of 50 at the UK offices in South London.
Background	This is a relatively young player in the satellite television business with a rapid expansion record to date. Strong base in German- and Dutch-speaking countries.
Benefits	Five weeks' holiday. Performance-related bonus. Clothing allowance and luncheon vouchers valued at about £30 per month.
Hours	0830–1800, though most evenings finish at 1930.
Staff turnover	High level of staff retention due to policy of internal promotion and job satisfaction. The company has retained 90 per cent of its original staff since its launch date in 1986.
Atmosphere	'Work hard and play hard.' The pace is fast and can be formal and glossy. Corporate culture is strong and the CEO instils much loyalty.
Educational requirements	Preferably a graduate or HND with secretarial competence at LCCI Private and Executive Secretary's Diploma level, but flexible, depending on age and experience.
Language requirements	Fluent French and German. Knowledge of Dutch is useful and a willingness to learn other languages is an advantage. Fluctuating level of language involvement on a day-to-day basis. Oral ability is more important for the higher degree of telephone and face-to-face work.
Secretarial skills	60 words per minute typing for own use. Some shorthand ability for own use. WP – Apple Macintosh. Model is due to be changed so there is some choice in WP used.
Start date	When the right person is found.
Reason for the vacancy	Current assistant is moving into sales within the same company.
Working with	A dynamic Scot in his early 40s. He has been at the head of the company since its inception and he speaks some German.
Responsibilities	Supervision of a junior secretary who handles the routine office secretarial workload. Administration of the company chauffeur,

company flat and chief executive's house in the south of France. Complete organisation and administration of European conferences and client lists. Some bookkeeping and administration of the chief executive's diary. Some drafting of correspondence. The PA has a vital management role and is a feedback point on subjects such as company morale and behaviour.

Most important quality sought	Integrity.
Age	Flexible, although the appropriate candidate is likely to be over 27 years of age.
Personality	A high-flyer who is prepared to work long hours. A good team player who inspires confidence and can relate to people at all levels. Tactful and calm but tough.
Prospects	The current personal assistant is moving into sales. The company policy is to promote from within. The CEO is looking for an assistant who is going to stay with him long term.

Secretarial responsibilities can vary wildly from level to level and from company to company. On accepting a job offer, the secretary at every level should always clarify and confirm the outline of the job specification so that there are no shocks for either side once a working partnership has begun and contracts are signed. This is insurance for both applicant and employer and forms the foundation of the communication launch pad from which to extend responsibilities and ultimately career prospects.

Carrying out this exercise sets the ground rules and demonstrates the intention for the working relationship from the start, involving a free flow of information and communication.

Whether working as a WP operator or team secretary or chairman's PA, the secretary must identify a unique element to that role and develop effective communication skills within that role. These cannot be done unless both sides of the recruitment equation are clear about the constituents and description of a job.

ADVERTISING FOR STAFF

Recruitment advertising is produced to elicit a response – it is a call to action. It should be considered from two points of view, that of the applicant and that of the recruiter.

Applicant   Wants to find a job that appeals to him or her, catches the eye and is different from others.

Recruiter   Wants to produce maximum response for minimum cost, to hit the right target market of suitable candidates.

Checklist for recruitment advertising

- *Logistics*
  Choose the right format and medium. A superb advertisement in the wrong publication is a waste of time and money. Research the circulation of magazines, journals or newspapers and the calibre or level of jobs they carry.
- *Target market*
  Word the advertisement to attract the type of candidate you require.

GERMAN 2ND JOBBERS
£14–15 000 + banking benefits

Genuine opportunity for young secretary who speaks good German and would like to improve it! A minimum of one year's experience is required for this unusually varied and interesting position. Lots of international telephone liaison, plenty of client contact and team environment. Professionalism and polish are very important prerequisites to success in this role.

Age: 20+

English shorthand essential
Banking background preferred.

Contact ABC Recruitment on 0812–2013

Fig 8.1 Example of a display advertisement

**SECRETAIRES EXPORT
BILINGUES ANGLAIS**

Rattachée aux Directeurs de Zone, vous assurerez le suivi administratif et commercial de nos lignes de produits destinées à l'exportation. Responsable de la réception des commandes, vous aurez un rôle d'interface permanent entre les clients, les commerciaux et les usines, et assurerez le secrétariat de votre zone.

De formation BTS secrétariat, bilingue anglais, vous êtes débutante ou justifiez d'une première expérience réussie dans la fonction et avez de bonnes connaissances en Allemand et/ou Espagnol. Rigoureuse, méthodique et autonome, vous avez un bon sens relationnel et êtes motivée par l'international. Ces postes sont à pourvoir à Paris.

Merci d'adresser votre candidature sous référence . . . à . . .

Fig 8.2a Example of a French display advertisement

Compañía de Seguros inicia la selección de:

Secretaria de Dirección

Las candidatas a considerar son personas de alto nivel profesional y cultural (preferiblemente con estudios universitarios), experiencia en puesto de secretaria de categoria similar y gran sentido de discreción y responsabilidad.

Se ofrece
Remuneración a convenir
Horario flexible
Puesto de alto nivel y ambiente
agradable

Se requiere
Experiencia en puesto similar
Manejo de tratamiento de textos
Conocimientos de inglés

Rogamos a las personas interesadas envíen curriculum y fotografía a . . .

Fig 8.2b Example of a Spanish display advertisement

**TV STAR £19,000.
Utilise your Italian
to mother-tongue
standard.
32–37 years old.
High-powered role.
SH/typing minimal.
Deputy MD Boss.
Ideally media exp.
Tel: ABC Co on
0812–2013**

Fig 8.3 Example of a lineage advertisement

- *Format*
  Consider the format of the advertisement against the cost – display versus lineage.
- *Cost*
  Monitor cost and number of responses for future strategy.
- *Avoid errors*
  Always fax a copy of the advertisement to the publication to avoid errors, especially if a foreign language is used in the copy or when liaising with foreign publications. If errors appear which are not your fault, negotiate discounts or replacement advertising.
- *Recruitment agents*
  If using a recruitment consultancy, ask them if they will advertise the vacancy for you. Do they charge a fee, do they mention your company name, can you clear copy before it appears?
- *Copy*
  Pick out the key points to the job. Is it skills, personality or experience? Do not add too

much detail, just enough to attract responses eager for more information. Use words sparingly and be clear.
- *Be honest*
  Never lie about any aspect of a vacancy.
- *Legal requirements*
  Ensure that you comply with employment legislation such as the Sex Discrimination Act (*see* page 179), Race Relations Act (*see* page 179), and so on.
- *Gain attention*
  Make the headline eye-catching, for example by referring to the salary and package, or by referring to some unusual or attractive element to the job, or by writing the headline in the foreign language required.
- *Who to contact*
  Always have a contact name/address.

PERSONAL ACTION PLAN 28

▶ **Draft advertisements for two of the full job specifications outlined earlier. Where would you advertise them and how?**

INTERVIEWING SKILLS

Interviewing skills cover a vast area of knowledge, expertise and experience. Before looking at how to interview well, either as recruiter or applicant, it is useful to consider the whole concept of self-marketing.

Principles of self-promotion and marketing

Consider the principles of self-marketing from two points of view: the philosophical and the functional. This can help to clarify the communication needs both of executive secretaries planning to market themselves and of the target market or potential new employer. How is self-marketing both a philosophy and a function?

The philosophy

In the philosophical context, self-marketing is creating an employer's desire to employ you above anyone else, by assessing your own attributes through the employer's eyes and by identifying and satisfying the potential employer's requirements better than anyone else. Similarly, an organisation has to make itself a desirable employer in the competitive market for good applicants.

In other words, you are marketing the potential benefits you can offer, not simply skills. Employers not only want to recruit a secretary with good shorthand and typing skills, and a good working knowledge of its specified software packages. They also want to employ a professional assistant who can clear the backlog of correspondence, and undertake tasks such as organise a conference, co-ordinate a production timetable with the Paris office (where little English is spoken) and take minutes of complex meetings where written confirmation of agreed action requires prompt circulation.

The marketing function

The marketing function is to implement the marketing philosophy. It is the anticipation, identification and satisfaction of the employer's needs through research, preparation, interview technique and the maintenance of consistently high levels of work. The self-marketing function is a continual process.

At all levels the principles of self-marketing are the same, for the senior PA as much as for the college leaver. Successful self-marketing requires effective communication of ability, intent and desire in a simple, step-by-step, logical format, involving:

- analysis of the current situation: where am I now?
- goal or objective-setting: where do I want to go?
- strategy: how will I get there?
- achievement/evaluation: how will I know I am getting there or have got there?

Previous sections have suggested ways in which you can analyse current situations and decide on goals based on personal strengths, weaknesses, wants, needs and desires. The strategy itself for achieving a goal merits closer attention. It will require some of the following:

Preparation
of yourself and your CV. Is the CV in response to an advertisement or an unsolicited application to a company?

Research
into the opportunities through the press,
recruitment consultancies,
personal and professional contacts,
networking library information,
computer data on companies or industry sectors.

Presentation and marketing
of your CV to employers and recruitment consultancies;
of yourself on interview with employers and consultancies.

It is vital to devote time to each of these areas in order to successfully reach your specific career goal.

Preparation of yourself

The words 'know thyself', from the Ancient Greek inscription in the Temple of Delphi, are never more important than when you are considering a career change or assessing career prospects and objectives.

The secretary or PA who has taken the time to think through their strengths and weaknesses, who knows their own mind, will present a more confident image when projecting to colleagues or potential employers.

PERSONAL ACTION PLAN 29

▶ **Cast your mind back to the personal SWOT analysis you carried out and compound that knowledge by considering the following:**

1 **Analyse the work experience which you have. What have been your main achievements over that time?**

2 **What achievements have you been proud of?**

3 **How have you learnt from your mistakes?**

4 **What are the reasons why you might want to leave your current job?**

5 **What can you offer a potential employer that other secretaries and personal assistants cannot?**

6 **What would you like to see yourself doing in five years' time?**

The worst answer that you could give to any of the questions in the Personal Action Plan 29 is: 'I don't know.'

It demonstrates a lack of preparation, a lack of direction and a lack of enthusiasm: enthusiasm is very important in a career, as it gives the individual the impetus and motivation to make progress. In other words: 'enthusiasm is knowledge brought to life.'

Preparation of your CV

This is the first impression a potential employer has of an executive secretary, and it must therefore look good and be professional.

Often a busy personnel manager may be able to devote no more than a minute or so to initial screening of CVs. The CV must therefore be clear, accurate and well-presented, with no typing errors.

There is no one correct way of preparing a CV, although there are a number of points to bear in mind when putting one together, such as:

- *Be concise*
  Try to keep your CV to a maximum of two pages and emphasise your main responsibilities – not a listing of everything you have ever done.

- *Be relevant*
  Try to think of your CV from the point of view of the potential employer reading it. Would your CV be of interest if you were the employer?

- *Chronology*
  When outlining your work experience, begin with your most recent work experience first, and then work backwards.

- *Complete your personal history*
  Do not leave gaps in your personal history. This will only prompt closer questioning on the reasons for the gaps and explanation of what was actually done in these interim periods.

- *Keep your options open*
  Try to avoid mentioning on paper either your salary requirements or your type of preferred industry as this could limit your possibilities and pigeon-hole you.

- *An outside opinion*
  Ask a trusted friend or relation to check your CV for an honest appraisal of its form and content.

Pre-interview

Preparation

- CV – always carry a copy of your CV, and be clear about dates, qualifications and previous employment so that you can present a consistent picture.
- Prepare as much information as you can about the organisation and the job description. Make a list of likely questions and prepare answers. Try to have access to a company report, product information or relevant newspaper articles. Keep abreast of current affairs. You may be called to comment on a recent event as a response to a general 'ice-breaker' question.
- Punctuality – arrive a little early for your appointment, especially if you are using public transport or do not know the route.
- Positive mental attitude – remain enthusiastic and optimistic on arrival and throughout the interview.
- Smile and keep eye-to-eye contact.
- You are 'on stage' even when waiting at reception. Remain consistent in your behaviour.
- Have a firm handshake – neither a 'wet fish' nor a vice-like grip.
- Presentation – make sure your presentation is in keeping with the company where you are on interview. A conservative appearance is appropriate. Consider your body language when communicating on interview as first impressions are, rightly or wrongly, very important.

Implementation

During the interview itself, which can be a stressful and nerve-racking experience, it is often helpful to try to consider the interview as a game, where you, as the interviewee, are attempting to find opportunities to demonstrate the reasons why you are the candidate best suited for the job. Play the game and create the impression that you are precisely the person that the interviewer wants to choose.

Consider the interview as a two-way process in which the candidate is as entitled to ask questions about the job description and the company as the interviewer is entitled to question the candidate about her or his CV. By the end of the interview, the candidate should have a clear picture of just what the job involves and whether it is something she or he is looking for.

Be honest and try to be yourself, because only then can you evaluate whether you can fit into a particular corporate culture or office environment, and only then can a potential employer do the same with you. This could avoid unpleasant shocks all round in the future as well as a wrong career move for you.

Interview techniques

The stress of an interview can cause secretaries, PAs and, indeed, anyone under scrutiny to react and behave in such a way that they do not reflect their true nature. This, of course, says something about how a person copes under pressure. In most cases, an interviewer will take this into account. The secretary needs to remember this, both as a candidate and also in the role of interviewer designated the task of recruitment of temporary or permanent junior staff. The added challenge of interviewer and interviewee having to converse in a foreign language may also cause reactions that are out of character. This is frequently also taken into account in the overall appraisal of a candidate.

Checklist for interview communication techniques

- *Adopt the attitude of a winner*
  Emphasise your successes and achievements in personal and professional life. You can be positive without being arrogant. Remember to create a realistic picture that you can live up to.
- *Be friendly*
  Try to convey personal details in a warm, accessible way. Be courteous and avoid arguing.
- *Don't be too wordy*
  If asked an open-ended question like, 'How would you describe yourself?', do not be afraid to pause for thought, and consider a short list of relevant characteristics which then give you the opportunity to focus on specific areas – but be concise.
- *Be enthusiastic*
  It counts for much. An interviewer will remember you for this and will also find you more interesting to listen to. It will make the interview more interesting for both of you if you can relate to the job for which you are applying.
- *Do not be afraid of the 'pause for effect'*
  An interviewer is only human and cannot assimilate an overload of information. Give yourself time to answer questions.
- *Watch for signals*
  Listen to the interviewer for cues either to laugh, show your sense of humour, or ask a question. By watching for signals you will avoid the irritating habit of interrupting.
- *Be positive*
  Make even your weaknesses seem like strengths. Give positive reasons for leaving your job, and avoid criticising your employers or colleagues. This will not reflect well on you.
- *Be aware of your body language*
  Avoid distracting mannerisms that become magnified through nerves, such as playing with your hair or wringing your hands (*see* Figs 8.4 and 8.5). Speak clearly and look the interviewer in the eye. Always thank the interviewer for their time.
- *Watch your posture and breathing*
  By sitting straight and regulating your breathing, you can control your stress level and not be thrown off balance by difficult questions.

The secretary/PA as interviewer

In companies both large and small, secretaries are responsible for interviewing and recruiting staff. They may or may not be called on to utilise their foreign-language skills in this task. Outlined below are some points to remember as an interviewer. These points will enhance the secretary's communication skills and force her or him to prepare communication objectives and criteria by which to judge the candidate's communication skills.

Fig 8.4 Bad
Negative body language conveys lethargy, anxiety, lack of purpose and lack of professionalism: all of these *impede* performance.

Fig 8.5 Good
Positive body language conveys enthusiasm, confidence, control and professionalism: all of these *enhance* performance.

Pre-interview preparation

- Know what you are looking for: have a clear job description, an idea of the candidate profile you are seeking, and an understanding of where priorities lie in terms of intellectual aptitudes versus proven track record and qualifications. Are you *au fait* with equivalent European secretarial qualifications?
- Plan your interview room so that it is not intimidating, but is conducive to discussion.

During the interview

- Retain control: listen, analyse, maintain a good atmosphere and rapport. Take notes discreetly for reference after the interview. It is impossible to remember all conversations with interviewees. Steer the interview in a subtle way to avoid creating the 'I am interrogating you' atmosphere.
- Initially ask easy questions which are specific and relevant to the applicant. This will create a good atmosphere and 'break the ice'. The aim at the start of the interview is to allow the candidate to relax and 'open up'.
- Use body language positively: nod, maintain eye contact, smile or display agreement. This will reassure the candidate and make her or him feel at ease.
- Watch the timing: gauge the right moment to ask probing questions or to test

language and secretarial skills. Within the limited framework of a first or second interview, it is particularly important to pace and alternate your questions in English and in foreign languages. Ensure that you have a selection of questions prepared in the relevant foreign language or languages, which are open-ended and will allow you to assess adequately the candidate's practical commercial ability.

- Indirect and/or open-ended questions give a candidate the chance to give a detailed reply. They are often more subtle questions and often elicit a more honest reply. Here are some examples of indirect and open ended questions:
  1 What do you feel have been your main achievements in your current job?
  2 What are your strengths and weaknesses?
  3 What kind of boss do you work with best?
  4 What kind of career challenge are you now seeking?
  5 Tell me about your academic career.
  6 What specific contribution do you think you can make to this company?
  7 What are your leisure interests?
  8 How are your language skills and work experience relevant to the job I have outlined to you?
  9 Why are you leaving your current job?
  10 What interests you about this job?
  11 How would you describe yourself?
  12 Describe a typical day.
  13 If you had to choose the colour that best suited your personality, which colour would you choose and why?
- Closed questions that require a one-word or short answer are useful for confirming facts and winding up the interview.

PERSONAL ACTION PLAN 30

▶ Many personnel managers refer to a system known as the Seven-point Plan when they are recruiting staff (see below). They are the main areas on which an assessment of suitability will be based for a particular candidate and job.

▶ Apply these selection criteria to yourself and evaluate your suitability to your current job, or jobs for which you are applying or for which you have an interview. On what areas could you improve?

▶ How can you utilise this plan when interviewing for juniors?

The seven-point plan is based on:

1 *Education/qualifications:* how relevant these are to the job.

2 *Physical characteristics:* health, general appearance and first impressions.

3 *Work experience:* relevance to the job under consideration, examples of initiative and future potential.

4 *Special abilities:* any abilities that are relevant, such as specific IT expertise, foreign-language skill, etc.

5 *Domestic background:* mobility, stability, flexibility and availability to start work.

6 *Interest:* hobbies that give an indication of personality type, whether any interests are relevant to the job under consideration, or an indication of a well-rounded personality.

7 *Personality:* a broad area which relates to the overall impression a candidate gives of their suitability for a job. Specific impressions from the other six points will combine with the candidate's many qualities and facets such as confidence, ability to learn quickly, stamina under pressure and whether she or he is fun to have within the working environment. This will establish whether the 'chemistry' of the candidate and the employer works. This is easy to specify but not so easy to judge in an applicant on interview. Honesty, determination, resourcefulness, enthusiasm and leadership skills are all important aspects to consider.

PERSONAL ACTION PLAN 31

▶ **Use the application form below (Fig 8.6) to carry out role-playing interview exercises with a colleague. As a recruiter, consider how second interviews should differ from initial interviews.**

▶ **Have you been involved with managing group interviews with either two or more candidates or two or more interviewers? What are the advantages and disadvantages of this kind of interview technique?**

It is important to understand the selection process from both sides of the interview table. With that skill the secretary can contribute towards more effective communication in international and domestic arenas and gain valuable personal and career-enhancing skills.

APPLICATION FORM

Registration No: Date:

(For internal use only)

General details

Surname: Forenames:

Address: Tel. no:

                                Work: Home:

Date of birth: Status:

                                Nationality:

Car owner/driver: Current salary:

Nearest Tube/BR Station: Salary required:

Availability/start date:

How did you hear of us?

Education summary

School: Qualifications:

University/further education: Qualifications:

Time spent abroad

Work/study:

Secretarial skills

Typing: WP packages:

Audio: Financial record-keeping:

Shorthand: English   Language ability: Spoken

           Other   Written

Career summary

Employer: Dates: Duties (current first):

What kind of work are you looking for and why?

Signature: Date:

Office use

Fig 8.6 Sample job application form

WORKING ABROAD

For those wanting to work abroad there are a number of points worth remembering:

- Be prepared to translate your CV accurately into a foreign language. Different countries may require emphasis on different areas of a CV. Research their requirements and tailor your CV to the market concerned. In Italy, for example, employers welcome a less formally-structured CV so that applicants have the opportunity to display their character and personality.
- Be aware of any work permit or visa restrictions that could complicate your application for work in another country.
- Finding the right job abroad can be a lengthy process. It requires self-analysis, research, planning, networking and determination. Try to avoid a situation where you give up work in one country without a guarantee of work in another, unless it is absolutely necessary.

PERSONAL ACTION PLAN 32

▶ Sample outlines for a CV are shown in Figs 8.7–8.11 in English, French, German, Spanish and Italian. Use the frameworks to compile your own CV in the relevant language or languages.

▶ The reference section could either include names and addresses of two referees whom you have already consulted and who have agreed to stand as referees, or could read: 'References: available on request'.

▶ You may also want to include a photograph of yourself with your CV. This is not always necessary and depends on whether you feel it would be an advantage or a disadvantage to your application for a job.

RECRUITMENT OPPORTUNITIES

A right decision is often a well-informed decision. Unless you are one of the lucky few who know exactly the type of company to join and the type of responsibilities to fulfil, then experience, discussion with others, and considerable research are required. These all contribute to knowledge, and in this case knowledge becomes power: power to consider all the possible options and make the right decision. Some of the research routes are outlined below.

Press

The recruitment pages of the daily newspapers abound with vacancies and job opportunities for secretaries. Some organisations advertise directly in the newspaper, and others utilise the services of general consultancies or specialist language recruitment consultancies, perhaps not stating the name of the prospective employer. Answering

CURRICULUM VITAE

Personal details

Name:

Address:

Telephone:

Date of birth:

Nationality:

Status:

Education and qualifications

Dates in full   Name of institution

                                           Type of qualification gained, with
                                           grades

Work experience
(*Starting with current work*)

Dates, in full, with name of organisation, position within organisation and summary
of main responsibilities.

If it is relevant, you might include a section on:

Vacation work/interests

If there is still relevant information or qualifications that you have not been able to
include in the other sections, then you may add a section:

Other information

References

Fig 8.7 Framework for a CV in English

Résumé/Curriculum Vitae

Nom: Brown

Prénoms: Alex

Adresse:

Téléphone:

Date de naissance:

Lieu de naissance:

Situation de famille:

Nationalité:

Diplômes:

Postes occupés: Du _____ 199– au _____ 199– secrétaire de direction, ABC Compagnie.

Autre renseignements: Bonnes connaissances de . . .

                       Permis de conduire:

                       Stage . . .

Fig 8.8 Framework for a CV in French

Lebenslauf

Alex Brown
41, Str. . .

Tel:

Geboren: in:

Familienstand:

Schulbildung:

Wehrdienst:

Studium: Juni 199 –   Mai 199 –

Berufliche Tätigkeiten: Mai 199 –   September 199 –
                               ABC London . . .

Kenntnisse: Gute mündliche und schriftliche Französisch

Fig 8.9 Framework for a CV in German

Curriculum Vitae

Apellidos: Brown

Nombre: Alex

Lugar de nacimiento:

Fecha de nacimiento:

Nacionalidad:

Estado civil:

Dirección:

Teléfono:

Estudios: 199 –

Información complementaria:

Cargos que ha ejercido: .... de 199 –
            a 199 –

Ocupación actual: Secretaria trilingue . . .

Fig 8.10 Framework for a CV in Spanish

Nome: Alex

Cognome: Brown

Data di nascita:

Nato a:

Stato civile:

Residenza:

Telefono: Ufficio . . .
            Abitazione . . .

Titoli di studio:
            Diploma istituto tecnico . . .

            Laurea in . . .

Lingue straniere:
            Francese . . .

            Conoscenza discreta de . . .

Esperienza professionale:

199 – /oggi   Responsabile . . .

Fig 8.11 Framework for a CV in Italian

an advertisement in the newspaper can therefore be an exciting or a harrowing experience, depending on the information given by the organisations and recruitment consultancies contacted.

It is worth staying in touch with the recruitment pages of the national daily newspapers on:

- Monday, Wednesday and Thursday, in *The Times* 'Crème de la Crème', and 'Multilingual opportunities';
- Monday for the *Guardian* Creative, Media, Marketing and Multilingual sections;
- Friday for the *Guardian*'s European Appointments section.
- *The Independent, The European* and *The Standard* also carry some relevant recruitment pages.

Specialist professional journals may also carry advertisements for secretaries with a knowledge of their subject or section of the market. Weekly magazines like *Ms London* and *Girl about Town*, and local newspapers are also worth consulting.

For those who want to work abroad, the media described above are equally relevant. It may also be worth reading the recruitment sections of *Le Figaro, Le Monde, El País, El Sol, Die Welt, Frankfurter Allgemeine Zeitung, Il Corriere della Sera* and national daily newspapers in other relevant markets.

Recruitment consultancies

You may choose to contact a recruitment consultancy as a result of seeing an eye-catching advertisement, or simply to 'register' for any vacancies that occur in the field that interests you.

Although the quality of recruitment consultancies varies enormously, it is worth-while treating every meeting with a consultant as a potential job interview. This may be the only opportunity for the consultant to assess you and your suitability for particular jobs. Be prepared to have your suitability and language skills tested for speed and accuracy. This is a vital part of the screening process, and should help the consultant to match the right secretary or PA to the right job.

Consultants work in different ways, and it is important to find out as much information as possible about potential job interviews and job specifications, so that you are only put forward for positions that are of genuine interest to you and for which you are suitable. The key point is not to waste any of your own time, or anyone else's. This may involve turning down an interview or just saying you are not interested in a particular job description.

Although relatively small, the language recruitment market is expanding all the time. It is worth contacting a number of consultancies in order to achieve the widest scope of different approaches and areas of expertise.

For those secretaries who want to work abroad, recruitment consultancies can usually be beneficial, or they can at least suggest other routes to explore. In markets where recruitment consultancies do not flourish, national press advertising should be examined. Unsolicited applications and relevant family/friend contacts can be used as a starting-point. They can also offer a valuable insight into working practices in certain markets. The Information Bank at the end of this book includes a list of addresses of recruitment consultancies for secretary-linguists and PAs, both in the UK and in other European markets.

Using recruitment consultancies as an employer

Advantages
- quality of service and personal contact;
- saves time: CVs are sifted and initial interviewing is carried out;
- only suitable candidates are presented for interview;
- advertising is placed for a client usually at no cost to the client;
- money-back guarantee period for the secretary and the possibility of taking 'temporary to permanent' adjustments easily;
- skills tested;
- long-term relationship with a consultant who understands your business and potential requirements;
- the consultant can act as adviser or sounding-board on other employment issues;
- temporary staff paperwork is handled at the recruitment consultancy;
- fast access to candidates.

Disadvantages
- a fee has to be paid;
- loss of control over initial checking of potential candidates;
- dealing with agencies can be a lottery: unscrupulous agencies exist which waste your time and money;
- it takes time to build up a solid relationship with a consultant you can trust;
- agencies can be a waste of time if appropriate candidates are not found;
- loss of confidentiality;
- you are dependent on the consultant's judgement and choice of applicants.

Contacts

Contacts, both personal and professional, are built up over a period of time, from a variety of sources. Family, friends, work colleagues, clients, suppliers and chance encounters can all be considered as contacts. In such a competitive world it is madness not to take advantage of opportunities that can help you to achieve your goal. However, it is important to acknowledge any assistance that has been given to you and to take on the responsibility of making the most of the advantage that has been afforded you. In some sectors, employers may choose not to advertise a job opportunity or to retain a recruitment consultancy to meet a language requirement. Contacts may prove to be helpful in such a situation and could make the difference between finding a good job and a great opportunity.

Networking

Networking is slightly different from 'using contacts', as it involves an active, systematic process of getting things done and getting ahead. This is often through being a part of a networking organisation, a professional body or organisation, or through membership of a 'social' meeting group. Networking can be the key to the job you seek, in your country or abroad. A starting-point for practising the art of networking could be to join the Institute of Qualified Private Secretaries (IQPS) or the European

Association for Professional Secretaries (EAPS) (*see* the Information Bank at the end of this book for further details).

Networking can help to build both your confidence and your personal directory of people you have met who could help you professionally or point you in the right direction. By the same token, you must be prepared to do the same for others where appropriate. Participation is the key here to self-development. Conferences, seminars, workshops and talks are set up by networking organisations.

Contact with a secretary in the company or country in which you would like to work is invaluable, and networking can afford this kind of opportunity.

Libraries and desk research

For information on particular companies or industry sectors, Companies House, or your local central reference library or the business and reference sections of local libraries can be useful. Publications like *Kompass*, *The Times Top 1000 Companies* and industry-specific directories are all worth consulting as background material for considering possible employers and preparing for interviews.

EXAMINE YOUR KNOWLEDGE

1 You are secretary to Mr Michael Vivoir (Case Study 3) and are required to deal with the note (Fig 8.12) which is in your in-tray.

> Will you now go ahead and ask the Employment Department to arrange to recruit the new Junior Secretary for you. As an initial step, please draft a job description for the position, as he/she will be responsible to you.
>
> M. Vivoir

Fig 8.12

(*PEI ASP*)

2 You are secretary to Mr Patrick Moreland (Case Study 2). As your workload has increased over the past year the personnel department has advertised for a young, newly-qualified secretary to assist you. You have been asked to form part of the interviewing panel.

(a) What personal qualities and qualifications would you look for when interviewing a college leaver?

(b) If given the opportunity to schedule the interviews, describe two methods you might use.

(LCCI PESD)

3 Your workload has increased considerably over the past 18 months. The personnel manager has suggested that an assistant secretary should be recruited to help you.

(a) State the personal qualities you would look for in an assistant.

(b) Give suggestions as to how your workload could be split to ensure that you are fully aware of the current situation at any time. (LCCI PESD)

4 You are secretary to Mr H Johnson, Company Secretary of Comlon International plc, civil engineering contractors.

Because of an increasing volume of work in Mr Johnson's office, it has been agreed that an assistant secretary should be recruited.

Draw up a draft advertisement, together with a job description, to pass to the appointments section of the personnel office. What personal qualities will you look for in candidates when you are invited to take part in the interviews? (LCCI PESD)

CHAPTER 9

Employment practices

ENGAGEMENT AND TERMINATION OF SERVICES

Once the selection process has produced the suitable candidate for employment (as seen in Chapter 8), and an offer of employment is made and accepted, a contract of employment comes into being and is enforceable. Terms of employment vary from one organisation to another and from country to country. There may be a time when harmonisation of employment procedures is implemented on a European scale within the European Union, but until such time procedures will vary. In general, when staff are employed, a new employee agrees to carry out certain responsibilities in return for a salary. A written statement of employment should be issued to full-time employees, normally within 13 weeks of the date on which service began with that employer, as required by the Employment Protection (Consolidation) Act 1978 (*see* page 179). This Act also stipulates the content of a basic contract of employment (*see* page 179).

Notice of termination of employment

Unless employees are dismissed without benefit of notice, they are entitled to receive notice of the termination of their contract, as laid down in the Employment Protection (Consolidation) Act 1978 (*see* page 179).

Advice should always be sought if you are drafting or receiving letters of this nature, especially if working or liaising over staff procedures abroad. For further information, see *Employment Contract Manual* by Desmond Payne and Keith Mackenzie (Gower), or contact the Department of Employment.

INDUCTION

New employees at any level need to know about the organisation for which they work. They should become acquainted with its mission statement, general objectives, policies and practices, and *modus operandi* as quickly and efficiently as possible. New employees must also gain a picture of where their job fits into the organisation and its importance to their department or section. This is called general induction and it should generate interest, enthusiasm for the job and the organisation, and a sense of loyalty. It aims at boosting morale and providing a confidence framework from which to grow. Specific induction concerns the detailed aspects of the new recruit's job, organisation charts, levels of authority and day-to-day procedures and administration. A staff handbook is a useful source of reference for induction courses, as it includes working procedures, personnel policy, terms of employment, promotion policy, welfare and recreation facilities.

Induction programmes may be prepared for one individual or on an annual basis for a group intake of staff. This varies according to company resources and policy. Some organisations prepare induction presentations or credentials presentations with flip charts, slides or films about the organisation's history and future.

One procedure which seems to work well in some companies is the 'aunty' concept, where new recruits to a company are assigned to a senior member of staff or 'aunty/mentor' for a month or so to provide guidance and information about the company and job. More general aspects of the company can be presented by lectures and formal group presentations at intervals, perhaps when other new recruits have joined the company.

Induction programmes may last an afternoon, a day, three days, a week or longer. This depends on the level of the new employee and the resources and time available.

PERSONAL ACTION PLAN 33

▶ **Have you prepared an induction programme or been exposed to one in the past? If so, how would you improve them?**

▶ **What would be your objectives if you had to experience an induction course?**

▶ **How would this affect the way you organise an induction course for a junior secretary?**

TRAINING

A personnel department in a large organisation will usually be involved with the setting up and implementation of training programmes. The format and substance of the courses will be based on the communication between personnel functions and operating functions. Some companies have a training manager who works alongside the personnel manager.

Business survival, success and future development are dependent upon a well-trained workforce at all levels from the clerical to the chief executive level, especially in the 1990s when business and technology changes are so rapid and competition so great within Europe. From a personal point of view, training is also important as it contributes to job satisfaction and incentive, earning power and career development. The Industrial Society Training Survey showed that less than 10 per cent of an organisation's training budget is spent on developing secretarial and administrative staff. The message is clear: secure your training needs and those of your juniors. Much persuasion is needed to secure adequate training for secretaries.

Checklist for providing effective training programmes

- Identify the training needs. Talk to people at all levels. Create an environment where ideas and suggestions are welcome.
- Plan training programmes based on current and future needs. Talk to colleagues abroad. Is there scope and a need for harmonisation of courses with staff mobility?

- Implement training in an appropriate manner. Consider timing, budget, time out of the office, shifting of workloads.
- Quantify the success of a programme.
- Review and evaluate past courses for future efficiency.
- Modify courses based on evaluation of the past.
- Consider how international and domestic aspects affect training needs:
  - language training
  - foreign culture briefings
  - foreign WP packages
  - staff movement/secondment to European subsidiaries
  - part-time workers
  - returners to work/maternity leave
  - manpower planning, such as the number of school leavers coming on to the market, natural wastage in the company, general levels of staff turnover in the company.

PERSONAL ACTION PLAN 34

▶ Which training courses have you attended in the last year? Which would you like to attend and why?

▶ Which training courses have you organised and which ones would you like to organise?

STAFF TURNOVER

Staff turnover is an important indicator of staff morale. It also reflects conditions of employment and general corporate philosophy.

Staff turnover is the number of staff who leave an organisation during a given period. It can be expressed as a percentage of the average number of full-time employees:

average number of employees = 100
number of staff who leave in one year = 10
staff turnover = 10%

High staff turnover can reflect poor job satisfaction, poor promotion prospects and training opportunities, or poor pay and work conditions. It may also reflect an ageing workforce. Low staff turnover is ideal, as it suggests effective employment procedures and a happy staff. This is not always the case, however – during a recession a lack of alternative employment opportunities locks employees into a company despite dissatisfaction with working conditions.

INCENTIVE SCHEMES

The quality of the incentive schemes in a company affects staff morale and can have a direct effect on turnover of staff. Examples of some incentive schemes are listed below.

- *Induction courses* They generate personal interest in an organisation and a desire to belong and contribute to their success. They can promote loyalty and boost morale.

- *Financial incentive* Calibre of work and loyalty to a company can be rewarded with a bonus, commission, share of profits or allowances.

- *Internal promotion* A policy or promise of internal staff promotion aims at encouraging staff loyalty through a defined career route or progression. This helps to maintain an organisation's philosophy and corporate culture. Great care is taken with the recruitment of junior staff with a view to long-term potential and high retention rate. This can, however, be negative and deprive a company of new ideas from outside the company and a fresh approach. The positive side lies in providing a stable company with employees who are committed to the company rather than, for example, gaining two years' experience and moving on.

- *Benefits* such as language training or health club membership offer added value to the employer and employee. This provides good PR for the company, which wants to invest in a skilled and fit staff, and is valuable for the staff.

- *Training courses* of any description show that a company is prepared to invest in an individual for the future.

- *Appraisals* are opportunities to discuss progress and plan for future career development. This is of benefit to both the employer and the employee.

- *Non-financial incentives* such as job security which may enhance performance.

- *Opportunity* to use skills, intelligence and initiative.

- *Goals and aspirations*.

- *A happy work environment*.

- *Recognition and status* for the individual.

- *Involvement* of staff.

- *Job satisfaction*.

PERSONAL ACTION PLAN 35

▶ **Which incentive schemes motivate you and why?**

JOB DESCRIPTIONS

As a PA or supervisor of junior staff you may be required to review job descriptions and contribute to evaluations and appraisals. A job description will normally state what a job entails, tasks to be performed, level of skills required, responsibility and authority to be assumed, type of working conditions and any particular features of the job. The job description for the PA to the editor of *Prima* magazine includes the following items:

JOB DESCRIPTION

Job title: PA to the Editor
Basic function: To assist the Editor with the co-ordination of her work and department

Main responsibilities:
1 organising the Editor's diary and appointments;
2 having a thorough knowledge of editorial objectives and priorities;
3 following through the Editor's initiatives;
4 ensuring that all correspondence and enquiries have been processed and actioned where necessary;
5 taking dictation and typing of memos, letters, reports, copy;
6 circulating information as instructed by the Editor;
7 co-ordinating and planning of all interdepartmental meetings;
8 co-ordinating and arranging special functions;
9 responsible for supervising the editorial office;
10 making UK and overseas travel arrangements for the Editor;
11 co-ordinating editorial photographic trips;
12 helping to co-ordinate travel pages;
13 researching and keeping information for special projects;
14 ensuring confidentiality where important;
15 on a monthly basis, arranging payment for published readers' letters;
16 when required, representing the Editor at press receptions, travel functions and product launches;
17 setting up organisational charts, forward planners, etc.;
18 continual update of files, documents and schedules;
19 be conversant with company policies;
20 assist in the implementation of the company's health and safety provisions.

PERSONAL ACTION PLAN 36

▶ **Fill in the blank job description given in Fig 9.1 with details of your job or your junior's job.**

JOB EVALUATION

Jobs vary according to the nature and degree of difficulty of the tasks involved, the skills required, degree of responsibility, experience needed, management skills involved, use of initiative and discretion. Job evaluation is the process of analysing and comparing these skills and qualities to assess the value of the job and provide the means by which a grading system can be used for setting salaries, assessing promotion prospects and recruiting staff. It is the job itself which is being evaluated, not the person doing the job – that is the appraisal. Typical methods of job evaluation are:

JOB DESCRIPTION

Job title

Location

Salary scale

Reports to

Responsible for staff

Job summary

Main duties and responsibilities

Special skills

Date

Fig 9.1 Sample job description form

- *Job grading*

  This is similar to job ranking. Grades are established with regard to specific criteria of responsibility and difficulty within jobs. Standard grades are selected, and jobs are given a grading based on an analysis of the job description.

- *Job ranking*

  Again from job description analysis, jobs are ranked according to difficulty and responsibility. Jobs of a similar status are ranked equally. This helps to confirm pay scales.

- *Points rating*

  Rather than looking at the job description as a whole, separate elements of a job description are given points which are allocated to each factor or skill. The points are added together and the job graded by points.

PERFORMANCE APPRAISAL

In any job some employees perform better than others and deserve more recognition, promotion, responsibility or pay or any combination of these. The process by which more efficient employees can be recognised and rewarded and given an incentive to do better is the performance appraisal. This is an evaluation of the way the job is performed for quality, quantity, reliability and potential. A job performance appraisal is usually an annual event carried out by the employee's immediate superior, manager, department head or supervisor. Records are usually held in the personnel department if there is one.

As an executive secretary you will be appraised and may well appraise others' work. The various aspects of performance are assessed and a rating or merit rating applied to specific criteria (*see* the performance plan in Fig 9.2).

Objective	*Performance criteria*	*Notes on attainment*	*Rating*
1 COMMUNICATION			
1.1 Ensure a polite and clear telephone manner	No complaints on manner and attitude		
1.2 Where possible ensure messages are clearly understood	No important misunderstandings		
1.3 Use systems to effect internal correspondence	Same-day transfer of notes and messages where possible		
1.4 Ensure a timely and accurate turnaround of typed letters	Same-day completion where possible		
2 PLANNING			
2.1 Maintain up-to-date diaries and plan to minimise last-minute changes	Avoid rearrangements due to overrun and non-attendance		

Objective	Performance criteria	Notes on attainment	Rating
2.2 Ensure effective preparation for meetings and discussions	Avoid last-minute preparation		
2.3 Administer an effective system of bring-up and follow-up	Timely responses to all requests and required action		
3 ADMINISTRATION			
3.1 Establish budget and monitor expenditure, highlighting potential out-of-line situations	Timely identification of potential problems to allow alternative corrective actions		
3.2 Meet the requirements of the company's safety and security policies	No violations		
3.3 Set up and maintain a secretarial will*/back-up file	Up-to-date record		
4 ADDED VALUE			
4.1 Advise on systems usage	Maintain state of the art usage as appropriate		
4.2 Handle correspondence and queries to the limit of knowledge and ability to research	Avoidance of passing on correspondence that could have been previously cleared		
4.3 Ensure that activities such as correspondence and presentations are of the highest quality	No errors and consistency of presentation format		
5 PERSONAL DEVELOPMENT			
5.1 Increase knowledge of external bodies and local and national issues	Demonstrate knowledge through increased added value		
5.2 Learn PC applications to develop efficient system usage	Maintain state of the art knowledge		

* A 'secretarial will' is a secretary's personal data file containing essential details about the manager: his/her preferences; checklists; office procedures; use of forms; distribution lists, etc., as a guide for a replacement secretary when required for cover or when a successor is appointed.

Fig 9.2 Performance plan/appraisal form

Appraisal forms can also ask open-ended questions regarding the last year's achievements and progress, such as:

- What do you consider to be your main achievement this year?
- What skills would you like to develop in the coming year?
- Where do you feel you need to improve your performance at work?
- What aspects of your job do you enjoy and why?

– What do you intend to achieve in the next year and how?

Appraisals usually have to be discussed, agreed and signed by the manager and the person assessed. Goals are set for the coming year to be assessed at the next appraisal. Job grade, salary increase and promotion prospects often result from this appraisal, so it is very important that both sides are happy with its content. It is usually the source of much heated discussion!

Scheduling staff appraisal interviews and other scheduling activities such as holiday rotas, maternity leave, training courses and the like can be maintained on card rack systems as illustrated in Fig 6.1.

Aspects likely to be covered in staff appraisals are:

- ability to recognise and solve problems;
- ability to plan and organise work programmes (for self and for juniors);
- ability to communicate effectively both vertically and horizontally;
- ability to create and maintain good relations with superiors, staff and colleagues, and to co-operate within the organisation;
- development of personal qualities such as leadership, decision-making, responsibility and positive attitude;
- technical skills;
- improvements compared against the last appraisal.

PERSONAL ACTION PLAN 37

▶ **Consider your appraisal system. Does it produce results for you and your staff? How could it be improved?**

EMPLOYMENT LEGISLATION

Below are some examples of UK legislation relating to office practices and employment.

Health and safety in offices

Health and Safety at Work Act 1974
(*See* details below.)

Data protection (computers)

Data Protection Act 1984
Protects individuals from misuse of personal information held about them on computer files and lays down codes of practice for those who use or process data relating to personnel. (*See also* page 52.)

Sex discrimination

Sex Discrimination Acts 1975 and 1986
Sex discrimination is unlawful in full-time and part-time employment, training and education, the provision of goods and services, and so on. Discrimination against married people on the grounds of marriage is also covered.

Race relations

Race Relations Act 1976
Discrimination on the grounds of race or colour is unlawful in employment (recruitment, terms of employment, promotion and dismissal); education; housing; membership of trade unions and professional bodies; and in advertising.

Employment protection

Employment Protection (Consolidation) Act 1978 (as amended by subsequent Employment Acts)
Employees must have:

- the right to belong to a trade union and take part in trade union activities;
- the right not to belong to a trade union;
- a contract of employment within 13 weeks of commencing employment;
- an itemised pay statement each pay day;
- full pay for a maximum of 26 weeks if suspended on medical grounds;
- maternity leave and maternity pay if certain laid-down conditions are met;
- minimum periods of notice to terminate employment:
  - at least one week's notice after four weeks' continuous service
  - at least two weeks' notice after two years' continuous service and thereafter one week for each completed year of service up to 12 weeks after 12 years' service;
- a written statement of reasons for dismissal;
- time off work for job hunting or training for new employment when they have been given notice of dismissal because of redundancy;
- time off work for trade union activities and public duties such as those of justices of the peace, members of local authorities, school governors, etc.

The employee must give at least one week's notice after continuous employment of one month or more, but this does not increase with length of service.

An employee cannot be unfairly dismissed if he or she has been continuously employed for at least two years.

A contract of employment should contain:

- job title;
- date when employment began and whether any previous employment is counted for 'continuous employment';
- minimum periods of notice;
- rate of pay and how this is calculated;
- hours of work, holiday entitlement and holiday pay;
- sick pay entitlement;
- conditions relating to a pension scheme;

- grievance procedure stating the person with whom any grievances should first be discussed, normally the employee's immediate superior;
- disciplinary rules indicating the means of appeal against disciplinary measures.

Financial services

Financial Services Act 1986
Protects investors by regulating the conduct of investment business involving shares, debentures, gilts, local authority securities, unit trusts, life assurance policies and so on. The investors' financial outlay is protected in the event of the insolvency of an investment business. Written agreements with investors are required to cover the basis for charging commissions or fees and explanations of the risks in the type of transaction undertaken.

Copyright

Copyright, Designs and Patents Act 1988
See page 63 for further details of this Act.

Consumer protection

Consumer Protection Act 1987
This Act establishes that a trader must not:

(*a*) display misleading information about goods or services, such as incorrect comparisons with recommended sale prices;
(*b*) supply goods in an unsafe condition.

HEALTH AND SAFETY IN OFFICES

New regulations and codes of practice governing health and safety in offices and display screen equipment work, implementing European Commission Directives, have been approved by the British government and came into operation on 1 January 1993.

Employers' duties

The new regulations require employers to:
- assess the risk to the health and safety of their employees and to anyone else who may be affected by their activity, so that the necessary preventive and protective measures can be identified;
- put into practice the health and safety measures that are identified in the risk assessment, covering planning, organisation, control, monitoring and review;
- provide appropriate health surveillance of employees where necessary;
- consult employees' safety representatives and provide facilities for them – consultation must now take place on such matters as the introduction of measures that may substantially affect health and safety, arrangements for appointing competent persons, health and safety information and training required by law and health and safety aspects of new technology being introduced to the workplace;

- appoint competent people to help advise and apply the health and safety measures;
- set up emergency procedures;
- give employees, temporary employees and others working in their undertaking information about health and safety;
- co-operate with any other employers who share a work site;
- make sure that employees have adequate health and safety training and are capable enough at their jobs to avoid risk;
- take into account the working conditions and risks in the workplace when selecting equipment;
- make sure that equipment is suitable for the use that will be made of it, provide protection from dangerous parts and ensure that equipment is properly maintained;
- give adequate information, instruction and training on equipment.

Employees' duties

Employees are required to:

- follow health and safety instructions when using equipment, transport and safety devices;
- report any work situation which is considered to represent a serious and immediate danger to health or any matters considered to be a shortcoming in the employer's protection arrangements for health and safety.

The NVQ performance criteria for monitoring and maintaining health and safety within the work area are:

- The immediate working area (including all equipment, fixtures and fittings within the job holder's responsibility) is kept free from hazards.
- Any discrepancies, damage and potentially unsafe features of public and office areas are noticed and rectified or promptly and accurately reported to an appropriate authority.
- All accidents are reported and recorded accurately, completely and legibly, in accordance with laid-down procedures.
- Operating instructions relating to the safety of all equipment and fixtures are followed.
- Approved and safe methods for lifting and handling heavy or bulky items are followed.
- Regulations and guidelines for the use of keyboards and exposure to VDU screens are followed.

Maintenance of workplace, systems and equipment

The following are the key issues in the code of practice but fuller details are given in the new code of practice (*see* page 180).

Maintenance The workplace, systems and equipment must be cleaned and maintained in an efficient state, in efficient working order and in good repair.

Ventilation Effective and suitable provision must be made to ensure that every enclosed workplace is ventilated by a sufficient quantity of fresh or purified air.

Temperature During working hours, the temperature in all workplaces inside buildings must be reasonable. A temperature of 16°C will normally be considered appropriate unless the work involves severe physical effort, in which case the temperature should be at least 13°C. A sufficient number of thermometers should be provided.

Lighting Every workplace must have suitable and sufficient lighting. It should be sufficient to enable people to work, use facilities and move from place to place safely and without experiencing eye strain.

Cleanliness Every workplace and its furniture, furnishings and fittings must be kept sufficiently clean. Floors and indoor traffic routes should be cleaned at least once a week.

Space Every room where persons work should have sufficient floor area, height and unoccupied space for purposes of health, safety and welfare. The total volume of the room, when empty, divided by the number of people normally working in it should be at least 11 cubic metres. A room which is more than 3.0 m high should be counted as 3.0 m high. In a typical room, where the ceiling is 2.4 m high, a floor area of 4.6 m^2 (e.g. 2.0 × 1.85 m) will be needed to provide a space of 11 m^3. Where the ceiling is 3.0 m high or higher the minimum floor area will be 3.7 m^2 (e.g. 2.0 × 1.85 m).

Workstations Workstations should be arranged so that each task can be carried out safely and comfortably. The worker should be at a suitable height in relation to the work surface. Work materials and frequently used equipment or controls should be within easy reach, without undue bending or stretching (*see* the section 'Workstations with display screen equipment' opposite on page 183).

Washing, drinking and toilet facilities Suitable and sufficient washing facilities, drinking water, accommodation for clothing and sanitary conveniences must be provided at readily accessible places. Facilities must also be provided for changing clothing, resting and eating meals.

Additional guidance on the new regulations, obtainable from the Health and Safety Executive or the HMSO, is contained in the following publications:

> *Management of health and safety at work*
> *Work equipment*
> *Manual handling*
> *Workplace health, safety and welfare*
> *Personal protective equipment at work*
> *Display screen equipment work*

The Health and Safety Executive also publishes a booklet entitled *Working with VDUs* which answers the questions that are most commonly asked about VDUs and health; it gives a brief summary of the new regulations, and suggests some simple adjustments that can be made to workstations and screens to make them more comfortable and easier to use.

The conditions outlined above help to prevent the phenomenon known as the sick building syndrome in which staff are absent as a result of unhealthy conditions.

Workstations with display screen equipment

The minimum safety and health requirements for work with display screen equipment, illustrated and numbered in Fig 9.3, are as follows:

1 Adequate lighting: ensure satisfactory lighting and an appropriate contrast between the screen and the background environment.

2 Co-ordinate the workplace and workstation layout with the positioning and technical characteristics of the light source in order to eliminate glare or distracting reflections.

Fig 9.3

3 Minimise noise from nearby equipment.

4 The chair should be stable and allow the operator freedom of movement and a comfortable position.

5 Windows should be fitted with a suitable system of adjustable covering to attenuate the daylight that falls on the workstation.

6 Software should be appropriate for the task; adapted to the needs of the user; provide feedback on performance; display information in a format and at a pace appropriate for the user.

7 The characters on the screen should be well defined and clearly formed, of adequate size and with adequate spacing between the characters and lines.

The image on the screen should be stable, with no flickering.

The brightness and the contrast between the characters and the background should be easily adjustable by the operator and also easily adjustable to ambient conditions.

The screen must swivel and tilt easily and freely to suit the needs of the operator.

The screen should be free of reflective glare and reflections liable to cause discomfort to the operator.

8 The keyboard should be tiltable and separate from the screen in order to allow the operator to find a comfortable working position and avoid fatigue in the arms or hands.

The space in front of the keyboard should be sufficient to provide support for the hands and arms of the operator.

9 The work surface should have a sufficiently large, low-reflectance surface and allow a flexible arrangement of the screen, keyboard, documents and related equipment.

10 The chair seat should be adjustable in height and the chair back should be adjustable in both height and tilt to provide good lumbar support.

11 A footrest should be made available to any operator who wishes for one.

Hazards and remedies

Display screen equipment

Hazards	*Remedies*
● Posture fatigue	● Apply ergonomic principles to the design, selection and installation of equipment; use approved methods for the design of the workplace and the organisation of the task. Example: use adjustable chairs to provide the correct seat height and back rest positions as laid down in British Standards specifications.
● Upper limb pains and discomfort	● Use only properly-designed equipment and furniture, with correct techniques of operation, job design and work planning.
	● Job variation and rotation will help to relieve this.
● Eye and eyesight effects	● Avoid siting the VDU in a brightly lit area where the lights are reflected in the screen; but the light must be adequate for reading the copy and the screen image.
	● Do not look directly at windows or bright lights.
	● Use task lighting specially designed for VDU operation – avoid unshielded fluorescent lights.
	● Use the brightness controls to suit the lighting conditions in the office.
	● Keep the screen clean, removing dirt and 'grease' finger marks from it.
	● Operators wearing glasses or contact lenses may have to have them corrected to the range of focus required.

Hazards   *Remedies*

Contact lens users may be affected by the dry environment resulting from the heat generated by VDUs. If so, they may have to blink more often or use tear substitute drops. Alternatively, they may be advised to wear glasses instead of lenses for VDU work.

● As a VDU ages, it is inclined to develop more faults such as drift and jitter of the images, and it is possible that the brightness control will need to be turned up. Regular servicing is essential to correct deterioration of the visual image.

Note: Under the new regulations employees may ask their employers to provide and pay for an eyesight test at regular intervals and also to provide spectacles if special ones are needed.

● Fatigue and stress

● Careful design, selection and use of equipment.
● Correct design of the workplace, environment and task.
● Training in correct techniques of operation.
● Consultation and involvement of operators in work practices.
  (*See also* page 188.)

Advice is given by the Health and Safety Executive on other concerns of VDU users.

Epilepsy

VDU operation does not affect most people with epilepsy. Even those who suffer from the rare photosensitive epilepsy and are susceptible to flickering lights and striped patterns can usually work successfully with VDUs.

Skin disorders

A small number of VDU users have experienced irritation, skin rashes or had existing skin problems aggravated by the use of VDUs. These may be associated with environmental factors, such as low humidity or the electrostatic charge near the VDU. In this case the solution may be to increase the humidity and reduce the electrostatic charge.

Electromagnetic radiation

The Health and Safety Executive has consulted the National Radiological Protection Board on the effects of radiation emissions from display screen equipment and possible effects on pregnant women. The levels of electromagnetic radiation which are likely to be generated by VDUs are well below those set out in international recommendations for limiting risk to human health created by such emissions, and the NRPB does not consider such levels to pose a significant risk to health. Neither does reasearch show any link between miscarriages or birth defects and working with VDUs, and there is no need for pregnant women to stop working with them.

Fire precautions

Hazards	*Remedies*
● Obstruction of fire exit	● Keep all fire exits clear to ensure that they are immediately available for use in an emergency.
● Inadequate or missing fire-fighting/ evacuation notices	● Make sure that all personnel know what to do should a fire break out: – how to raise the fire alarm; – how to use fire-fighting equipment if required to do so; – where to assemble outside the building; – which is the shortest escape route to the assembly point and what other routes might be used if the shortest route is blocked.
	● When dealing with a fire: – if a person's clothing is on fire, wrap a blanket, rug or similar article closely round them and lay them down on the ground to prevent flames from reaching the head; – if electrical appliances are on fire, switch off the current before dealing with the fire; – shut the doors and, if possible, the windows of the room in which the fire is discovered.
● Fire doors locked or propped open	● Keep fire doors closed, except in situations where the Fire Brigade has given permission for the doors to be held open by an automatic device.
● Use of wicker wastepaper baskets as ashtrays	● Do not allow smoking in any part of the building where there is a risk of fire. Ensure that smokers use ashtrays and not the waste-paper bin or the floor.
● An open can of cleaning fluid left around in an office	● Make sure that bulk quantities or large cans of highly flammable correcting and cleaning fluids are locked away in a well-ventilated store room or metal cabinet when not in use.
● A quantity of waste paper piled up in the corner of an office	● Insist upon combustible materials such as papers and envelopes being placed in waste bins and that they are removed regularly for disposal.
● Fire alarm/fire-fighting equipment not working when required	● Ensure regular maintenance and checking of fire alarms and fire extinguishers.
● Delay and uncertainty when required to evacuate the building	● Arrange regular fire drills for all personnel.

▶ How effective are the health and safety procedures in your office? Is this an area where you could become involved?

▶ Suggest three ways in which your work in text processing could be made more comfortable.

ERGONOMICS AND THE WORKING ENVIRONMENT

Staff perform at their best when office furniture, equipment and decor are designed to support the work environment. This is enhanced when:

- there is a pleasing blend of wall colours, fabrics, floor coverings, furniture and equipment reflecting the company's image and functions;
- desks and chairs are ergonomically designed with the person and their job in mind (ergonomics is a science concerned with the relationship between human beings, the machines they use and the working environment – *see* 'Ergonomically designed chairs' below);
- each workstation is designed individually to accommodate the needs of the job and the person performing it;
- work surfaces are adequate for the job and blend in with the rest of the decor;
- multiple workstation configurations facilitate the collaboration and interaction of staff in joint projects;
- the furniture interfaces with computers and provides panels below the work surface for the necessary cables;
- appropriate task lighting supplies light exactly where it is needed.

Ergonomically designed chairs

The Equa chair, illustrated in Fig 9.4, is advertised as offering the following ergonomic characteristics to achieve the right seating position and comfort:

- The seat and back sections adjust to your size, weight and the way your body moves.
- The seat and backrest are contoured for your comfort with a space between which allows air to circulate around your body.
- Wide, soft arms sloped at the front allow you to push out of the chair more easily, pull up to the work surface and move around more freely.
- Tension of tilt can be set to suit your body weight.
- The chair has soft and rounded edges for your comfort.
- Double-wheel castors or glides are used for easy movement.
- When you sit on an Equa chair the seat moves down and the backrest moves out creating a pocket to receive your body. As you recline the knee tilt allows you to keep your feet on the floor. As you recline further for brief periods, the top of the backrest flexes out as the bottom flexes in to support your lower back.

Fig 9.4 The Equa chair

PERSONAL ACTION PLAN 39

▶ **Carry out a survey of your workstation to test whether you are working comfortably and at optimum rate. Are your surroundings inspiring or hindering your performance? Why?**

▶ **If they are hindering, how could you change this?**

STRESS IN THE OFFICE

Stress in the office is a major problem in business, largely resulting from the increase in the pace of business, deadlines, cost cutting and competition creating the need for higher levels of productivity from smaller, leaner, multidisciplinary teams. Such pressures can be self-destructive and costly and cause absenteeism, high labour turnover, poor quality of work, accidents and apathy.

As a supervisor the executive secretary must be aware of signs of stress in others as well as her or himself. According to the CBI, illness caused by stress in the workforce has increased by 500 per cent since the mid 1950s. The annual cost of stress to British industry is said to be in the range of £4.6 billion.

Checklist for spotting stress in secretarial work

- Too much or too little work.
- Too much or too little direction from management.
- Too many or too few decisions to make.
- Fear of making mistakes.
- Time pressures.
- Inability to cope/adapt to change.
- Job instability.
- Too much competition.
- Inability to ask for help or delegate work.
- Frustration at lack of career development.
- Personal problems.
- Poor office layout, systems, decoration, etc.

How to minimise the effects of stress

Routine

- Prioritise work.
- Use time wisely.
- Monitor movement of information and files.
- Write information down; do not rely on memory alone.
- Ensure the office environment is conducive to work and results; change an uncomfortable chair, for example.
- Keep regularly used information at hand for quick reference.
- Remember balance.

Communication

- Establish a good working relationship with your boss.
- Involve your team in decisions.
- Express your wants, needs and desires to create a happy environment.
- Be flexible.

Attitudes

- Be positive.
- Be receptive to challenges.
- Act confidently.
- Keep sight of your goals and be determined to achieve them.
- Develop your desire to learn new skills.
- Talk to others and if in doubt, ask. Seek advice when necessary.
- Be prepared to listen to others.

PERSONAL ACTION PLAN 40

▶ **What are your own stress triggers?**
Name three ways in which you could avoid them.

EXAMINE YOUR KNOWLEDGE

1 You are personal assistant to Mrs Sylvia Fairbanks (Case Study 4). Make the necessary preparations for the induction programme as requested in the following note:

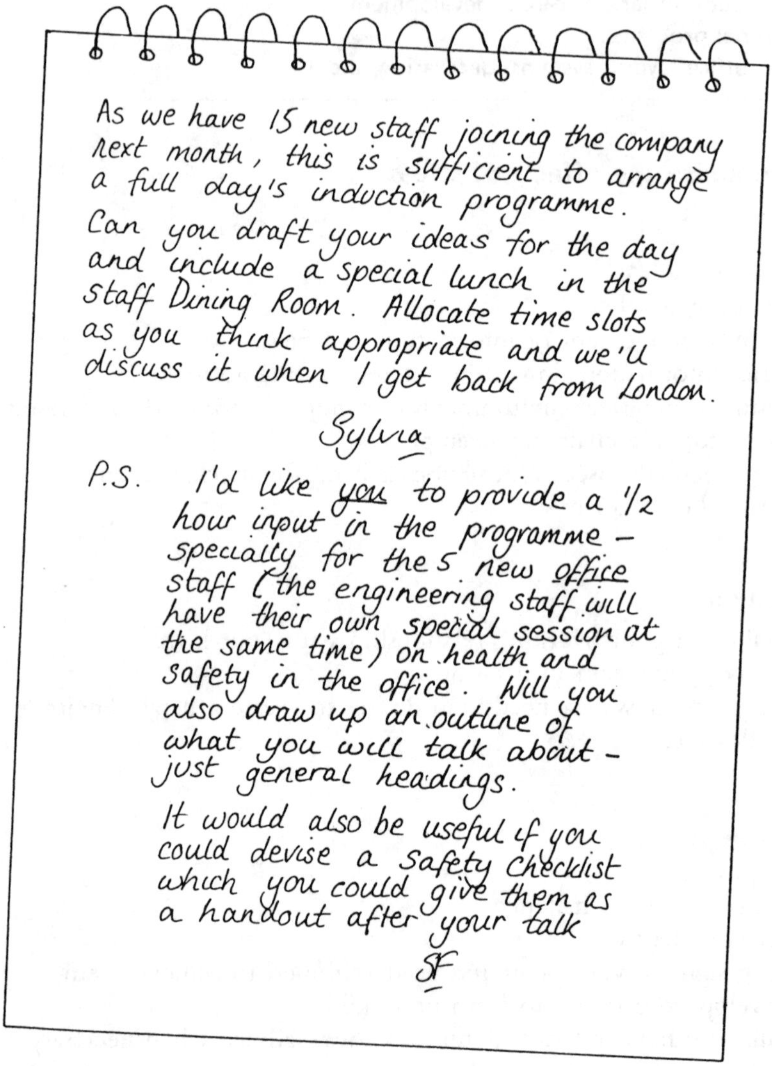

> As we have 15 new staff joining the company next month, this is sufficient to arrange a full day's induction programme.
> Can you draft your ideas for the day and include a special lunch in the Staff Dining Room. Allocate time slots as you think appropriate and we'll discuss it when I get back from London.
>
> Sylvia
>
> P.S. I'd like you to provide a ½ hour input in the programme – specially for the 5 new office staff (the engineering staff will have their own special session at the same time) on health and safety in the office. Will you also draw up an outline of what you will talk about – just general headings.
>
> It would also be useful if you could devise a safety checklist which you could give them as a handout after your talk
>
> SF

Fig 9.5

(PEI ASP)

2 You are secretary to Mr Patrick Moreland (Case Study 2). You are concerned that over the past six months work output in the office generally seems to be falling. Many of the staff have been complaining about feeling unwell. You feel this may be due to the sick building syndrome.

(a) Explain what the sick building syndrome is and prepare a report for the health and safety representative of the company.

(b) What general safety precautions should staff take for themselves? (*LCCI PESD*)

3 You have been asked to take on the responsibilities of safety representative for the office staff of Comlon International plc. What do you consider to be the duties of a safety officer? How can office staff contribute towards a safe working environment? (*LCCI PESD*)

4 (a) What information would you expect to be given in a contract of employment and when would you expect to receive it?

(b) How much notice should (i) an employee give to terminate employment and (ii) an employer give to terminate employment?

(c) In what ways can an employer assist staff who are made redundant?

WORK TASKS

Assessment of competence for Element 10.1
Monitor and maintain health and safety within the work area

Performance criteria

- *The immediate working area (including all equipment, fixtures and fittings within the job holder's responsibility) is kept free from hazards.*
- *Any discrepancies, damage and potentially unsafe features of public and office areas are noticed and rectified or promptly and accurately reported to an appropriate authority.*
- *All accidents are reported and recorded accurately, completely and legibly, in accordance with laid down procedures.*
- *Operating instructions relating to the safety of all equipment and fixtures are followed.*
- *Approved and safe methods for lifting and handling heavy or bulky items are followed.*
- *Regulations and guidelines for the use of keyboards and exposure to VDU screens are followed.*

Range statement

Competent performance must be demonstrated across a range of:
- *Potential hazards:*
  those identified in two public areas within a building; those identified in three separate offices.
- *Environments:*
  one office equipped with new technology; one open plan office.

Personal action plans 38, 39 and 40 relate to this work.

CHAPTER 10

Public relations

THE ROLE AND IMPORTANCE OF PUBLIC RELATIONS

The Institute of Public Relations describes PR practice as: 'the deliberate, planned and sustained effort to establish and maintain goodwill and mutual understanding between an organisation and its publics'.

Developing good PR now plays a very important role in both the public and private sector. It applies to the relationship between an organisation and its publics and also the relationship between an organisation and its employees at all levels. On a personal level it is crucial that the executive secretary effects good PR practice with colleagues, friends and superiors. Good PR seeks to promote a two-way communication process.

How do you achieve good PR?

To cultivate the support and goodwill of the many publics an organisation has, a programme of information and events is organised which is calculated to sustain and develop the desired image of the organisation.

The importance of good PR

Whatever the method used, establishing and maintaining good public relations on behalf of your organisation and yourself is paramount in international business. The public, that is, clients, colleagues and anyone with whom you come into contact in professional life, will judge your credibility and that of the company you represent by the service you deliver and the image you project. At any level, discourtesy, inefficiency, sloppiness and lack of professionalism in business are not readily overlooked because of youth, inexperience or the excuse that 'you are a nice person'. The international business climate is highly competitive and tough. Expectations of professionalism and competence must be high. Without the confidence and belief of clients and investors in a business there is little job security.

Building up a good reputation and engendering goodwill takes time and effort. However, a good reputation can be destroyed overnight and will take a long time to rebuild. To promote confidence takes time, and the need for special attention to PR is vital: a rude telephone operator, or an unprofessional junior secretary could be the first and perhaps only contact a potential customer or client has with a company. Even relatively minor incidents can have far-reaching effects.

Macro/micro PR

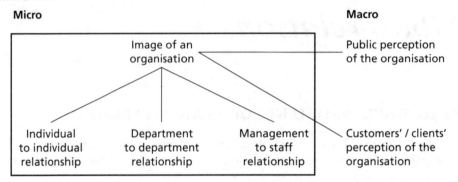

Fig 10.1 Macro/micro PR

PR can be used to present one appropriate image of an organisation to the general public; this is the macro or broader image. It can also be used to present another different yet specific image to customers and existing users, and in another way PR can be used by senior management within the organisation to generate good morale and team work; this is the micro image, i.e. moving from the general and overall to the specific and smaller. At the micro level, departments and indeed individuals within departments use PR skills to present themselves or their departments in a positive and favourable light with the aim of influencing others through good relations.

Some of an organisation's 'publics' or PR targets are shown in Fig 10.2. However, public relations are established by most companies with three main groups in mind:

1 Their employees for discussing, negotiating and communicating such matters as:
- pay and working conditions;
- career structures, promotion and training;
- industrial relations.

2 Their customers, clients and business associates:
- to maintain effective personal business relationships;
- to elicit a response to advertising and the presentation of goods and services;
- to provide an awareness of the reliability of products and services;
- to maintain contacts with an after-sales service.

3 The community:
- to be a respected and desirable contributor to the welfare of the community;
- to cultivate useful and amicable contacts with dignitaries in local public administration organisations and other businesses/traders;
- to demonstrate a practical concern for people within the area and for people in need.

THE BENEFITS OF GOOD PUBLIC RELATIONS

- Promotes a good local, national and international reputation for the company, encouraging confidence in its products or services.

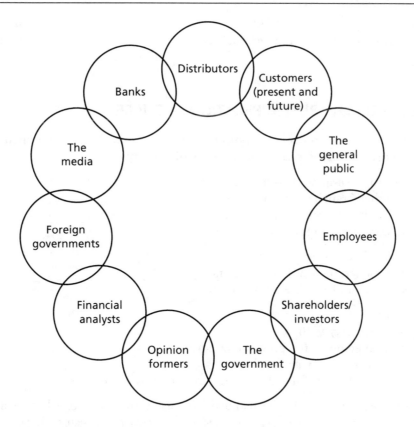

Fig 10.2 Possible PR targets for an organisation

- Increases business by advertising goods and services locally, nationally or internationally.
- Establishes a sound financial base, making the company attractive from an investment point of view.
- Gains public approval and support for its policies.
- Fosters and maintains good morale among the company's workforce.
- Creates a sound reputation by marketing reliable products or services, and by showing a genuine desire to help the public in an active and practical way.
- Demonstrates a desire to be active in helping and supporting the public on occasions when the need arises.

Promoting and protecting image

Public relations can be handled by different people in an organisation, depending on the size of the company and the emphasis placed on marketing in general. It can be handled by senior management who are charged with the responsibility of 'managing' an organisation's reputation, corporate image and credibility: developing, moulding, protecting and promoting it. More usually, however, a member of the marketing team will be responsible because PR forms part of the promotion element to the marketing mix, the four Ps:

Promotion	*Product*	*Place*	*Price*
Advertising and PR	Design quality	Channels of distribution	Pricing policy

THE ROLE OF THE PUBLIC RELATIONS OFFICER

A public relations officer is responsible for securing the benefits outlined above; these will normally involve three main areas of activity:

1 External company liaison with:
  - other branches and subsidiaries;
  - media sources;
  - community organisations.

2 Internal company liaison:
  - production of house magazine;
  - social and welfare organisations.

3 Media:
  - interviews with reporters;
  - arrangements for press conferences;
  - preparation of press releases;
  - arrangements for exhibitions and demonstrations.

Public relations can also be handled by outside specialists or PR consultancies who may have niche market expertise and contacts with journalists. If you are involved in the process of choosing a PR consultancy, the PRCA (Public Relations Consultants Association) will be of assistance (*see* the Information Bank for further details). The three rules to remember if using outside consultancies are:

1 know what you want – for example, increased sales or a shift in company image;
2 know who can deliver;
3 find out if it is working – agree your own performance criteria.

PR takes many forms (*see* Fig 10.3) and many channels:

- national press for advertisements and new items (press releases);
- local and provincial newspapers;
- magazines, journals and internal publications including company house magazines;
- television and teletext;
- radio and TV, both national and local;
- leaflets, handbills, brochures and posters;
- special offers in conjunction with any of the above, including promotion campaigns, free samples of goods, competitions, etc.;
- exhibitions and demonstrations;
- open days and visits to firms' premises.

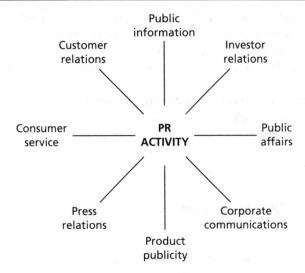

Fig 10.3 Types of PR

Promoting image

Attacking

Enhancing the image of a company (corporate identity) by sponsorship of social or sports activities such as the arts or golf tournaments. This can involve considerable amounts of money and is a way of advertising a company's name with added value. In this way the company is seen to be helping the community and perceived to be socially responsible and motivated not purely by profit. The overall message implies that the company has its customers' interests at heart and is socially aware, for example, *The Times'* sponsorship of the Office Secretary of the Year Award or Business Pages' sponsorship of the seminars at the London Secretary and Office Management Show, and the involvement of *Prima* magazine in a project to help mentally handicapped teenagers by decorating and furnishing a flat in a London care home. Various firms associated with the magazine decorated and furnished the flat. By this means they informed the public about the company's actions, products and policies which might affect the physical and social environment.

Protecting image

Defensive

A large part of the work of a PR executive, officer or executive secretary specialising in PR is to deal with complaints and criticisms from customers and the general public. How well these are dealt with will influence the customer's perceptions of the company or product under scrutiny and how effectively changes are implemented to improve the service or product.

Damage limitation

This involves planning responses to difficult situations or scenarios that may occur with a product. Volkswagen, the car manufacturer, for example, took conscientious steps and positive action in support of its customers when fans of a particular pop group were stealing the famous VW roundel car logo. Volkswagen offered free replacement roundels to all its customers, which reflected very well on VW and its many dealers.

Protecting the organisation's reputation in general

This can involve such things as pacifying initiatives from pressure groups raising objections to a company's actions and finding compromises. In these cases it pays to avoid rumours, be factual, admit a mistake instead of 'covering up', and be positive with defensive PR showing how the situation can be resolved.

Advertising and PR: the differences

Advertising

Aims to inform, persuade and convince a target market to buy a product or service.

Public relations

Aims to influence public opinion favourably with a general positive image of a company or individual. There are many different types of PR, ranging from sponsorship, publicity stunts and celebrity appearances to public speaking and editorial in newspapers and magazines. All are designed to publicise who you are and what you do, and suggest that you have something worthwhile and new to offer.

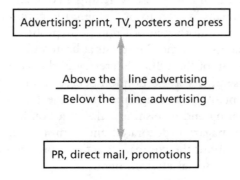

Fig 10.4 The place of PR in the organisation's advertising

PROTOCOL

Protocol is defined as 'the rules of diplomatic etiquette and procedures'. This means knowing what to do and when – in other words:

- being professional;
- making the effort to find out the correct titles of people with whom you may deal, especially abroad where business etiquette can be more formal and cultural differences may affect business procedure;

prima

Portland House
Stag Place, London SW1E 5AU
Telephone: 071-245 8700
Telefax: 071-630 5509

12 August 19_ _

Miss Lesley Partridge
18 Crossways
Dublin 1
Ireland

(1) Dear Miss Partridge

Many thanks for your letter regarding our travel
article on Kenya. I'm so glad you enjoyed reading
all about the Safari. Our fashion department went on
a photographic trip to Kenya and had a wonderful
time there. It's a real holiday of a lifetime.

(2) The travel company we used, African Tours and
Hotels, were extremely helpful. They can be
contacted at their Sales Office, 30 Old Bond Street,
London W1X 3AD. Telephone number: 071-491 7431.

(3) I do hope you manage to visit Kenya, and if so we
would love to hear how you got on.

Yours sincerely

DSaker

Dee Saker
PA to Editor

prima is published monthly by Gruner + Jahr (U.K.)

(1) Correct form of address.

(2) Professional passing-on of information in response to request.

(3) Conversion of an enquiry into a possible contact for a future article.

Fig 10.5 An example of good public relations

- acquainting yourself with the correct procedures for approaching and dealing with contacts.

Contact with anyone outside the office is an opportunity to practise and foster good public relations, as demonstrated in the letter from the editor's PA of *Prima* magazine (Fig 10.5). In short, protocol is:

- saying the right thing
- to the right people
- in the right manner
- at the right time.

PLANNING A PUBLIC RELATIONS EXERCISE

It is important to try to find a new angle, something different about your product or service or the way you promote it – in other words, its 'unique selling point', such as the jeans manufacturer that wrapped a whole building in denim as a publicity stunt, Rolex's sponsorship of Wimbledon, celebrity endorsement of a designer label of clothes, or a recruitment consultancy's sponsorship of a student's study at secretarial college.

When Perrier were forced to withdraw stocks of their mineral water due to benzene contamination, this could have had a life-threatening effect on the brand. However, Perrier used clever defensive PR and withdrew the water for a period of time and then relaunched the whole brand in a highly successful campaign. Perrier were completely honest, and in the use of their PR presented the image of a totally responsible company that would only relaunch the product when it was sure that the public was not at risk. A combination of direct advertising, press releases and editorial in newspapers was used to communicate the message to the public.

At a different level, using language skills to communicate with customers, such as a multilingual receptionist or sending faxes in a foreign language or employing staff in a retail outlet who can sell in three languages, are examples of the value added, the good PR, being prepared to make that extra effort for the customer. These additional features to a service may be the difference between improving business and standing still.

Collection and dissemination of information

This is a vital and highly responsible managerial part of the PR function. Knowing how to store PR information – releases, articles, contacts, names and addresses and their relevance, timing of PR events and activity in different markets, keeping abreast of costs, analysis of benefits and performance criteria – are complex issues which require an understanding of the business and PR objectives. For the secretary to make a valuable contribution in this area, she or he must be given access to strategy information and be part of the team.

Checklist when planning a public relations exercise

- *Purpose*   Decide on the objective of the exercise, such as sales promotion, dissemination of a new item, community services: analyse problems and opportunities (this should remind you of the SWOT analysis in Chapter 1).

- *Image*   Decide on the image that needs to be presented.
- *Target group*   Decide on the target group that should be reached.
- *Content*   Decide on the information to be conveyed.
- *Approach*   Decide on the appropriate approach to be used to attract attention to the purpose.
- *Media*   Decide on the medium or combination of media to use for the exercise.
- *Cost*   Estimate the cost and be satisfied that it can be met from the budget resources.
- *Date/duration*   Decide on the date and duration of the campaign. A press conference publicising a news item should be arranged so that the journalists can report the news back to their newspapers in time for the next edition of the paper.
- *Evaluation*   Set evaluation criteria to assess results against objectives.
- *Assign tasks*

DEALING WITH THE MEDIA

Positive PR can often result from free coverage in the editorial of trade journals, local or national newspapers. This comes about largely due to having contacts within the media and by sending press releases to mark events such as new product launches or new business openings. Key points to remember when dealing with the media, whether it is for TV or print coverage, are:

1 The media are only interested in 'news'. The mere fact of opening a business or presenting a new service may not be of interest or newsworthy enough. A unique angle is vital to keeping a constant presence in the media, and much depends on timing and contacts. Develop and maintain good working contacts.

2 When dealing with enquiries from reporters:

   (*a*) be approachable, friendly and co–operative, as press reports influence a company's public image for good or evil;
   (*b*) if information is freely available, give it without 'hedging';
   (*c*) guard against divulging any information which is secret or confidential;
   (*d*) if pressed to give confidential information, be diplomatic in evading the question and explain the company's procedures in such matters;
   (*e*) if a request is made for an appointment with your executive, allow him or her sufficient time to prepare their response.

3 When writing press releases, try to create an air of excitement and mystery. Embargo it, prohibit its use until the date that suits you best, and send it to publications or journalists who are most likely to use it. Always follow up your work and be determined. For examples of press releases, see Figures 10.6 and 10.7. The Institute of Public Relations issues guidelines and recommended practice papers which may be helpful.

4 The following list will help you to prepare a press release for your company in terms of format and manner required by the press. Check that:

   (*a*) the heading is clear and indicates what the subject is about;
   (*b*) the opening paragraph summarises the main points of the message;

Patron:
HER MAJESTY THE QUEEN

15 Queen's Gate Terrace
London
SW7 5PR
Telephone: 071-584 9315
Fax: 071-581 0410

WINSTON CHURCHILL MEMORIAL TRUST

PRESS RELEASE   *Organisation's logo* →

For Immediate Release   ← *When the release Should be issued*   15 February 1993

Eye-catching headline ←

Churchill does not surrender, his spirit lives on!

As modern historians reassess Sir Winston Churchill's contribution to the nation, 95 Britons are showing the world that the Churchillian spirit of determination, initiative and adventure is very much alive. These men and women have won prestigious Churchill Travelling Fellowships. ＼

Newsworthy subject ↓   *1½ or double spacing*

Selected from 1600 applicants from all parts of the United Kingdom, they have been given the chance of a lifetime to travel abroad on a project of their own choice to gain experience which will benefit their work. Originated as a "Living Memorial", the Winston Churchill Memorial Trust was endowed by the nation in 1965 in gratitude for Churchill's leadership and inspiration. The competition to become a "Churchill Fellow" is always keen and this year has been no exception.

The youngest is a 16-year-old schoolboy wheelchair tennis champion; the oldest is a 70-year-old travel writer who will be cycling from the Baltic to the Black Sea. A young mother from Kent with her baby will buy a caravan to join an Italian circus on tour; a scientist from Northern Ireland will study the detection of veterinary drugs in animals; a Scottish tree nurseryman will investigate renewable organic materials in horticulture; an adventure trainer from Gwynedd will assess outward-bound schemes in America.

Fig 10.6a Winston Churchill Memorial Trust press release (page 1)

Benzodiazepine withdrawal guidelines, fish gene transfer, multicultural dance and choreography, plastic jewellery moulding, computer-based learning in veterinary education, a biography of Primo Levi, psychiatric care in the community - those are amongst the fascinating projects to be studied by Fellows travelling to every corner of the globe.

Quotation - breaks up the copy and gives an opinion

Sir Richard Vickers, Director General of the Trust, is very impressed by this year's winners. He says, "While academics conjecture about the possibility of Churchill making peace with Hitler and Nazi Germany, these Churchill Travelling Fellows epitomise the British spirit of no surrender - to the recession, to unemployment, to disability, to injustice. On their return with new knowledge, skills and enthusiasm, they will do their best to make a more effective contribution to the community and the country. Sir Winston would have been proud of them."

Please note:

The enclosed list gives the names, addresses and projects of the 1993 Award winners. The regional and category index will enable you to pick out your own area of special concern. Hopefully their stories will interest your readers/viewers/listeners so that they will be inspired to apply for their "Chance of a lifetime" in 1994.

The attached leaflet gives information about the Churchill Trust and the opportunites offered for 1993. Information on how to apply for future awards can be obtained from the Winston Churchill Memorial Trust, 15 Queen's Gate Terrace, London SW7 5PR.

Contact name and number

For further information please telephone Miss R Conner on 071-584 9315 (office hours).

ENDS *← Indicates no pages are missing*

Fig 10.6b Winston Churchill Memorial Trust press release (page 2)

Headline
↓

LaserMaster® introduces A3 format 1200 dpi, multi-platform, Plain-Paper Typesetter

Newsworthy
↓

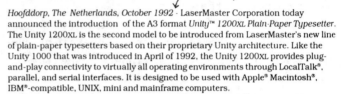

Contact: *Contact name*

Marian Westland
(31) 2503 - 22000
(31) 2503 - 31240 (fax)

For Release:

October 1, 1992

When Release should be issued

Hoofddorp, The Netherlands, October 1992 - LaserMaster Corporation today announced the introduction of the A3 format *Unity™ 1200XL Plain-Paper Typesetter*. The Unity 1200XL is the second model to be introduced from LaserMaster's new line of plain-paper typesetters based on their proprietary Unity architecture. Like the Unity 1000 that was introduced in April of 1992, the Unity 1200XL provides plug-and-play connectivity to virtually all operating environments through LocalTalk®, parallel, and serial interfaces. It is designed to be used with Apple® Macintosh®, IBM®-compatible, UNIX, mini and mainframe computers.

The Unity 1200XL prints 1200-dpi, camera-ready output on plain paper up to A3 format. Other features include an internal hard disk with 135 pre-installed Type 1 typefaces, 1200 x 1200 TurboRes® quality, SmartSense™ automatic emulation sensing, superior font handling, an optional Ethernet expansion port, HotPorts™ automatic port switching, and TurboGray™ halftone-enhancement technology. The Unity 1200XL has a list price of UK £7,695 excl. VAT. *Quotations break up copy and give opinions*

"The introduction of the Unity 1000 last April marked a major product transition for LaserMaster from that of bus-based technology to the most sophisticated network-compatible technology in our history," says Mel Masters, LaserMaster CEO. "By offering multi-platform, plug-and-play connectivity in A3 format, the Unity 1200XL is yet another major step forward in our quest to deliver high-quality, low-cost typesetting devices to a wide segment of the market."

Large-Format Versatility
The Unity 1200XL prints on plain paper up to A3 format, allowing users to print camera-ready two-page spreads, oversized graphics, A4 page layouts with crop marks, and more. The Unity 1200XL comes standard with one paper cassette that holds 250 sheets and can be adjusted to any of its supported paper sizes (US letter, legal, A4, A3, B4 and B5 sheets). Users may purchase an additional cassette feeder as an option to hold an additional 250 sheets. A multi-purpose feeder is also available for feeding up to 150 odd-sized sheets or up to 20 envelopes.

1200 x 1200 TurboRes Quality
The Unity 1200XL features LaserMaster's patented TurboRes resolution-enhancement technology for high-resolution, camera-ready copy on plain paper. By controlling the position and height of individual dots on the page, the Unity 1200XL is able to print text and line art at a resolution of 1200 x 1200 TurboRes. Users also have the option to select the faster proof mode that prints at 600 x 600 dpi.

TurboGray
TurboGray improves the appearance of halftone images by providing contour smoothing for increased gray levels at higher screen frequencies. Users have both high image resolution to show fine detail and smooth gray-level control to achieve contour smoothing.

Organisation's logo →

LM EUROPE **LASERMASTER™** E U R O P E L t d .

Debbemeerstraat 12, 2131 HE Hoofddorp, The Netherlands
Tel: (+) 31 2503 22000 FAX: (+) 31 2503 31240

Fig 10.7a LaserMaster Europe press release (page 1)

Target Markets

The Unity 1200XL provides A3 format, camera-ready output on plain paper. Target markets include graphic art and design studios, quick-printers, in-plants, and newsletter publishers.

Availability

The Unity 1200XL is priced at UK £7,695 excl. VAT (list price). It will begin shipping October, 1992. It is available through LaserMaster's network of Authorized Resellers and International Value-Added Distributors.

Additional Information

Additional reference documents about LaserMaster's new Unity 1200XL Plain-Paper Typesetter are included in this press packet. See LaserMaster *Unity 1200XL: Editor's Quick Reference* for a general listing of key Unity 1200XL features. See also the LaserMaster *Unity 1200XL: Technology Overview* for detailed explanations of the unique hardware and software of the Unity 1200XL.

LaserMaster is a world leader in high-resolution, high-performance printing systems for microcomputers and microcomputer networks. For more information about the large-format Unity 1200XL, contact Marian Westland at LaserMaster Europe, tel. (31) 2503 - 22000.

©LaserMaster Corporation. The LM logo, LaserMaster and TurboRes are registered trademarks and Unity, SmartSense, HotPorts, TurboGray and Reconfigurable Resident Fonts are trademarks of LaserMaster Corporation. Adobe Type Manager, ATM and PostScript are trademarks of Adobe Systems, Incorporated. This product incorporates TrueImage v.1 software with proprietary LaserMaster enhancements for performance and resolution. Microsoft is a registered trademark and Windows and TrueImage are trademarks of Microsoft Corporation. All other product names or brand names are trademarks or registered trademarks of their respective holders. Specifications and prices subject to change without notice.

Fig 10.7b LaserMaster Europe press release (page 2)

Fig 10.7c LaserMaster Unit 1200XL printer

(c) facts are accurate and presented logically;

(d) style, content and vocabulary are appropriate to the audience and overall requirements of the selected publication;

(e) supporting illustrations such as photographs, diagrams or leaflets are available;

(f) the final paragraph gives the name and address of the organisation together with telephone and fax number where appropriate;

(g) copy is made available in time to meet the deadline;

(h) the name of the author/contact and the date of issue are stated.

5 Write succinctly. Overlong, badly written releases find their way to the waste-paper basket.

6 Keep up-to-date lists. Incorrect names, addresses and titles can be offensive and lose business.

7 Research all media possibilities and try to maximise coverage.

8 Always send press releases to a particular person with their job title. There is more chance of it reaching a decision-maker if you research who the decision-makers are: news editors, business editors, local editor, and so on.

9 Remember the value of a photograph, especially where language may be a problem.

VISITORS AND TELEPHONE CALLERS

The overriding first impression a visitor gains of an organisation is influenced by the manner in which he or she is received at reception or on the telephone. The receptionist or secretary must possess the necessary business skills and personal qualities to greet all visitors pleasantly and efficiently and to deal with their enquiries appropriately. As an executive secretary, this is at the heart of your day-to-day work. As a supervisor, you must be able to recognise these requirements in others and foster them. This is a PR opportunity for you and for the company (see Fig 10.8).

PERSONAL ACTION PLAN 41

▶ **Role play three situations where you receive, screen and assist 'difficult' visitors, for example:**
  a) non-English speaker
  b) irate client
  c) suspicious individual asking for your boss
  d) two double-booked appointments
  e) unexpected customer.

▶ **How do you know where your authority begins and ends with visitors? Have you clarified this with your boss or reviewed your progress? When and how frequently?**

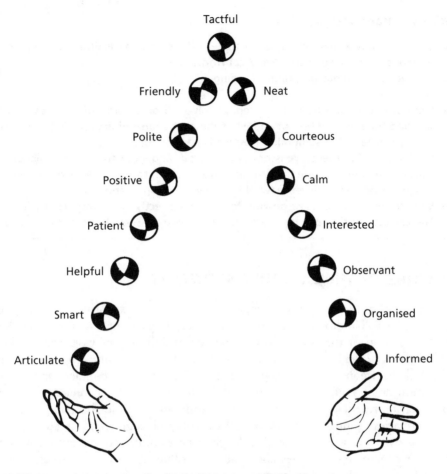

Fig 10.8 You are your organisation's PR opportunity package!

How to deal with external calls

There are times when managers must be 'screened' from telephone calls and visitors
– for example, when they are attending meetings, appointments and when working
to an urgent deadline. As a general rule, the secretary should act as a 'filter', not a
barrier, in keeping that vital channel of communication open between managers, their
colleagues and the public. The secretary who knows the manager's contacts and is
knowledgeable about the business will be equipped to handle the many enquiries
received and will shield the manager when appropriate. The key to success is the
identification of important issues. By establishing good relations with the contacts, the
executive secretary can anticipate and satisfy the needs of the manager and callers.

Problems, complaints, complex questions and sensitive issues are areas of
communication that confront the executive secretary every day. Each is an opportunity
to practise good PR for yourself and the company you represent. Turn a potential
negative experience into a positive opportunity. Being able to deal with these types
of problems successfully in a foreign language or with people whose mother tongue
is not English provides tremendous positive PR in itself.

Checklist for handling problems

- Listen – allow a client or customer to 'let off steam'. This is often all the person needs, someone to listen to them. Avoid confrontation.
- Always be courteous and understanding.
- Obtain all the facts.
- Suggest a form of action. If you cannot solve a problem immediately, explain how you will find the person who can and what the next course of action will be. This will make the person feel that something positive is happening.
- Be discreet where sensitive issues are involved. Engender trust in your actions.
- Take control and manage the situation. Agree when to follow up with the answer to the complaint or query. Never leave the conversation open-ended.
- Be clear and concise. Take down information correctly and always clarify it if in doubt. The correct decision can be made only when you possess all the relevant facts.

THE PR ROLE OF THE EXECUTIVE SECRETARY

At the heart of the secretary's success and value to the executive and the organisation is her or his skill in dealing with people and in creating an impression which will enhance the reputation of the organisation. The responsibilities are vast, and the key is the PR element of the job as it extends to all areas of responsibility. The secretary provides the link between the executive and his or her various contacts and ensures that communication is effective or enhanced. In this capacity the secretary is the executive's personal representative and ambassador inside and outside the company.

Secretaries cannot play this vital full PR role unless given complete understanding of their own and the executive's role. Secretaries must acquire sufficient knowledge of their executive's activities and sphere of influence to be able to ask for work to be delegated to them. Secretaries make decisions, give instructions and represent the executive on business occasions. To some extent they manage their own and their boss's general PR by exerting a positive influence over the behaviour and reactions of others. In this respect they are managers and leaders. This is discussed further in the next chapter. However, there are limits to a secretary's responsibility. When the executive is away the secretary is the guardian of the office, not the acting deputy. This is where the executive and the secretary must communicate and clarify the limits or boundaries to responsibility in order to avoid negative PR or operational errors.

Checklist of the PR opportunities for the executive secretary

- *Telephone manner*
  Handling telephone calls and messages courteously and efficiently so that they satisfy the needs of the caller.

- *Personality*
  Making visitors feel welcome, attending to their individual needs so that they feel special.

- *Quality of work*
  Ensuring that correspondence and all documents leaving the company are accurate, well presented, and convey the correct meaning and tone.

- *Method of work*
  Organising the office efficiently to cope with changing priorities and demands.

- *Ability to plan meetings and conferences*
  Anticipating the needs of all participants and ensuring a successful outcome.

- *Willingness to be of assistance*
  Responding positively to requests for assistance and advice from customers, clients and colleagues.

- *Interpersonal skills*
  Creating and maintaining professional relationships with customers, clients and colleagues.

- *Diplomacy and tact*
  Using diplomacy and tact in handling the press and other agencies to enhance the company's reputation.

- *Personal effectiveness*
  Setting yourself high standards of personal appearance and effectiveness when representing the firm at external functions.

PERSONAL ACTION PLAN 42

▶ How are you involved with PR work in your company?

▶ At a personal level how would you implement your own image development campaign in the office?

▶ For which skills would you like to be known and recognised?

PERSONAL ACTION PLAN 43

▶ A survey undertaken by Cranfield School of Management with the Institute of Public Relations showed that the following qualities were necessary for success in PR. As an executive secretary, which of these skills do you utilise and how?

- Ability to analyse management needs.
- Ability to counsel management.
- Ability to identify causes of problems.
- Ability to plan, organise and co-ordinate tasks and to bring them to a successful conclusion.
- Ability to monitor and follow up on tasks.
- Ability to set goals and objectives.
- Ability to motivate and influence others.
- Ability to work effectively with media personnel.
- Presentation skills.
- Ability to establish financial controls.
- Ability to prepare news releases, special reports and to arrange news conferences.

- **Ability to identify major social issues affecting organisations and to resolve conflict.**
- **Ability to work with others.**

EXAMINE YOUR KNOWLEDGE

1 You are PA/secretary to Mrs Catherine Walsh (Case Study 1). Prepare a note of the requirements for press releases for a new secretary in marketing. Elisabeth Ford wishes to obtain some good publicity in the trade magazines with an article on the design chosen for the new extension to the museum. *(LCCI PESD)*

2 Write a brief note on the difference between public relations and advertising. How can a secretary enhance her company's public relations? *(LCCI PESD)*

3 You are secretary to Mr Patrick Moreland (Case Study 2). Assume that Janet Cantrell, secretary to Martin Fletcher, has been notified that she has been awarded the top place nationally in the London Chamber of Commerce Private and Executive Secretary's Diploma examination. Supply details of this successful achievement in a press release for your local newspaper. Take the opportunity to provide details of the course she attended and draw attention to the relevance of the management skills the students acquired on the course for successful employment at executive secretarial level in today's offices.

4 The following is a transcript of a telephone conversation of a customer with Paul, a telephonist at Delta Bakeries.

PAUL: Good morning, Delta Bakeries.

CALLER: I'd like to speak to the Sales Manager.

PAUL: Just one moment, I'll see if he's available. (*Pause*)

PAUL: I'm sorry, he's not available at the moment. Would you like to speak to someone else?

CALLER: No thanks. When will he be back?

PAUL: I'm sorry, I've no idea.

CALLER: Well, what am I supposed to do, then? He promised to make a delivery this morning and there's no sign of it. This isn't the first time it's happened either! My customers rely on fresh bread and cakes and I've just about had enough of it.

PAUL: Well, if you won't speak to anyone else, there's nothing I can do about it.

CALLER: Look here, young man, you were recommended to me as providing a good service and high-quality goods. So far the service has been abysmal – whenever I ring there's no one available to speak to me – and here you are telling me there's nothing you can do about it. Someone ought to tell you that it's the customers who pay and if you can't give them what they want, they'll go somewhere else, which is just what I intend to do!

PAUL: Well, it's a free country! There's plenty more people who *do* want our goods!

CALLER: That's what you think, *you jumped-up little upstart!* I'll make sure word gets around not to do business with *you!*

PAUL: Don't you speak to me like that! (*Slams receiver down.*) Who the hell does she think she is, anyway?

(Reproduced from *An Integrated Approach to Business Administration* by Valerie Bell and John Harrison, Pitman Publishing.)

(*a*) Discuss the implications of this telephone call for Delta Bakeries.
(*b*) As Paul's supervisor, suggest:
  i) how the call should have been handled;
  ii) what action should be taken to improve Paul's telephone technique.

WORK TASKS

Assessment of competence for Element 3.1
Receive, screen and assist visitors

Performance criteria

- *Visitors are received courteously and their identity is established.*
- *The nature of the visit and the needs of the visitor are identified and matched to the products and/or services of the organisation.*
- *Visitors within own scope of responsibility are dealt with directly.*
- *Other visitors are referred or redirected in accordance with laid down procedures.*
- *The structure, products and/or services of the organisation are accurately described and promoted to the visitor.*
- *Non-routine and emergency demands are dealt with promptly and effectively.*
- *The principal is protected from unnecessary interruptions at all times.*
- *Any protective clothing or equipment required for the visit is provided.*
- *Records are kept up to date, legible and accurate.*
- *Safe working practices are always followed and implemented.*
- *Security and confidentiality procedures are always followed and implemented.*

Range statement

Competent performance must be demonstrated across a range of:

- *Visitors:*
  expected and unexpected; internal to own organisation; both senior and junior to principal; external including foreign nationals.
- *Visitor needs:*
  both routine and complex queries; both within and beyond own scope of responsibility.
- *Visitor behaviours:*
  pleasant and positive; demanding and negative; uncertain or confused; complaining and angry.
- *Contingencies:*
  several visitors at once; telephone or other interruptions; conflicting demands of internal and external visitors.

Personal action plan 41 relates to this work.

CHAPTER 11

The management support role of the secretary

THE QUALITIES REQUIRED IN AN INTERNATIONAL ENVIRONMENT

The good secretary/PA working in the international environment is a delicate balance and melding of disparate skills and personality traits. Qualities such as tact, determination, strength of character, diplomacy and the ability to anticipate needs and responses to different situations play important roles in the business life of the executive secretary. Allied to these 'life' skills are the solid operational skills such as text processing, shorthand and administration.

Analysing the concept of success within the context of 'being good at the job' is not an easy task. There are ingredients that contribute to moulding a successful professional secretary, and these are outlined below. Importantly, all these skills contribute towards a secretary's managerial skills and the ability to support management. Being able to motivate, supervise and negotiate well in English, and increasingly in foreign languages, are areas in which secretaries should take the initiative and develop the mantle of 'executive assistant'.

What makes a good executive secretary in the international environment?

- Understanding and agreeing aims and objectives.
- Creating effective working relationships.
- Professional manning of the office in the absence of others.
- Technical skills based on training, natural talent and experience.
- Foreign-language ability.
- Personality and interpersonal skills, that is to say, the ability to relate to people at many different levels. This is the area where a certain *je ne sais quoi* or indefinable special something makes each executive secretary unique and different.
- Positive self-image and motivation.
- The ability to understand different cultures. This is drawn from personal experience, time spent abroad in foreign countries learning the language and assimilating the culture and mores.

AIMS AND OBJECTIVES

Many of the secretary's day-to-day routine responsibilities involve making decisions, actioning them herself or himself, or obtaining a colleague's agreement to action them. This is essentially a 'managing' role, which is achieving results through people.

Management is the process or act of managing which involves skill in controlling and handling. As a dictionary definition it is not very helpful. It requires expansion.

Management involves the guidance and motivation of staff within an organisation (*see* Chapter 1 for corporate objectives) and the supervision of personnel in carrying out and fulfilling tasks and achieving objectives.

Executive secretaries in most organisations are not labelled as managers, although they have authority to use discretion in making decisions and are often party to highly confidential information and responsible for its circulation. This is where much of the challenge, enjoyment and frustration of being an executive secretary can lie. Perhaps Norway and Sweden can set a good example, where research has confirmed that the secretary is a member of the management team and treated as such; two or three languages are essential, personal development is stressed and management support is emphasised.

At the heart of the secretary's management support role is being involved with the setting of aims and objectives. It is vital to be part of the team right from the start.

Do you set yourself objectives? What is more important, are you able to achieve them? Perhaps you have used the objectives set in the Personal Action Plans in this book. If so, you are now well on target to accomplish your objectives!

Objectives can be thought of as targets to be reached which, when prescribed realistically, encourage us to work more effectively with greater purpose. Sometimes we fail to accomplish our objectives because we are deflected in other directions and pay inadequate attention to the activities which matter. It is then that we need a gentle prod, such as the advice given in this card displayed prominently on an executive's desk:

> ## IS WHAT I AM DOING
> ## OR ABOUT TO DO
> ## CONTRIBUTING TO MY OBJECTIVES?

Apparently that technique saved the executive from making many useless trips, lunch dates, meetings and conferences.

Objectives are important for everyone in business, as was shown in Chapter 1. For the executive secretary the prime objective is to assist senior management in achieving their objectives as given below.

Senior management objectives

Some examples:

- Contribute, along with other senior executives, to achieving the corporate objectives.
- Develop and contribute towards the implementation of more efficient and cost-effective administrative, marketing and production systems.
- Increase the company's market share.
- Identify new market niches (e.g. in Eastern Europe) and tailor the company's products and methods of business to their needs.
- Investigate ways of expanding sales in all European markets, in order to become more strategically balanced.

Executive secretary's objectives

Some examples to assist senior management to achieve their objectives are:

- Co-ordinating and planning the administration of the senior executive's office; accounting for priorities and planning to minimise last-minute changes.
- Ensuring effective preparation for meetings, appointments and discussions.
- Controlling a budget and monitoring expenditure according to prescribed limits.
- Maintaining up-to-date diaries and arranging appointments, travel reservations and itineraries to meet the needs of the senior manager.
- Using the information processing system to effect internal correspondence and ensure timely and accurate turnround of letters and reports.
- Supervising and supporting junior staff to assist in the achievement of these objectives.

The boss is responsible for involving the executive secretary, but he or she may need to be prompted. Manage your boss: ask to be involved, for you cannot contribute fully unless you are given a full and clear understanding of what is expected of you, ask about the executive's role, his or her objectives and the part they play in the organisation as a whole. Your greater understanding of the reasons why certain projects are undertaken will prove invaluable to your boss when you make a concrete contribution to its fulfilment.

A task- or objective-oriented approach to work can be highly productive for both the executive secretary and the boss. Rather than having tasks imposed or handed down in an authoritarian manner, setting objectives as a team leads to consultation, and aims are agreed rather than orders being passed on. This is both motivating (making you want to perform at a high level) and provides more job satisfaction and self-development. If you are closely involved with setting objectives it is only human nature to be motivated to achieve those goals. By working with the boss in setting aims and objectives you are motivating both yourself and your boss. The personal involvement of a boss at all levels in setting targets and agreeing workloads is vital for the boss's own positive motivation and management development as well as the secretary's. Managers are responsible for the activities and success of their juniors as well as being accountable to their own bosses for agreed aims and objectives.

Checklist for aims and objectives

- Be clear about the corporate objectives, the departmental objectives, and those of your own job description.
- Agree, through discussion with your boss, targets for your own job. If necessary, outline the benefits to the boss of involving you at an early stage.
- Take the initiative. Ask to be present at meetings and suggest projects and responsibilities you could shoulder.
- Clarify boundaries to responsibility.
- Agree timing and performance criteria for projects.
- Agree evaluation processes.
- Agree some form of recognition of personal achievement, such as appraisal.
- Agree some form of management development programme – courses or specific project work, for example.

WORKING RELATIONSHIPS

When the executive secretary has clear work objectives and aims, the correct course of action in any situation usually becomes clearer also. The secretary should have clear intentions for specific working relationships. At the root of these is the boss/secretary relationship. If it is good and based on a free flow of information and good rapport, then other working relationships should flourish. If the basis of the relationship is bad and communication partial, or there is no feeling of working towards common goals, this can affect how the secretary relates to other colleagues and is perceived by others. It can also affect the quality of co-operation and help from others.

Today's managers/bosses are becoming more teamwork-oriented, but both the secretary and the boss must be prepared to take their part in creating an effective and cohesive management unit based on mutual understanding. The secretary may need to go some way towards understanding business economics or accounting in order to have a clearer perspective of the organisation's role in the business market. Likewise, the boss may need to recognise that the secretary should attend training courses. They are as vital for the secretary as for the manager. The boss must allow the secretary to show problem-solving skills and to adapt to and master new technology, to systemise and process information, and to acquire foreign-language skills. By developing the boss/secretary relationship, the secretary's management support role will be enhanced and grow. Secretaries can carry out more research, manage information more effectively, liaise more professionally at all levels and generally ease the burden while their bosses concentrate on the more pressing aspects of their jobs.

Checklist for creating effective working relationships

- *Appropriate communication*
  It is vital to allow a free flow of information between boss/secretary and colleagues. Tell people what you are doing where appropriate. However, learn to know where and when to stop and maintain confidentiality. Be professional.

- *Confidentiality/diplomacy*
  Recognise where information-passing boundaries lie. Avoid 'office gossip' and err on the side of diplomacy. Any information you pass on to others will reflect on you well or badly, depending on the nature of the information. Remember, the art of good management often lies in knowing when *not* to say something. If you want to be trusted you must learn when to be discreet.

- *Priorities*
  Do not allow yourself to be sidetracked. Keep to your goals, be single-minded. This suggests professionalism.

- *Loyalty*
  A good boss values and engenders loyalty in his or her secretary and *vice versa*. Remember the unique nature of the boss/secretary relationship and the give and take involved. If you work together as a team with common goals, then loyalty will grow on both sides, with mutual respect for the different and complementary skills both parties bring to the working relationship.

- *Listen to others*
  Take into account the other person's point of view. Listen and allow others to express their views and arguments.

PERSONAL ACTION PLAN 44

▶ Consider your working relationship with your boss.

▶ Do you carry out your work in a helpful and willing manner?

▶ Do you keep your boss informed in an appropriate level of detail about activities, progress, results and achievements?

▶ Is information about problems and opportunities clear, accurate and provided with an appropriate degree of urgency?

▶ Do you seek information and advice from your boss as and when necessary?

▶ Do you present clear proposals for action at an appropriate time and with the right level of detail?

▶ Where proposals are not accepted, do you consider the reasons for their rejection and do you put forward alternative proposals?

▶ Where you have disagreements with your boss, do you make an effort to avoid damaging your relationship with him or her?

▶ How could your relationship with your boss be improved?

▶ Now discuss your findings and recommendations with your boss.

STAFFING THE OFFICE IN THE ABSENCE OF OTHERS

When the boss is absent, whether on holiday, on a business trip or at a meeting or conference out of the office, the secretary is the guardian or trustee but *not* the replacement or deputy for the boss. This again refers back to the understanding of the nature of the boss/secretary relationship. Limited or ineffective communication between the two may result in the secretary being unclear about the limits to responsibility and information-passing requirements, and this could result in lack of diplomacy or confidentiality. The secretary has the responsibility to apprise herself or himself of the line of command and authority in the boss's absence, possible scenarios and how to anticipate and deal with them, especially in international business where time differences and lack of availability make it difficult to gain access consistently to the right person at the right time. This is, in fact, an opportunity for the secretary to show management support skills to the full and the highest levels of professionalism. Set an example!

Checklist for staffing the office in the boss's absence

- Decide what matters are urgent and important and should be dealt with by the executive's deputy; what matters you can deal with, as agreed with the executive; and what matters should await the executive's return. These are the decisions which you must learn to make wisely; under no circumstances should you attempt to act as the executive's deputy.
- If ever in doubt, ask the executive's deputy for help. Know the chain of command. If you cannot understand something, ask someone who does know. Remember what Confucius had to say about this: 'He who asks a question is a fool for a moment. He who does not ask a question is a fool for life.'
- Always be aware of confidentiality and security.
- Always keep close at hand contact numbers for the executive who is absent should you need to contact him or her quickly. You are the executive's point of contact during his or her absence and must be available to supply information or to implement action which is requested.
- Be one step ahead by anticipating the needs of the executive and the deputy by having information at your fingertips.
- When the executive returns, brief him or her on all the developments which have taken place. Keep an accurate record of them as they occur and be prepared to summarise them.
- Instil confidence in the executive that you can be trusted to represent him or her, make wise decisions and be relied upon to hold the fort during their absence.
- Develop the ability to convey essential facts succinctly, both face to face and over the telephone. Can you summarise the contents of reports and journals so that your boss does not have to waste time reading non-essential data?

TECHNICAL SKILLS

The quality of the training a secretary receives, allied to the desire to learn, largely determines the quality of skills attained and the overall calibre of a secretary. The raw materials, or talents, are also relevant. There will always be people who are more or less talented than ourselves. This knowledge must be accepted in a positive way in order to be utilised to the secretary's advantage. Take this self-awareness, capitalise on it, develop your strong areas and ask for help to improve on the weak areas.

Experience, or 'laps around the track', also develops the standard of technical skills. There is no substitute for experience, for it develops interpersonal skills and contributes to good judgement. The perfect partner to training is the opportunity to put that training into practice.

Technical skills refer not only to text processing, shorthand, making correct travel arrangements or accurate financial records; they can also refer to personal efficiency, time management or exercising a positive mental attitude. The greater the variety of technical skills secretaries have at their disposal, the greater and more influential a management support role they can effect and the greater the job satisfaction they will derive. In Sweden, some secretaries control budgets and are responsible for administration, areas that managers in the UK would traditionally handle. Managers have trained themselves to look at secretaries in a different light, and some even spend part of their own training courses with their secretaries.

Checklist for developing technical skills

- Find relevant training courses that fulfil your training needs, such as those preparing students for the LCCI Private and Executive Secretary's Diploma, the PEI Level 3 Administration and Secretarial Procedures examination or the RSA Higher Diploma in Administrative and Secretarial Procedures.
- Be practical when implementing the course. Involve your boss in the decision process and always ask for feedback.
- Always give feedback after a course or ask for it if you are supervising staff undertaking training courses.
- Find a mentor or close ally who can be honest with you in discussing your training needs.
- Role playing can hone new technical skills if practical experience is lacking.
- Do not be afraid to fail. This is how we learn.
- Do not give up if results are not immediate. Set yourself evaluation times and stick to them.
- Be prepared to adapt and change your ideas. Office technology is changing rapidly. The secretary with a future is the secretary who can adapt to change and derive satisfaction from the challenge of updating skills.
- Simplify systems where possible. This way it is easier to see the real requirements and needs.
- Make things happen and develop a bias for action. This involves knowing your own mind, goal-setting, taking advantage of opportunities and creating your own luck.

PERSONAL ACTION PLAN 45

▶ **Who could act as your mentor at work? Why is that person suitable for the role?**

▶ **Give two examples of situations at work which you would now handle differently as a result of new technical skills you have acquired.**

FOREIGN-LANGUAGE SKILLS

Foreign-language ability is valuable for the following reasons:

- Personal achievement and enjoyment. Voltaire's Candide says, 'Il faut cultiver notre jardin' – 'We must make our garden grow.' We must be active, busy, set tasks and achieve goals in order to be happy and fulfilled.
- It is good PR for yourself and the company for which you work.
- It can help increase business. Croner's *Europe* says in its business strategy in the Single Market Section: 'There is a direct relationship between trading success and the ability to speak the customer's language.'
- It can increase your exposure to and dealings with clients and senior management and increase your management support role.
- It can make a job more interesting.
- It can increase the possibility of taking on more senior-level roles in an international company.

- It may enable you to travel and work abroad.
- It will provide you with a management skill in advising or assessing language requirements in a company.

The benefits of being able to communicate in a second language are undeniable, and are both personal and professional.

Personal benefits of foreign-language learning

- Builds confidence levels.
- Makes the secretary/PA more interested in other cultures and broadens the outlook. This leads to a greater understanding of what motivates people, along with greater tolerance of other cultures and flexibility in dealing with them.
- Time spent abroad is interesting and satisfying.
- Offers more potential to make contact with people abroad on a social level or with a view to working abroad.
- Makes the secretary/PA more interesting, and adds another dimension to their personality.
- It is fun!
- Attracts attention and ensures that the secretary is noticed.
- Allows a broader appreciation of culture, history and literature of your own country and that of the country whose language is studied.

Professional benefits of foreign-language training

- Additional technical skill in the secretarial repertoire.
- Can lead to being earmarked for special projects.
- Can lead to being regarded as a specialist and consulted for your skill.
- Contributes to career advancement within a company.
- Increases career opportunities abroad and in the domestic market.
- Can lead to salary improvement.
- Can lead to improved status.
- Can make a job more interesting, challenging and varied.
- Offers the opportunity to practise and improve a language skill. If you do not use it you lose it.
- Incentive to stay with a company if it invests time and money in offering in-house language training. Fosters the feeling that the company is prepared to invest in the secretary in the long term.

The benefits to the company of employing secretaries with competent language skills

- They are excellent representatives for the company and provide solid PR value.
- If they are allowed to make a positive contribution in the workplace this can boost morale, contributing to fulfilled staff who have the opportunity to develop.
- Increased morale and confidence contribute to increased productivity, and less absenteeism and lethargy.

- Competent linguists contribute to a company's professionalism and quality of work and demonstrate the company's commitment to Europe and international business development.
- Linguists can help create and maintain the competitive advantage by putting clients at their ease and carrying out business in the client's mother tongue.
- Having a language resource in a company can provide valuable feedback to personnel and human resources functions on future language needs. It can act as an early warning system. This fosters positive communication flow between the linguists and management and exposure to senior management of the value of employing linguists.

FOREIGN-LANGUAGE TRAINING

Once the decision has been taken to provide language tuition or the secretary has decided to suggest language training for others, then certain priorities must be considered:

- language needs;
- costs;
- timing;
- the logistics of training, daytime versus evening or lunch–hour course.

PERSONAL ACTION PLAN 46

▶ **Carry out a language audit in your company and consider the following:**
  1 **What is the specific language requirement: oral, written, translating, greetings?**
  2 **Which language or languages are required?**
  3 **What skills and abilities are already available in house?**
  4 **What level of language ability is needed and on what timescale?**

PERSONALITY AND INTERPERSONAL SKILLS

Personality is made up of that wonderful combination of 'nature and nurture'. It is this element of the total 'secretary' package more than any other that makes each secretary unique. It is therefore the element of the total package that employers consider most seriously when assessing the suitability of candidates for jobs. Will the chemistry between the secretary and the boss be right? Will the candidate 'fit in' with the company culture? For many secretaries and bosses the working relationship is like a marriage. For there to be any scope for the marriage to succeed and for both partners to develop and grow professionally, there has to be a compatible personality mix to serve as the communication foundation or platform from which to build.

Different personalities suit different bosses. Some secretaries will look for certain characteristics in their bosses, and this is a matter of personal taste. It is also important, particularly if working within a multicultural environment, to know how to deal with different personalities and to relate effectively. The key to this is the ability to adapt and build a rapport at all levels of seniority in a company while retaining a strong personal character. Be yourself.

Listed below are some of the personal qualities which bosses seek in their executive secretaries for working in the international environment:

- 'confidence'

- 'an understanding of human psychology and what makes people tick . . . the ability to build a rapport equally well with my clients in Chile and the newly recruited junior secretary in accounts'

- 'a sense of humour'

- 'a logical approach to problem-solving'

- 'the flexibility to take on a range of tasks – good time management'

- 'the ability to see a job through . . . someone I can rely on'

- 'resilience under pressure'

- 'the ability to think on their feet'

- 'emotional and intellectual maturity'

- 'able to articulate thoughts clearly'

- 'plan and think ahead unprompted'

- 'enthusiasm and willingness to learn'

- 'anticipate my needs and speak up – I am not a mind reader'

PERSONAL ACTION PLAN 47

▶ Are you still thinking and acting like a manager at all times? Which of the qualities listed above do you possess?

▶ Ask someone, your mentor or a colleague who knows you well, to describe your personality honestly, both positive and negative features. How does this differ from your own perceptions of yourself? The ability to marshal your personal qualities, positive outlook and all your technical skills can contribute towards the elusive *je ne sais quoi* that gives you management potential.

▶ Who do you admire at work and why?

▶ Define the elements that make that person a success.

Interpersonal skills

The ability to relate to people at different levels is at the heart of good interpersonal skills, along with the ability to articulate in an assertive manner your wants, needs and desires for a relationship. Being a good manager depends heavily on good interpersonal skills and achieving results with the help of others, i.e. through other people. The executive secretary must employ leadership and management skills every day to obtain results and motivate others, either directly or indirectly. This applies to one-to-one as much as to group situations. The balance has to be kept between:

- achieving a goal or task;
- maintaining the team momentum and motivation;
- developing the individual.

In the management support role the secretary's leadership skills will involve:

- *Self-confidence*
  Belief in yourself and the ability to solve problems and difficult situations and deal with difficult people. Self-confidence itself is made up of:
  - drive: urge and enthusiasm to stimulate action
  - initiative
  - willingness to accept responsibility and accountability
  - organising skills

- *Clarity of thought and expression*
  Articulating ideas and feelings clearly and concisely.

- *Decision-making*
  Making decisions based on objectives and situations, positive thinking and analysis of the situation.

- *Being assertive*
  Controlling and directing the actions of others and yourself in a positive way.

- *Being tactful*
  Treating colleagues firmly yet carefully and fairly and being sensitive to moods and attitudes.

- *Listening*
  Giving colleagues the time and the opportunity to express their views, and taking those views into account in the decision-making process.

- *Motivating*
  Encouraging, and harmonising, delegating and making others feel good about their tasks, and being a focus for feedback and information-passing alongside and sometimes instead of the boss.

- *Stamina*

- *Integrity*
  Being loyal and trustworthy, having emotional maturity and human understanding.

- *Adaptability*

- *Educational standards*
  Adequate educational and training standards and qualifications.

SELF-IMAGE AND MOTIVATION

The areas of self-image and motivation have been discussed in depth in Chapter 7. They are important in the context of the secretary's management support role as self-image affects personal motivation and, in turn, the successful motivation of others. This is vital, as successful management revolves fundamentally around the ability to motivate others. Secretaries must first work on their own motivation before they are able to motivate others successfully. This is as relevant in the domestic as in the international business arena.

UNDERSTANDING DIFFERENT CULTURES

The final element within the total package for the successful secretary as management support is the ability to understand different cultures and to utilise that knowledge to improve business practice and effectiveness. Mastery of language alone is not enough.

The cosmopolitan and international dimension that a secretary-linguist can bring to a job can afford greater understanding of a client's business, smooth client relations and facilitate more efficient international liaison, whether as part of an extended internal network or as part of the corporate image projected in the market-place.

On the one-to-one level of boss and secretary working together, the secretary's understanding of foreign cultures can be invaluable in relating to a boss who does not speak the foreign language. At the functional level the executive secretary can act as an interpreter and can provide a valuable insight into foreign customs, mores and even business etiquette.

The run-up to the European Single Market in 1992 saw a plethora of articles written about the understanding of our fellow Europeans, how national characteristics are reflected in the way business is conducted, and so on. There has been a surge in the demand for courses giving international briefings, training in international business practices and crash courses in foreign-language learning through immersion in the culture.

Many executive secretaries with different levels of foreign language skill and international experience have at their fingertips the type of knowledge mentioned above. If their knowledge is partial they can often suggest sources or contacts for further information. The key message lies in the realisation that there is unfulfilled potential and under-utilised ability in many a secretary.

The ability to understand different cultures is closely associated with the 'personality' section of this chapter, with being able to relate to people on many different levels, for culture is formed by the language, customs, history, geography, religion and contemporary social structures of a country. These are all factors that affect the lives of everyone and are elements of experience common to all that can be picked up and used as tools with which to relate to others.

Understanding the language of another culture will assist secretaries and executives alike on two levels: firstly, on the purely linguistic level it will lower a communication barrier, and secondly, language is a living thing. It changes to reflect changes in society. The ability to understand and to speak a language allows the individual to 'get behind' the language itself and understand the motivation behind actions, beliefs and behaviour.

PERSONAL ACTION PLAN 48

▶ Consider the ways in which you can enhance your understanding of foreign cultures.

▶ Are there any specific projects where your international experience could be utilised? What are they and how would you go about discussing them with your boss?

Checklist for assisting in your understanding of other cultures

- Spend time abroad whenever possible. Immerse yourself in the culture, make contact with native speakers and their different outlooks on life.
- Acquaint yourself with foreign newspapers, literature, art, history and general cultural influences.
- Analyse the sense of humour of the country whose language you speak. What does this tell you about the people?
- Keep an open mind and be patient. Preconceptions and hasty conclusions are a waste of time and can reflect personal inadequacies and insecurities.
- Keep developing your language skills. Make the learning process enjoyable. More information is absorbed by the brain when it is in a relaxed, 'having fun' mode. Learn card or board games, listen to songs and watch films in the foreign language.

CONCLUSION

To sum up, for the role of the executive secretary working in the international environment to evolve further it is clear that the secretary must be regarded as an essential member of the management team. The executive secretary has come a long way – understanding of the business, information technology, foreign-language skills and an understanding of foreign cultures enable the secretary to be the guardian of quality, an internal and external communicator, a team player, and responsible for seeing that the service to top management is professional. The executive secretary can and will progress much further in the run-up to the year 2000 and beyond. It is hoped that the material within this book, the strategies and *aides-mémoire*, will assist the executive secretary in facing unpredictable events, in coping with stressful conditions, and in managing communication challenges with confidence and strong personal and corporate identification.

EXAMINE YOUR KNOWLEDGE

1 As a supervisor you are required to maintain effective relationships with staff. What skills do you think are required for ensuring this and why? Illustrate your answer with practical examples. *(PEI ASP)*

2 You are secretary to the office manager. While she is on holiday you are left to deal with emergencies, although you are able to ask the advice of executives. A junior secretary does not turn up for work for three days and neither telephones nor writes. What would you do in these circumstances?

3 In response to an advertisement for an executive secretary in a company abroad, write a letter of application (with your CV) offering your services and referring especially to the foreign-language skills which you could contribute to the company. Explain how you consider the company would benefit from these language skills.

4 You work for an architect who is an official of his professional association. He has been asked to represent his association at an international conference in Paris. He decided to combine the conference with a holiday in France, and is therefore travelling in his own car. The day before the conference, he telephones from a small French village to say that he has crashed his car and, although not seriously hurt, he is feeling very shaken and quite unable to continue his journey to Paris. He asks you to take whatever action you consider appropriate with regard to the conference. What action would you take in the circumstances?

5 You are PA/secretary to Mrs Catherine Walsh (Case Study 1).

(*a*) Name and describe two services which may be suitable for the transportation of pieces of jewellery or high-value gems.

(*b*) Mrs Walsh has recently become more concerned about security in the office. Outline a procedure for her to put into action.

(*c*) The Brantwood Gallery extension to the Comlon Jewellery Museum in Amsterdam is to be ready for opening in October. What type of opening ceremony do you suggest? Draw up an appropriate checklist of all actions from initial planning to conclusion appropriate to your suggestion.

(*d*) Mrs Walsh will be travelling to Amsterdam for the opening of the Brantwood Gallery extension in October. She will be accompanied by her husband and they will stay for three or four nights. Her husband will return to England while she travels on to the Singapore office for a week.
(i) What preparations will you make on her behalf for these visits?
(ii) How will you ensure the smooth running of the office in her absence?

(*e*) In August a group of school and college leavers will join the company. What are the advantages of an induction course? Also include in your answer the topics and aims which should be covered in such a course.   (*LCCI PESD*)

INFORMATION BANK

Section 1 MULTILINGUAL ABBREVIATIONS AND ACRONYMS

1 ENGLISH (including Latin)

AA	Automobile Association; Alcoholics Anonymous
aar	against all risks
ab initio	from the beginning
abt	about
a/c	account
AC	alternating current
ACAS	Advisory, Conciliation and Arbitration Service
AD	In the year of the Lord (Anno Domini – Latin)
ad; advt	advertisement
ad hoc	for this purpose
ad infinitum	to infinity
ad lib	at pleasure (ad libitum, Latin)
ad valorem	according to the value
afft	affidavit
AGM	Annual General Meeting
agst	against
agt	agent
amicus curiae	a friend of the court
amp.	ampere
amt	amount
A/N	advice note
anon.	anonymous
ans.	answer, answered
a/o	account of
AOB	any other business
AP	Associated Press
APEX	Advance-purchase Excursion
APR	annual percentage rate
AR	advice of receipt; all risks (marine)
arr.	arrivals, arrived
A/S	account sales
a.s.a.p.	as soon as possible
ASLIB	Association for Information Management (formerly Association of Special Libraries and Information Bureaux)
assn	association
assoc.	associate
asst	assistant

ATM	automatic teller machine
au fait	to be well informed
A/V	according to the value (ad valorem – Latin)
av.	average
AWOL	absent without (official) leave
B.; b.	born
BA	Bachelor of Arts; British Airways
BAA	British Airports Authority
BACS	Bankers' Automated Clearing Service
bal.	balance
BB	bill book
BBC	British Broadcasting Corporation
BC	Before Christ
BCL	Bachelor of Civil Law
BD	Bachelor of Divinity
bd	board, bond
b/d	brought down
B/D	bank draft
B/E	bill of exchange
b/f	brought forward
BIM	British Institute of Management
BIS	Bank for International Settlements
B/L	bill of lading
BMus	Bachelor of Music
bona fide	of good faith
bon voyage	wishing a traveller a good journey
B/P	bills payable
Br.; Brit.	British
B/R	bills receivable
B/S	balance sheet; bill of sale
BSc	Bachelor of Science
BSI	British Standards Institution
BST	British Summer Time
bt	bought
BTEC	Business and Technology Education Council

C	Celsius
c.	circa (approximate), cents, copyright
CA	current account; Chartered Accountant
CAA	Civil Aviation Authority
CAL	computer-assisted learning
CAP	Common Agricultural Policy (EC)
CAR	computer-assisted retrieval
carte blanche	full discretionary power
caveat emptor	let the buyer beware
CB	cash book
CBD	cash before delivery
CBI	Confederation of British Industry
CC	County Council; County Councillor
cc	copies
CD	Civil Defence
c/d	carried down
CERN	European Laboratory for Particle Physics (formerly European Organisation for Nuclear Research)
CET	Central European Time
c.&f.	cost and freight
cf	carried forward; compare
CFP	Common Fisheries Policy (EC)
cg	centigram
CGT	capital-gains tax
chq.	cheque
c.i.f.	cost, insurance and freight
CILT	Centre for Information on Language Training and Research
CIR	Commission on Industrial Relations
cl	centilitre
cm	centimetre
C/N	credit note
CNAA	Council for National Academic Awards
Co.	company; county
COBOL	computer language – common business-oriented language
COD	cash on delivery
C of E	Church of England; Council of Europe
com., comm.	commission
COM	computer output on microfilm
COMECON	Council for Mutual Economic Assistance

COMETT	Community in Education and Training for Technology (EC)
con.	against (*contra* – Latin)
contg	containing
contr.	contract
CPU	central processing unit
C/R	company's risk
CRAC	Careers Research and Advisory Centre
CRE	Commission for Racial Equality
crs	credits; creditors
C/T	credit transfer
CTT	capital-transfer tax
cum. pref.	cumulative preference
CV	curriculum vitae
c.w.o.	cash with order
DA	deposit account
dag	decagram
dal	decalitre
dam	decametre
DB	day book
DC	direct current; district council
DCL	Doctor of Civil Law
DD	direct debit; Doctor of Divinity
d.d.	days after date
deb.	debenture
def.	deferred
de facto	in fact
dep.	depart
d.f.	dead freight
DFE	Department for Education
dft	draft
DG	By the Grace of God (*Dei gratia* – Latin); thanks to God (*Deo gratias* – Latin)
dg	decigram
diam.	diameter
dis.	discount
div.	dividend; division
dl	decilitre
dm	decimetre
DM	Deutschmark
D/N	debit note
DN	dispatch note
do.	ditto, the same
DO	delivery order
d.o.b.	date of birth
DP	data processing
D/P	deferred payment; documents against payment
Dr	doctor

dr, drs	debtor, debtors
DTP	desktop publishing
DV	God willing (*Deo volente* – Latin)
D/W	dock warrant
dy., dely.	delivery
E	east
ea.	each
EAPS	European Association of Professional Secretaries
EC (now EU)	European Community
ECGD	Exports Credits Guarantee Department
ECSC	European Coal and Steel Community (EC)
ECU	European Currency Unit
ed., eds	editor, edition, editors, editions
EE	errors excepted
EFTA	European Free Trade Association
EFTPOS	electronic funds transfer at point of sale
e.g.	for example (*exempli gratia* – Latin)
EGM	extraordinary general meeting
EIB	European Investment Bank
EMF	European Monetary Fund
EMS	European Monetary System
EMU	economic and monetary union (EC)
enc.	enclosure
Eng.	English
eng.	engineer
en masse	all together
en route	on the way
entd	entered
EOC	Equal Opportunities Commission
E&OE	errors and omissions excepted
e.o.m.	end of month
EP	European Parliament
EPU	European Payments Union
ERASMUS	EC programme to promote student mobility
ERDF	European Regional Development Fund
ERM	Exchange Rate Mechanism
ERNIE	Electronic Random Number Indicating Equipment
ESA	European Space Agency
Esc	Escudo
ESPRIT	European strategic programme

	for research and development in information technology
ETA	estimated time of arrival
et al.	and others (*et alii* – Latin)
etc	and so on (*et cetera* – Latin)
ETD	estimated time of departure
et seq.	and the following (*et sequens* – Latin)
ETUC	European Trade Union Confederation
EU	European Union
EURATOM	European Atomic Energy Community
EUROPMI	European Committee for Small and Medium-sized Industries
EUROSTAT	The EU's statistics office
ex div.	exclusive of dividend
ex gratia	as a favour, voluntary
ex int.	exclusive of interest
ex officio	by virtue of office
exch.	exchange
F	franc, francs, fahrenheit
fait accompli	a thing already completed
f.a.q.	fair average quality
faux pas	an error or indiscreet action
fax	facsimile transmission
FBI	Federation of British Industries; Federal Bureau of Investigation
FCO	Foreign and Commonwealth Office
fcp	foolscap
FIFO	first in, first out
FIPMEC	International Federation of Small and Medium-sized Enterprises
f.i.t.	free of income tax
fm	fathom
fo., fol.	folio
f.o.b.	free on board
f.o.c.	free of charge
f.o.q.	free on quay
for.	foreign
f.o.r.	free on rail
FORTRAN	computer language – formula translation
f.p.	fully paid
Fr., FF	French franc
frt	freight
FTI	Financial Times Index
f/u	follow up
f.y.i.	for your information

g	gram
GATT	General Agreement on Tariffs and Trade
GDP	gross domestic product
GMT	Greenwich Mean Time
GNP	gross national product
GP	general practitioner
GRN	goods received note
gr. wt.	gross weight
g.v.	gross value
ha	hectare
HE	His (or Her) Excellency, His Eminence
hg	hectogram
HICA	high interest cheque account
hl	hectolitre
hm	hectometre
HMC	Her Majesty's Customs
HMIT	Her Majesty's Inspector of Taxes
HMSO	Her Majesty's Stationery Office
HNC	Higher National Certificate
HND	Higher National Diploma
Hon.	Honorary, Honorable
h.p.	hire purchase
hp	horsepower
Hr	Herr
hrs	hours
HSE	Health and Safety Executive
ib./ibid.	in the same place (*ibidem* – Latin)
IBRD	International Bank for Reconstruction and Development (the World Bank)
i/c	in charge
ICAO	International Civil Aviation Organisation
ICFTU	International Confederation of Free Trade Unions
ID	identification
id./idem	the same
IDD	international direct dialling
i.e.	that is (*id est* – Latin)
IF	insufficient funds
IFAD	International Fund for Agricultural Development (UN)
ILO	International Labour Organisation (UN)
IMF	International Monetary Fund

IMO	International Maritime Organisation
inc.	increase; including; incorporated
Inmarsat	International Maritime Satellite Service
ins., insce	insurance
inst.	institution
int.	interest
inter alia	among other things
Interpol	International Criminal Police Organisation
intra vires	within one's powers
inv.	invoice
IPS	international paper sizes
ipso facto	by the very fact
IPSS	International Packet Switchstream Service
IQPS	Institute of Qualified Private Secretaries
IRO	Inland Revenue Office; International Refugee Organisation
ISBN	International Standard Book Number
ISO	International Standards Organisation
iss.	issue
IT	information technology
ital.	italics
ITB	Industry Training Board
ITU	International Telecommunications Union
J.	Judge
J/A	joint account
JP	Justice of the Peace
kg	kilogram
kl	kilolitre
km	kilometre
kW	kilowatt
l	litre
LAN	local area network
l.c.	lower case (printing)
L/C	letter of credit
LCCI	London Chamber of Commerce and Industry
LCM	lowest common multiple
LEA	Local Education Authority
LIFO	last in, first out
LILO	last in, last out

LIP	life insurance policy		*non seq.*	it does not follow logically (*non sequitur* – Latin)
LLB	Bachelor of Law		NP	Notary Public
LOB	Location of Offices Bureau		n.p.	net proceeds; new paragraph
locum tenens	a deputy		NR	no risk (insurance)
LS	the place of the seal (*locus sigilli* – Latin)		NVQ	National Vocational Qualification
Ltd	Limited			
LV	luncheon voucher		o/a	on account (of)
			ob.	died (*obiit* – Latin)
m	metre; million		obit.	obituary
M	Monsieur		OCR	optical character recognition/ reader
MA	Master of Arts			
MB	Bachelor of Medicine		o/d	on demand; overdraft; overdrawn
MD	Managing Director; memorandum of deposit; Doctor of Medicine		OECD	Organisation for Economic Co-operation and Development
m/d	months after date			
mdse	merchandise		OFT	Office of Fair Trading
MEP	Member of the European Parliament		O&M	organisation and methods
			o.p.	out of print
mfg	manufacturing		op. cit.	in the work cited (*opere citato* – Latin)
mg	milligram			
mgr	manager; Monsignor		OPEC	Organisation of Petroleum-Exporting Countries
MICR	magnetic–ink character recognition		OR	owner's risk; operational research
MIS	management information system		o/s	on sale; out of stock; outstanding
ml	millilitre		OS	Ordnance Survey
MLA	Member of the Legislative Assembly			
Mlle	Madamoiselle		p.	page
MLR	minimum lending rate		PA	power of attorney; private account; Press Association; personal assistant
mm	millimetre			
MM	Messieurs			
Mme	Madame		p.a.	per annum
Monsig.	Monsignor		PABX	private automatic branch exchange
MP	Member of Parliament			
MS	manuscript		PAYE	pay as you earn
MSS	manuscripts		PC	Police Constable; Privy Council(lor); personal computer
n/a	not available; not applicable			
N/A	no account; no advice		P/C	petty cash; price current
NATO	North Atlantic Treaty Organisation		PCB	petty cash book
			PEI	Pitman Examinations Institute
NB	note thoroughly (*nota bene* – Latin)		per capita	for each person
			per se	by itself
NCR	no carbon required		PhD, D.Phil	Doctor of Philosophy
n.d.	no date		PIN	personal identification number
nem. con.	no one contradicting, unanimously (*nemine contradicente* – Latin)		P/L	profit and loss
			PLC, plc	public limited company
N/F	no funds		PMBX	private manual branch exchange
n/m	no mark (on a bill of lading)		PN	promissory note

PO	Post Office; postal order
POP	Post Office preferred (size of envelopes, etc.)
P&P	postage and packing
pp	*per pro* – by the authority of
pp.	pages
prima facie	on the face of it
PRO	public relations officer
pro forma	as a matter of form
pro rata	in proportion
pro tem	for the time being (*pro tempore* – Latin)
PSS	Packet Switch Stream
QC	Queen's Counsel
QED	which was to be proved (*quod erat demonstrandum* – Latin)
qlty	quality
quid pro quo	something in return
q.v.	which see (*quod vide* – Latin)
qy	query
R&D	research and development
R/D	refer to drawer
re	with reference to, relating to
recd	received
rect	receipt
ref.	reference
rev. a/c	revenue account
RIP	rest in peace
rm	ream
ROM	read-only memory
RP	reply paid
RPI	retail price index
RRP	recommended retail price
RSA	Royal Society of Arts
RSVP	please reply (*répondez s'il vous plaît* – French)
RV	rateable value
SAE	stamped, addressed envelope
SALT	Strategic Arms Limitation Treaty
s.a.v.	stock at valuation
SAYE	save as you earn
SB	sales book
Scd, DSc	Doctor of Science
SCOTVEC	Scottish Vocational Education Council
SE	Stock Exchange
SEA	Single European Act
seq.	the following (*sequens* – Latin)
sgd	signed

SHAPE	Supreme Headquarters of the Allied Powers in Europe (NATO)
sic	so written
sine die	without an appointed day
SMEs	small and medium-sized enterprises
S/N	shipping note
SO	standing order; seller's option
SOR	sale or return
SOS	save our souls (distress message used in morse code)
spec.	speculation, specification
SSP	statutory sick pay
status quo	existing state of affairs
STD	subscriber trunk dialling
std	standard
stet	let it stand
stg	sterling
stk	stock
STMS	short-term monetary support (EC)
sub judice	under judicial consideration
SWIFT	Society for Worldwide Interbank Financial Transmissions
t.	tonne
T/A	trading as
TB	trial balance; tuberculosis
TEC	Training and Enterprise Council
TM	trademark
t.o.	turn over
Tr	trustee
TT	telegraphic transfer
TUC	Trades Union Congress
u.c.	upper case (printing)
u/c	undercharge
UDI	unilateral declaration of independence
ultra vires	beyond legal authority
UHF	ultra high frequency
UNESCO	United Nations Educational, Scientific and Cultural Organisation
UNICEF	United Nations Children's Fund (formerly United Nations International Children's Emergency Fund)
UNO	United Nations Organisation
UPU	Universal Postal Union (UN)
u/w	underwriter

v.	versus, against		VTR	videotape recorder
var.	various			
VAT	value added tax		w/e	week ending
VDU	visual display unit		w.e.f.	with effect from
Ven.	Venerable		WEU	Western European Union
VHF	very high frequency		WHO	World Health Organisation
via	by way of		w/o	write off, written off
VIP	very important person		WORM	write once, read many (times)
viz.	namely (*videlicet* – Latin)		w.p.	without prejudice
VN	voucher number		WP	word processor
VSO	Voluntary Service Overseas			

Further sources of information on abbreviations:

Acronyms, Initialisms and Abbreviations Dictionary
Penguin Dictionary of Abbreviations, Penguin Books Ltd
The Secretary's Desk Book, Harrison, Pitman Publishing

2 FRENCH

Abréviations et sigles (Abbreviations and acronyms)

a.	accélération, *acceleration*			d'industrie, *Association of French Chambers of Commerce*
A2	Antenne 2, *Channel 2, television station*		Appt	Appartement, *flat*
abrév	abréviation, *abbreviation, abbreviated*		Ardt	Arrondissement, *district*
			AS	Assurances sociales, *National Insurance*
a.b.s.	aux bons soins (de), *care of*		Asc.	Ascenseur, *lift*
act.	action, *share, stock, security*		A.S.L.V.	assurance sur la vie, *life assurance*
ADEF	Agence d'Evaluation Financière, *credit reference checking agency*		ASSEDIC	Association pour l'emploi dans l'industrie et le commerce, *business development agency*
AF	Allocations familiales, *family allowance*		auj.	aujourd'hui, *today*
AFP	Agence France-Presse, *French Press Agency*		av.	Avenue, avant, *Avenue, previous, before*
AG	Assemblée générale, *general assembly*		Av.	avoir, *credit, asset*
A.&M.	école des arts et métiers, *technical institute*		B. de F.	Banque de France
amort.	amortissable, *redeemed*		Bac, bac, bacc	Baccalauréat, *leaving examination taken in lycées (less specialised A level equivalent for entry into higher education)*
ANPE	Agence nationale pour l'emploi, *job centre*			
AOC	Appellation d'origine contrôlée, *classification of wine guaranteeing origin and type of grape stated on label*		banl.	banlieu, *suburb*
			Bat	Bâtiment, *building*
			BC	Brevet de College, *secondary level qualification*
A.P.	Assistance publique, *national assistance*		bd	Boulevard
APCCI	Assemblée Permanente des Chambres de Commerce et		BE	Brevet élémentaire, *equivalent to GCSE*

B.E.	Bureau d'études, *research department*
BEP	Brevet d'Etudes Professionnelles, *equivalent to a BTEC qualification*
BEPC	Brevet d'études du premier cycle, *secondary level school qualification*
BNP	Banque Nationale de Paris *(one of France's three largest banks)*
BP	Boîte postale, *PO box number*; Brevet Professionnel, *qualification*
BT	Brevet de technicien, *qualification at secondary level allowing university admittance*
bte	breveté, *patent, licensed*
BTn	Baccalauréat de Technicien, *qualification*
BTS	Brevet de Technicien Supérieur, *two-year post-Bac qualification equivalent to a higher BTEC*
burx	bureaux, *offices*
C.	Celsius, *centigrade*
CA	Crédit Agricole *(one of France's three largest banks)*
C.-a-d.	c'est-à-dire, *that is to say*
CAF	coût, assurance, fret, *cost, insurance and freight*
CAO	Conception Assistée par Ordinateur, *CAD or computer-aided design*
CAP	Certificat d'Aptitude Professionnelle, *craft qualification equivalent to City and Guilds*
CAPEGC	certificat d'aptitude au professorat de l'enseignement général de collège
CAPES	certificat d'aptitude au professorat de l'enseignement du second degré
CAPET	certificat d'aptitude au professorat de l'enseignement technique
CC	corps consulaire, *consular service*
CCP	Compte Courant Postale *(Giro bank run by the French Post Office*
CCIP	Chambre de Commerce et d'Industrie de Paris corps diplomatique, *diplomatic service*

CE	Conseil de l'Europe, *Council of Europe*
CEDEX	Courrier D'Entreprise à Distribution Exceptionnelle *(special sorting code to speed delivery of mail)*
CEE	Communauté Economique Européenne, *EEC*
CEG	Collège d'enseignement général, *general training college*
CEGEP	Collège d'enseignement général et professionnel, *general and vocational college*
CEP	Caisse d'épargne et de prévoyance, *savings bank, building society*; Certificat d'études primaires, *primary school leaving certificate*; certificat d'éducation professionnelle
CERN	Conseil européen de recherches nucléaires, *European Nuclear Research Council*
CES	Collège d'enseignement secondaire, *secondary modern school*
CET	collège d'enseignement technique
C&F	Coût et fret, *cost and freight*
CFA	Communauté française d'Afrique, *French African community*; centre de Formation d'Apprentis, *centre for vocational training*
CFCE	Centre Français de commerce extérieur, *French Export Office*
CFDT	Confédération Française et Démocratique du Travail, *left-wing trade union*
CFES	certificat de fin d'études secondaires *(qualification obtained if the Bac is failed but the course of study has been completed)*
CFF	Chemins de fer fédéraux, *Swiss railways*
CGC	Confédération Générale des Cadres, *general staff trade union*
CGT	Confédération Générale du Travail, *trade union*
CH	Confédération Helvétique, *Switzerland*
Chbre	Chambre, *room*
Ch. comp	Charges comprises, *cost included*
Chf. cent.	Chauffage central, *central heating*

Cial	Commercial, *commercial*
CIO	Comité International olympique, *International Olympic Committee*
CL	Crédit Lyonnais *(one of France's three largest banks)*
commerct	commerçant, *merchant, trader, shopkeeper, retailer*
c/n.	compte nouveau, *new account*
CNAM	Confédération National de l'Artisanat et des Métiers *(union representing self-employed in business and crafts)*
CNPF	Conseil National du Patronat Français *(employers' federation equivalent to the CBI)*
CNRS	Centre national de la recherche scientifique, *National Scientific Research Centre*
CNTE	Centre national de télé-enseignement, *Centre for televisual learning*
Constr.	Construction, *building*
Cpt	Comptant, *cash, in cash*
C.Q.F.D.	ce qu'il fallait démontrer *(see English QED)*
cr.	crédit, *credit*
C.R.	compte rendu, *record, proceedings*
CROUS	Centre régional des oeuvres universitaires et scolaires
curr. vitae	Curriculum Vitae
DATAR	Délégation du Territoire et de l'Action Régionale, *Regional Development Agency*
DEA	Diplôme d'études approfondies *(academic qualification)*
DES	Diplôme d'études supérieures *(academic qualification)*
DEUG	Diplôme d'Etudes Universitaires Générales *(a general two-year university degree qualification)*
DOM-TOM	Départements d'Outre-mer-Térritoires d'Outre-mer *(French overseas departments like Martinique and Guadeloupe)*
DPLG	Diplômé par le gouvernement *(government-recognised qualification)*
DUT	Diplôme Universitaire de Technologie *(qualification from the equivalent of a polytechnic or college of technology)*
dz.	douzaine, *dozen*
e.a p.	effet à payer, *bill payable*
e.a r.	effet à recevoir, *bill receivable*
EDF	Eléctricité de France *(state-run electricity monopoly)*
eg, ex	par example, *for example*
empl. de bur.	employé de bureau, *clerical worker*
EN	Ecole normale, *teachers' training college*
ENA	Ecole Nationale d'Administration, *National Administration School (business school: one of the Grandes Ecoles, elite institutes of higher education ranking above universities)*
ENI	Ecole nationale d'ingénieurs, *National engineering school*
ENSAE	Ecole Nationale de la Statistique et de l'Administration Economique *(Grande Ecole specialising in economics)*
en tte ppte	en toute propriété, *freehold*
e.o.o.e.	erreur ou omission exceptée, *errors or omissions excepted*
equival.	equivalent à, *equivalent to*
ESSEC	Ecole Supérieure des Sciences Economiques et Sociales *(a Grande Ecole)*
Et.	étage, *floor*
F	Francs, *Francs*
FAB	Franco à Bord, *free on board*
FB	Franc Belge, *Belgian Franc*
FC	Football club
FF	Frères, *Brothers*; Franc français, *French franc*
FLN	Front de libération nationale, *National Liberation Front*
F.M.	Fréquence modulée
FMI	Fonds monétaire international, *the IMF*
FNSEA	Fédération nationale des syndicats d'exploitants agricoles, *Farmers' Union*
FO	Force Ouvrière *(left-wing trade union)*
FPLP	Front populaire pour la libération de la Palestine, *PLO*

FR3	France Régions Trois *(TV station)*
FS	Franc suisse, *Swiss Franc*
GDF	Gaz de France *(state-run gas supply monopoly)*
GO	Grandes Ondes, *long-wave*
gr. coup.	grosses coupures, *big denominations*
h.	heure, *hour;* hier, *yesterday;* hypothèque, *mortgage*
Ha	Hectare *(metric unit of area)*
HEC	Hautes Etudes Commerciales *(a Grande Ecole for MBA courses*
HF	Haute fréquence, *high frequency*
HLM	Habitation à loyer modéré *(council house/building equivalent)*
h.s., H.S.	hors de service, *out of use*
HT	hors taxe, *excluding tax, duty-free*
IFOP	Institut Française d'Opinion Publique
Imm.	Immeuble, *building*
IN . . .	Institut national . . .
INSD	Institut National de la Statistique et de la Demographie
INSEE	Institut National de la Statistique et des Etudes Economiques
IPES	Institut de préparation aux enseignements du second degré *(preparation for secondary level of education)*
I.R.P.P.	Impôt sur le revenu des personnes physiques, *income tax*
IUT	Institut Universitaire de Technologie, *polytechnic or college of technology*
J-C	Jésus–Christ
J.F.	jeune fille, *young lady*
J.H.	jeune homme, *young man*
JO	journal officiel, *official journal, gazette*
j/v.	jours de vue, *days after sight*
Km	Kilometre, *kilometre*
LC	lettre de credit, *letter of credit*
LEGT	Lycée d'enseignement général et technologique

LEP	Lycée d'Enseignement Professionnel *(technical college with 2–3 year courses leading to CAP and BEP qualifications*
L ès L	Licence ès Lettres *(BA equivalent)*
L ès Sc	Licence ès Sciences *(BSc equivalent)*
liq. cte	liquidation courante, *current account*
liq. pro	liquidation prochaine, *next account*
loc. comm. et ind.	locaux commerciaux et industriels, *business property, business premises*
M.	Monsieur, *Mr, Sir*
M6	Métropole 6 *(TV station)*
MATIF	Marché à Terme des Instruments Financiers, *Futures Exchange (opened in 1987)*
Max.	maximum
Me	Maître, *Master*
Messrs	Messieurs, *Sirs, Gentlemen*
MF	Modulation de Frequence, *FM*
M.G.	médecin generaliste, *GP*
Mgr	Monseigneur, *Monsignor*
Min.	minimum
MLF	Mouvement de libération des femmes, *The Women's Movement*
Mlle	Mademoiselle, *Miss*
M.M.	messageries maritime, *shipping company*
MM	Messieurs, *Gentlemen*
Mme	Madame, *Mrs, Madam*
Mo	Métro, *Underground railway*
MONEP	Marché des Options Negociables de Paris, *Paris Options market (which opened in 1987)*
MRG	Mouvement des Radicaux de Gauche *(centre-left political party)*
NB	Nota Bene, *NB*
o/a	à l'ordre de, *to the order of*
OC	Ondes courtes, *short wave*
OCDE	Organisation de coopération et de développement économique, *OECD*
OM	Ondes Moyennes, *medium wave*
OMM	Organisation météorologique

	mondiale, *World Meteorological Organisation*
OMS	Organisation mondiale de la santé, *World Health Organisation*
ONU	Organisation des Nations Unies, *UN*
OPA	Offre Publique d'Achat, *take-over bid*
OPEP	Organisation des pays exportateurs de petrole, *OPEC*
OS	ouvrier spécialisé, *semi-skilled worker in industry*
OTAN	Organisation du Traité de l'Atlantique Nord, *NATO*
OUA	Organisation de l'unité africaine, *Organisation for African Unity*
ouv.	ouverture, *opening*
OVNI	Objet volant non identifié, *UFO*
p.	pièce, *room*
P.A.	propriété assurée, *insured property*
PAL	Phase alternation line *(colour TV system developed by AG Telefunken and used in UK and Germany)*
Park.	parking
p.c.	pas coté, *not quoted*; pour cent, *per cent*; pourcentage, *percentage*
PC	Parti Communiste, *Communist Party*
PCC	Pour copie conforme, *certified accurate*
PCV	Percevable à l'Arrivée, *a reverse charge call*
PDG	Président-Directeur Général *(company head)*
per.	premier, *first*
p. et m.	poids et mesures, *weights and measures*
PIB	produit intérieur brut, *Gross Domestic Product*
P.J.	pièce jointe, *enclosed, attached*
Pl.	Place, *Square*
pl. temps	à plein temps, *full-time work*
PME/PMI	Petites et Moyennes Enterprises/Industries *(most french companies fall into these two categories: PME is a company with less than 50 employees; PMI has 50–500 employees)*
PMU	Pari mutuel urbain, *Tote*
PNB	Produit National Brut, *Gross National Product*
PO	Petites Ondes, *short wave*
Ppte	Propriété, *property*
PR	Parti républicain, *Republican Party*
prec.	précédent, *previous, preceding*
PS	Parti Socialiste
PSU	Parti Socialiste Unifié, *socialist party*
Pte	Porte, *door*
PTT	Postes Télégraphes Téléphones *(French postal service)*
P.-V.	Procès-verbal, *minutes*
Px	Prix, *price*
px tot.	prix total, *total price*
QG	Quartier général, *Headquarters*
QI	Quotient intellectuel, *IQ*
qn	quelqu'un, *someone*
qq	quelques, *some*
qqch	quelque chose, *something*
qqf	quelquefois, *sometimes*
r.	route, *road*; rue, *street*; reçu, *received*
®	marque déposée, *registered trademark*
R.A.	Régie autonome, *public corporation, Authority*
RATP	Régie Autonome des Transports Parisiens *(company operating the Paris Métro)*
RD	Route départmentale, *secondary road*
R.d.C.	Rez-de-Chaussée, *ground floor*
Ref.	Référence, *with regard to*
remuner	rémunération, *salary*
rens.	renseignements, *information*
RER	Réseau Express Régional, *Paris suburban express rail service, part of SNCF*
RF	République Française
RMC	Radio Monte Carlo
RN	Route nationale, *main/primary road*
RPR	Rassemblement pour la République *(right-wing Gaullist party)*
RSVP	Répondez s'il vous plaît *(see English RSVP)*
Rte	Route, *Road*
RTL	Radio Télévision Luxembourgeoise

RU	Royaume Uni, *UK*
R-V	Rendez-vous, *meeting*
SA	Société Anonyme *(a large company or corporation)*
SARL	Société à Responsabilité Limitée, *limited liability company*
SDN	Société des Nations, *League of Nations*
SECAM	Séquentiel à Mémoire *(French colour-TV system)*
SEITA	Service d'exploitation industrielle des tabacs et allumettes *(trade body for development of tobacco industry)*
s.e. & o.	sauf erreur et omission, *errors and omissions excepted*
SFAC	Société Française Assurances Crédit *(agency like ADEF providing credit information for verification of credit references)*
SGDG	Sans garantie du gouvernement, *without government guarantee of quality*
SGEN	Syndicat général de l'éducation nationale *(education trade union)*
SMAG	Salaire minimum agricole garanti, *guaranteed minimum wage for farm workers*
SMIC	Salaire minimum interprofessionnel de croissance, *legal minimum wage adjusted in line with current economic factors and retail prices*
SOFIRAD	Société Financière de Radiodiffusion *(state-owned company holding shares in private radio and television stations)*
SNCB	Société Nationale des chemins de Fer belges, *Belgian railways*
SNCF	Société Nationale des Chemins de Fer Français, *French State Railway Company*
SNES	Syndicat national de l'enseignement secondaire, *secondary teaching union*
SNE sup	Syndicat national de l'enseignement supérieur, *higher education union*
SNI	Syndicat national des instituteurs *(teachers' union)*
SOFRES	Société française d'enquêtes pour sondage *(Gallup Poll equivalent)*
SOS	Message de détresse, *SOS*
S.P.	service de presse, *PR department*
SPA	Société protectrice des animaux, *society for the protection of animals*
SS	Sécurité sociale, *social security*
Ste	Société, *society*
SVP	S'il vous plaît, *please*
T.C.	taxe complémentaire *(added value)*
TEE	Trans-Europe-Express
Tel.	Téléphone
Telev.	télévision
TF 1	Télévision Française Un *(TV station)*
TGV	Train à Grande Vitesse, *high-speed train*
TIR	Transit International Routier, *road haulage association*
TNP	Théâtre national populaire, *National Theatre company*
tr. urg	très urgent
T.S.	tarif spécial, *special rate*
TSF	Telegraphie sans Fil, *wireless*
TSVP	Tournez s'il vous plaît, *please turn*
TTC	toutes taxes comprises, *including/include taxes*
Tt cft	tout confort, *all mod cons (modern conveniences)*
TUC	Travaux d'Utilité Collective *(government youth employment scheme)*
TVA	Taxe sur la Valeur Ajoutée, *VAT*
UDF	Union pour la Démocratie Française *(centre alliance political party, Giscardian in nature)*
UEBL	Union Economique de la Belgique et du Luxembourg
UER	Unité d'enseignement et de recherche, *a teaching establishment*
un.	unité, *unit*
UNEF	Union nationale des étudiants de France, *French Students' union*
U.P.U.	Union Postale Universelle
URSS	Union des Républiques Socialistes Soviétiques, *USSR, Soviet Union*

US	Union sportive, *sports club*	virt	virement, *transfer*
UTA	Union de Transports Aériens *(long-haul French airline)*	VPC	Vente par Correspondence, *mail order*
UV	ultra-violet, *ultra-violet*; unité de valeur, *unit of value*	v/Ref	votre référence, *your reference*
		VRP	Voyageur Représentant Placier, *travelling salesman/representative*
v.	vendeur, *seller*; vendez, *sell*; velocité, *speed*; voir, *see*; volume, *volume*	VSOP	très vieil alcool supérieur, *very superior old alcoholic beverage*
v/.	valeur, *security/share*; votre, *your*	WC	water closet
vac.	vacances, *holiday*		
v/c	votre compte, *your account*	ZAC	Zone d'aménagement concerté, *special development area*
Vd	vend, *sale*		
VDQS	Vins Délimités de Qualité Supérieur *(wine classification similar to AOC, usually local wines)*	ZUP	Zone à Urbaniser en Priorité *(state-funded urban development scheme for housing and office buildings)*

3 GERMAN

Abkürzungen (Abbreviations and acronyms)

AA	Auswärtiges Amt, *Foreign Office*	a. O.	an der Oder, *on the Oder (river)*
a.a.O.	am angeführten Ort, loc. cit., *in the place cited*	APO	Außerparlamentarische Opposition, *extra-parliamentary opposition*
Abb.	Abbildung, *illustration, figure*		
Abf.	Abfahrt, *departure*	App.	Apparat, *apparatus*
Abk.	Abkürzung, *abbreviation*	a. Rh.	am Rhein, *on the Rhine (river)*
Abs.	Absatz, *paragraph*; Absender, *sender*	Art.	Artikel, *article*
		ASTA	Allgemeiner Studentenausschuß, *general students committee*
Abschn.	Abschnitt, *paragraph, chapter*		
Abt.	Abteilung, *department*	A.T.	Altes Testament, *Old Testament*
a. Chr.	ante Christum, *BC*	atü	Atmosphärenüberdruck, *excess atmospheric pressure*
a. D.	außer Dienst, *retired*		
ADAC	Allgemeiner Deutscher Automobil-klub, *General German Automobile association*	Aufl.	Auflage, *edition*
		Az	Aktenzeichen, *file number*
ADN	Allgemeiner Deutsche Nachrichtendienst, *General German News Service*	b.	bei, *with, near, care of*
		Bd.	Band, *volume*
		beif.	beifolgend, *herewith*
Adr.	Adresse, *address*	beil.	beiliegend, *enclosed*
AEG	Allgemeine Elektrizitäts-Gesellschaft, *General Electric Company*	Bem.	Bemerkung, *comment, note, observation*
		bes.	besonders, *especially*
AG	Aktiengesellschaft, *corporation/joint stock company*	Best.Nr.	Bestellnummer, *order number*
		betr.	betreffend, betrifft, betreffs, *regarding, concerning*
allg.	allgemein, *general*		
amtl.	amtlich, *official*	bez.	bezahlt, *paid*; bezüglich, *with reference to*
Anh.	Anhang, *appendix*		
Ank.	Ankunft, *arrival*	BFH	Bundesfinanzhof, *Federal Finance Court*
Anl.	Anlage im Brief, *enclosure*		
Anm.	Anmerkung, *note*		

BGB	Bürgerliches Gesetzbuch, *German Civil Code*	DIN	Deutsche Industrie-Norm, *German Industrial Standards*
BGH	Bundesgerichtshof, *Federal Supreme Court*	Dipl.	Diplom, *diploma*
Bhf.	Bahnhof, *station*	d.J.	dieses Jahres, *of this year,* der Jüngere, *junior*
bisw.	bisweilen, *sometimes*	DKP	Deutsche Kommunistische Partei, *German Communist Party*
Bkl.	Beklagte, *defendant*		
Bl.	Blatt, *sheet*	DM	Deutsche Mark, *German Mark*
Bln.	Berlin	d.M.	dieses Monats, *instant*
BP	Bundespost *(Federal Postal Administration)*	DNA	Deutscher Normenausschuß, *German Committee of Standards*
BRT	Brutto-Register-Tonnen, *gross register tons*	do.	dito, *ditto (the same)*
B.w.	Bitte wenden, *please turn over,* PTO	d.O.	der (die, das) Obige, *the above-mentioned*
Bw	Bundeswehr, *Federal Armed Forces*	Doz.	Dozent, *university lecturer*
		dpa	Deutsche Presse-Agentur, *German Press Agency*
bzgl.	bezüglich, *with reference to*		
bzw.	beziehungsweise, *respectively*	Dr.	Doktor, *Doctor*
		Dr. jur.	Doktor der Rechte, *Doctor of Law*
C	Celsius	Dr. med.	Doktor der Medizin, *MD*
ca.	circa, etwa, *about, approximately*	Dr. phil. nat.	Doktor der Naturwissenschaften, *DSc*
cal.	Kalorie, *calorie*		
cand.	candidatus, Kandidat, *candidate*	Dr. theol.	Doktor der Theologie, *Doctor of Divinity*
cbm	Kubikmeter, *cubic metre*	DRK	Deutsches Rotes Kreuz, *German Red Cross*
ccm	Kubikzentimeter, *cubic centimetre*		
CDU	Christlich-Demokratische Union, *Christian Democratic Union*	dt(sch).	deutsch, *German*
		Dtschld.	Deutschland, *Germany*
		Dtz., Dtzd.	Dutzend, *dozen*
Cie.	Kompanie, *Company*	d. Verf.	der Verfasser, *the author*
cm	Zentimeter, *centimetre*	D.V.O.	Durchführungsverordnung, *Implementing Ordinance*
Co.	Kompagnon, *partner,* Kompanie, *company*		
		dz	Doppelzentner, *100 kilogrammes*
CSU	Christlich-Soziale Union, *Christian Social Union*	D-Zug	Durchganzug, *fast through train*
c.t.	cum tempore, mit akademischem Viertel, *with a quarter of an hour's allowance*	E	Eilzug, *fast train*
		ebd.	ebenda, *in the same place*
		Ed.	Edition, Ausgabe, *edition*
C.V.J.M.	Christlicher Verein Junger Männer, *YMCA*	EDV	elektrische Datenverarbeitung, *electronic data processing*
		e.h.	ehrenhalber, *honorary*
d.A.	der Ältere, *senior*	ehem., ehm.	ehemals, *formerly*
DAG	Deutsche Angestellten-Gewerkschaft, *Trade Union of German Employees*	eig., eigtl.	eigentlich, *really, properly*
		einschl.	einschließlich, *including*
		EKD	Evangelische Kirche in Deutschland, *Protestant Church in Germany*
den	Denier, *denier*		
DGB	Deutsche Gewerkschaftsbund, *trade union*		
		EKG	Elektrokardiogramm, *electrocardiogram (ECG)*
dgl.	dergleichen, desgleichen, *the like*		
		entspr.	entsprechend, *corresponding*
d. Gr.	der Große, *the Great*	erg.	ergänze, *supply, add*
d.h.	das heißt, *that is to say, ie*	Erl.	Erläuterung, *explanation*
d.i.	das ist, *that is, ie*		

Euratom	Europäische Atomgemeinschaft, *European Atomic Community*
ev.	evangelisch, *Protestant*
e.V.	eingetragener Verein, *registered society, association*
evtl.	eventuell, *perhaps, possibly*
EWG	Europäische Wirtschaftsgemeinschaft, *European Economic Community*
exkl.	exklusive, *except, not including*
Expl.	Exemplar, *sample, copy*
EZU	Europäische Zahlungsunion, *European Payments Union*
F	Fahrenheit
Fa.	Firma, *firm, Sirs (in a letter)*
Fam.	Familie, *family*
FAZ	Frankfurter Allgemeine Zeitung *(newspaper)*
F.D.G.B.	Freier Deutscher Gewerkschaftsbund, *Free Federation of German Trade Unions*
F.D.P.	Freie Demokratische Partei, *Liberal Democratic Party*
FD-ZUG	Fernschnellzug, *long-distance express*
ff.	folgende Seiten, *following pages*
fig.	figürlich, *figurative*
fm	Festmeter, *cubic metre*
fortl.	fortlaufend, *running, successive*
Forts.	Fortsetzung, *continuation*
Fr.	Frau, *Mrs*
frdl.	freundlich, *kind*
Frhr.	Freiherr, *Baron*
Frl.	Fräulein, *Miss*
frz.	französisch, *French*
F.U.	Freie Universität, *Free University (of Berlin)*
g	Gramm, *gramme*
geb.	geboren, *born*; gebunden, *bound*
Gebr.	Gebrüder, *Brothers*
gegr.	gegründet, *established*
gek.	gekürzt, *abbreviated*
Gen.	Genitiv
Ges.	Gesellschaft, *association, company*; Gesetz, *law*
ges. gesch.	gesetzlich geschützt, *registered*
gest.	gestorben, *deceased*
gez.	gezeichnet, *signed*
GG	Grundgesetz, *Basic Constitutional Law*
GmbH, G.m.b.H	Gesellschaft mit beschränkter Haftung, *limited liability company*
ha	Hektar
Hbf.	Hauptbahnhof, *main station*
Hbg	Hamburg
h.c.	honoris causa, ehrenhalber, *honorary*
HG	Handelsgesellschaft, *trading company*
HGB	Handelsgesetzbuch, *commercial code*
hl.	heilig, *holy*
höfl.	höflich, *kindly*
Hp.	Haltepunkt, *halt, stop*
hpts.	hauptsächlich, *mainly*
Hr., Hrn.	Herr(n), *Mr*
hrsg.	herausgegeben, *edited*
Hrsg.	Herausgeber, *editor*
HTL	Höhere Technische Lehranstalt, *polytechnic, college*
Hz.	Hertz
i.	im, *in*
i.A.	im Auftrag, *for, by order*
i.allg.	im allgemeinen, *in general*
i.b.	im besonderen, *in particular*
i.D.	im Durchschnitt, *on an average*
i. Fa.	in Firma, *care of*
IG	Industriegewerkschaft, *Industry Trade Union*
i.J.	im Jahre, *in the year*
i.L.	in Liquidation
Ing.	Ingenieur, *engineer*
Inh.	Inhaber, *proprietor*; Inhalt, *contents*
inkl.	inklusive, *inclusive*
Interpol	Internationale Kriminalpolizei-Kommission, *International Criminal Police Commission*
I.O.K.	Internationales Olympisches Komitee, *IOC*
i.R.	im Ruhestand, *retired, emeritus*
IRK	Internationales Rotes Kreuz, *IRC*
i.V.	in Vertretung, *by order, on behalf of*
i.W.	in Worten, *in words*
J.	Joule, *joule (SI unit of work)*
jhrl.	jährlich, *annual*
jr., jun.	junior
jur.	juristisch, *legal*

Kap	Kapitel, *chapter*	möbl.	möbliert, *furnished*
kath.	katholisch, *catholic*	mod.	modern
kcal	Kilocalorie	Mrd.	Milliarde, *thousand millions,*
Kfm.	Kaufmann, *merchant*		*billion*
kfm.	kaufmännisch, *commercial*	mtl.	monatlich, *monthly*
Kfz.	Kraftfahrzeug, *motor vehicle*	m.W.	meines Wissens, *as far as I*
kg	Kilogram		*know*
KG	Kommanditgesellschaft, *limited*	MWSt	Mehrwertsteuer, *VAT*
	partnership		*equivalent*
Kgl.	Königlich, *Royal*		
Kl.	Klasse, *class, form*	N	Norden, *north*; Leistung, *power*
Km/Std.	Kilometer pro Stunde, *miles per*	Nachf.	Nachfolger, *successor*
	hour	nachm.	nachmittags, *in the afternoon*
KP	Kommunistische Partei,	NATO	Nordatlantikpakt-Organisation,
	Communist Party		*NATO*
kr.	Krone	n. Chr.	nach Christus, *after Christ, AD*
Kripo	Kriminalpolizei, *Criminal*	N.N.	Name unbekannt, *name*
	Investigation Department		*unknown*
Kto.	Konto, *account*	NO	Nordosten, *north-east*
		NOK	Nationales Olympisches
l	liter, *litre*		Komitee, *NOC*
LDP	Liberal-Demokratische Partei,	Nom.	Nominative
	Liberal Democratic Party	NPD	National-Demokratische Partei
led.	ledig, *unmarried*		Deutschlands, *National*
Lekt.	Lektion, *lesson*		*Democratic Party of Germany*
lfd.	laufend, *current, running*	Nr.	Numero, Nummer, *number*
lfd. Nr.	laufende Nummer, *current*	N.T.	Neues Testament, *New*
	number		*Testament*
Lfg., Lfrg.	Lieferung, *instalment, delivery*	NW	Nordwesten, *north-west*
LG	Landgericht, *District Court*		
Lit.	Literatur, *literature*	O	Osten, *east*
Lkw.	Lastkraftwagen, *lorry, truck*	o.	oben, *above*; oder, *or*; ohne,
Lok.	Lokomotive, *engine*		*without*
lt.	laut, *according to*	o.ä.	oder ähnlich, *or the like*
ltd.	leitend, *managing, chief*	OB	Oberbürgermeister, *Chief*
Ltg.	Leitung, *management, direction*		*Burgomaster (equivalent to*
luth	lutherisch, *Lutheran*		*Mayor)*
		o.B.	ohne Befund, *without findings*
m.	Meter, *metre*		*(medical)*
max.	maximal, *maximum*	Obb.	Oberbayern, *Upper Bavaria*
m.b.H.	mit beschränkter Haftung, *with*	od.	oder, *or*
	limited liability	OEZ	Osteuropäische Zeit, *Eastern*
Mdb, M.d.B.	Mitglied des Bundestages,		*European time*
	Member of the Bundestag	öff., öffentl	öffentlich, *public*
	(equivalent to MP)	offiz.	offiziell, *official*
mdl.	mündlich, *verbal*	OHG	Offene Handelsgesellschaft,
MdL,	Mitglied des Landtages, *Member*		*general commercial partnership*
M.D.L.	*of the Landtag*	o.J.	ohne Jahr, *no date*
m.E.	meines Erachtens, *in my opinion*	OLG	Oberlandesgericht, *Higher*
MEZ	Mitteleuropäische Zeit, *Central*		*Regional Court*
	European Time	o.Prof.	ordentlicher Professor, *Professor*
Mill.	Million	Orig.	Original
Min., min.	Minute, *minute*; minimal, *minimal*	orth.	orthodox

p.A.	per Adresse, *care of*
Pf	Pfennig
Pfd.	Pfund, *pound (weight)*
PH	Pädagogische Hochschule, *teachers' training college*
PKW, Pkw.	Personenkraftwagen, *car*
Pl.	Platz, *square*
p.p, p.pa., ppa	per procura, *by proxy*
Prof.	Professor
Prov.	Provinz, *province*
PS	Pferdestärke, *horsepower*; postscriptum, *PS*
qm	Quadratmeter, *square metre*
®	Warenzeichen, *registered trademark*
rd.	rund, *roughly, in round figures*
Reg. Bez.	Regierungsbezirk, *administrative district*
Rel.	Religion
Rep.	Republik
resp.	respektive, *respectively*
Rhld	Rheinland
rk.	römisch-katholisch, *Roman Catholic*
rm	Raummeter, *cubic metre*
röm.	römisch, *Roman*
S	Süden, *south*
S.	Seite, *page*
S-Bahn	Schnellbahn, *city railway*
SDS	Sozialistischer Deutscher Studentenbund, *Association of German Socialist Students*
sec	Sekunde, *second*
sen.	senior
SO	Südosten, *south-east*
s.o.	siehe oben, *see above*
sog.	sogenannt, *so-called*
SPD	Sozialdemokratische Partei Deutschlands, *Social Democratic Party*
St.	Stück, *piece*; Sankt, *Saint*
Std., Stde.	Stunde, *hour*
stdl.	stündlich, *every hour*
stellv.	stellvertretend, *assistant*
StGB	Strafgesetzbuch, *Penal Code*
Str.	Straße, *street*
StVO	Straßenverkehrsordnung, *road traffic regulations*
s.u.	siehe unten, *see below*

SW	Südwesten, *south-west*
s.Z.	seinerzeit, *at that time*
t	Tonne
tägl.	täglich, *daily*
TEE	Trans-Europ-Expreß
Tel.	Telephon, *telephone*; Telegramm, *telegram*
TH	Technische Hochschule, *technical college* or *university*
Transp.	Transport
TU	Technische Universität, *Technical University*
TÜV	Technischer Überwachungsverein, *Association for Technical Inspection*
u.	und, *and*
u.a.	und andere(s), *and others*; unter anderem, *among others*
u.ä.	und ähnliche(s), *and the like*
u.A.w.g.	um Antwort wird gebeten, *please reply, RSVP*
u.dgl.	und dergleichen, *and the like*
u.d.M.	unter dem Meeresspiegel, *below sea level*
ü.d.M.	über dem Meeresspiegel, *above sea level*
UdSSR	Union der Sozialistischen Sowjetrepubliken, *USSR*
u.E.	unseres Erachtens, *in our opinion*
UKW	Ultrakurzwelle, *ultra-short wave, vhf*
U/min	Umdrehungen in der Minute, *revolutions per minute*
urspr	ursprünglich, *original(ly)*
USA	Vereinigte Staaten von Amerika, *USA*
usw.	und so weiter, *and so forth*
u.U.	unter Umständen, *circumstances permitting*
UV	ultaviolett, *ultra-violet*
u.v.a.(m.)	und viele(s) andere mehr, *and many others more*
u.zw.	und zwar, *that is*
v.	von, vom, *of, from, by*
V	Volt, *volt*; Volumen, *volume*
V.	Vers, *line*
VB	Verhandlungsbasis, *o.n.o.*
v. Chr.	vor Christus, *BC*
Verf., Vf.	Verfasser, *author*
verh.	verheiratet, *married*

Verl.	Verlag, Verleger, *Publishing company*		WS	Wintersemester, *winter term*
vgl.	vergleiche, *compare*		Wwe.	Witwe, *widow*
v.g.u.	vorgelesen, genehmigt, unterschrieben, *read, confirmed, signed*		Wz	Warenzeichen, *registered trade mark*
v.H.	vom Hundert, *per cent*		Z.	Zahl, *number;* Zeile, *line*
v.J.	vorigen Jahres, *of last year*		z.	zu, zum, zur, *at, to*
v.M.	vorigen Monats, *of last month*		z.B.	zum Beispiel, *for example, e.g.*
V.N.	Vereinigte Nationen, *UN*		ZDF	Zweites Deutsches Fernsehen, *German television broadcasting*
vorm	vormittags, *a.m.;* vormals, *formerly*		z.E.	zum Exempel, *e.g.*
Vors.	Vorsitzender, *chairman*		z. H(d).	zu Händen, *attention of, to be delivered to*
VR	Volksrepublik, *People's Republic*		ZPO	Zivilprozeßordnung, *Code of Civil Procedure*
v.T.	vom Tausend, *per thousand*		z.T.	zum Teil, *partly*
v.u.	von unten, *from below*		Ztg.	Zeitung, *newspaper*
			Ztschr.	Zeitschrift, *periodical*
W	Westen, *West;* Watt, *watt*		zus.	zusammen, *together*
WE	Wärmeeinheit, *thermal unit*		zuz.	zuzüglich, *plus/in addition*
WEU	Westeuropäische Union, *WEU*		zw.	zwischen, *between, among*
WEZ	Westeuropäische Zeit, *Western European Time, GMT*		z.Z(t).	zur Zeit, *at the time, at present*

4 SPANISH

Abreviaturas y siglas (Abbreviations and acronyms)

a.c.	año corriente, *current year*		Art.arto	Artículo, *article*
a/c	a cuenta, *on account*		atmo.	atentísimo, *(Yours) truly*
adj.	adjunto(s), *enc(s)*		Atto.atta	Atento, atenta, *your letter*
Admon.	Administración, *Administration*		Avda	Avenida, *Avenue*
Admor.	Administrador, *administrator*			
AEB	Asociación Española de Banca, *Spanish banking Association*		Bco.B	Banco, *Bank*
			BEI	Banco Europeo de Inversión, *European Investment Bank*
AECOC	Asociación Europea de Codificación Comercial		Bo	Beneficio, *profit*
a/f	a favor, *in favour*		BOCM	Boletín Oficial de la Comunidad de Madrid *(Madrid's official journal)*
Afmo.Affmo	Afectísimo, *dear/yours faithfully*			
A.I.	Amnistía Internacional, *Amnesty International*		BOE	Boletín Oficial del Estado, *Official State journal*
ALALC	Asociación Latinoamericana de Libre Comercio, *Latin American Free Trade Association*		BUP	Bachillerato Unificado y Polivalente *(school leaving equivalent of O levels; Bachillerato superior is the equivalent to A Levels)*
AMA	American Marketing Association			
AME	Acuerdo Monetario Internacional			
ANGED	Asociación Nacional de Grandes Empresas de Distribución		c.	capítulo, *chapter*
			C.	compañía, *company*
			c/	calle, *street*
Apdo.Aptdo	Apartado, *PO Box*		C.A.E.	cóbrese al entregar, *cash on delivery*
Arch	Archivo, *file*			

CAMP	Caja de Ahorros y Monte de Piedad de Madrid *(Savings Bank)*
CAMPSA	Compañía Arrendataria del Monopolio de Petróleos *(state-owned petrol company)*
CAP	certificado de Aptitud Pedagógica *(teacher training qualification)*
cap. capo	capítulo, *chapter*
CARICOM	Mercado Común del Caribe, *Caribbean Common Market*
CARIFTA	Caribbean Free Trade Association
CAT	Compañía Arrendataria de Tabacos *(state-owned tobacco company)*
c/c, cta. cte	Cuenta corriente, *current account*
C.D.	Club deportivo, *sports club*
c/d	con descuento, *discounted, reduced*
Cdad.	Ciudad, *town*
C/e	Conocimiento de embarque, *bill of lading*
CECA	Comunidad Europea del Carbón y del Acero, *European Coal and Steel Community*
CED	Comunidad Europea de Defensa
CEDIN	Centro de Documentacion e Informacíon del Comercio Exterior, *Export agency*
CEE	Comunidad Económica Europea, *EEC*
cent, cents, cts	Céntimo, Céntimos, *hundredth*
CEOE	Confederación Española de Organizaciones Empresariales *(CBI equivalent)*
CEPYME	Confederación Empresarial Pequeña y Mediana Empresa *(small and medium sized business association)*
cert.	certificado, *registered*
CES	Comité Económico y Social, *Economic and Social Affairs Committee*
CESCE	Compañía Española de Seguro de Crédito a la Exportación, *Spanish Export Credit Insurance Company*
C.F.	club de Fútbol, *football club*
cg	centigramos, *centigram*
ch/. ch.	cheque
Cia	Compañía, *company*

C.I.F., c.i.f.	costo, seguro y flete, *cost, insurance and freight*
cje.	corretaje, *brokerage*
cl	centilitro, *centilitre*
cm	centímetro, *centimetre*
CN	colegio Nacional, *state school*
Cnel	Coronel, *Colonel*
co	Cambio *(facility to change currency)*
Cod.	código, *code*
COI	Comité Olímpico Internacional, *International Olympic Committee*
Com.	Comisión, *Commission*
COMECON	Consejo de Asistencia Económica mutua, *Council for mutual economic assistance*
COPA	Comité de Organizaciones Profesionales Agrícolas, *Farmers' Trade Association*
COREPER	Comité de Representantes Permanentes
C.P.	contestación pagada, *reply paid*
CSB	Consejo Superior Bancario
cta	cuenta, *account*
cta./ab.	cuenta abierta, *open account*
cta/n	cuenta nueva, *new account*
cte.	corriente, *current (month)*
c/u	cada uno, *each*
C.V. H.P.	Caballos de Vapor, *horsepower equivalent*
d/	día, *day*
D., Da.	Don, *Mr*; Doña, *Mrs*
dcha.	derecha, *right/on the right*
d/f.	días fecha, *holidays*
dg.	decigramos
Dg.	decagramos
D.G.T.	Dirección General de Turismo *(State Tourist Organisation)*
DGTE	Dirección General de Transacciones Exteriores, *General Directorate of Foreign Transactions*
dho	dicho, *aforesaid*
Dl.	decalitros
dm.	decímetros
Dm.	decámetros
D.m.	Dios mediante, *God willing*
Doc.	documento, *document*
dpto.	departamento, *department*
Dr., Dres.	Doctor, doctores
dto.	descuento, *discount*

Dtor.	Director
dupdo., dup., dupl.	duplicado, *copy*
d/v.	días vista, *days after sight*
e/	envío, *shipment, consignment, letter*
E.	Este, *East*
ECU	Unidad de Cuenta Europea, *European Currency Unit*
ed.	Edición, *Edition*; editor, *editor*; editorial, *editorial*
EE. UU.	Estados Unidos, *USA*
EFTA	Asociación Europea de Libre Comercio
efvo.	efectivo, *cash*
EGB	Enseñanza General Básica *(the elementary education system from 6-13 years of age)*
ej.	ejemplo, *example*
Ema.	Eminencia, *His eminence*
Emmo.	Eminentísimo, *Most Eminent*
entlo.	entresuelo, *mezzanine*
E.P.D.	en paz descanse, *RIP*
E.P.M.	en propia mano, *in one's own hand*
ES	Ejército de Salvación, *Salvation Army*
esq.	esquina, *corner*
etc.	etcétera, *etc*
EURATOM	Comisión Europea de la Energía Atómica
EUROSTAT	Oficina Estadística de las Comunidades Europeas *(official EC statistics office)*
E	Excelencia, *Excellency*
Excmo. Excma	Excelentísimo, Excelentísima, *Most excellent*
ext.	exterior
fa	factura, *bill/account*
fab.	fábrica, *factory/works*
f.c., ff. cc., FF. CC.	ferrocarril, *railway*; ferrocarriles, *railways*
fcha.	fecha, *date*
FDG	Fondo de Garantía de Depósitos
FED	Fondo Europeo de Desarrollo, *European Development Fund*
FEDER	Fondo Europeo de Desarrollo Regional, *European Fund for Regional Development*
FEOGA	Fondo Europeo de Orientación y Garantía Agrícola

f/f	fecha factura, *date of bill*
FMI	Fondo Monetario Internacional, *IMF*
f.o., fol.	folio, *folio, page*
fr., frs.	franco, francos, *French Franc*
fra.	factura, *bill/invoice*
FSE	Fondo Social Europeo
g., grs.	Gramo, *gram*; Gramos, *grams*
g/	giro, *draft/money order*
GATT	Acuerdo General sobre Aranceles y Comercio, *GATT agreement*
gde	guarde, que Dios guarde, *whom God protects*
G.P., g/p., g.p.	Giro postal, *postal order*
G.T., g/t., g.t.	Giro telegráfico, *telegraphic money order*
gta.	Glorieta, *Square*
gtos	gastos, *costs*
gtos. grles.	gastos generales, *general costs*
g.v.	gran velocidad, *high speed*
Ha.	hectárea, *hectare*
Hg.	hectogramo, *hectogram*
Hl.	hectolitro, *hectolitre*
Hm.	hectómetro, *hectometre*
Hno(s.)	Hermano(s), *Brothers*
IATA	Asociación Internacional de Transporte Aéro
ICO	Instituto de Crédito Oficial *(the official credit institute/organisation)*
Id.	idem, lo mismo, *the same*
IEME	Instituto de Moneda Estranjera *(foreign money exchange)*
IFEMA	Instituto Ferial de Madrid
IGTE	Impuesto General sobre el Tráfico de Empresas, *business tax*
IL	Instituto Laboral, *technical school*
Ilmo., Ilma.	Ilustrísimo, Ilustrísima, *most distinguished*
Iltre.	Ilustre, *distinguished*
IMAC	Instituto de Mediación y Arbitraje *(ACAS equivalent)*
Imp.	Imprenta, *printers*
Impte	Importe, *amount*
Impto.	Impuesto, *tax*
INDO	Instituto Nacional de Demoninación de Origen *(organisation for the classification of wine)*

INI	Instituto Nacional de Industria, *State Industrial Council*	Mod.	modelo, *model*
int.	interior	MS	manuscrito, *manuscript*
ITE	Impuesto Tráfico de Empresas, *business tax*	n/	nuestro, nuestra, *our*
IV	Instituto de la Vivienda, *housing office*	N.	norte, *north*
IVA	Impuesto sobre el valor añadido, *VAT equivalent*	n/ch.	nuestro cheque, *our cheque*
izdo., izda., izq	izquierdo, *left/on the left*	n/cta.	nuestra cuenta, *our account*
		NE.	nordeste, *north east*
Juzgo.	Juzgado, *court*	n/fra.	nuestra factura, *our bill*
		n/L.	nuestra letra, *our letter*
Kg., kg	kilogramo, *kilogram*	NN. UU.	Naciones Unidas, *United Nations*
Kl.	kilolitro, *kilolitre*	n/o.	nuestra orden, *our order*
km.	kilómetro, *kilometre*	NO.	noroeste, *north west*
km./h., km/h.	kilómetro por hora, *km per hour*	Nom.	nominal
		n/p.	nuestro pagaré, *our IOU*
l.	ley, *law*	n/r.	nuestra remesa, *our consignment*
L.	Liras, *Italian Lira*, letra (de cambio), *bill (of exchange)*	Num., n.o	número, *number*
Lic. en Fil y Let	Licenciado en Filosofía y Letras *(equivalent of a BA:* Titulo de . . . *is the equivalent of a BSC; university courses usually last a minimum of 5 years)*	o/	orden, *order*
		O.A.A.	Organización de Agricultura Alimentación, *Food and Agriculture Organisation*
Liq.o	líquido, *liquid*	OACI	Organización de Aviación Civil Internacional, *International Civil Aviation Organisation*
Ltd., Ltda	Limitada, *Limited*	ob. obpo	obispo, *bishop*
m.	minuto, *minute*	OCDE	Organización de Cooperación y Desarrollo Económico, *OECD*
m/.	meses, *months*; mi(s), *my*	OECE	Organización Europea de Cooperación Económica
m., mts.	Metro, Metros, *Underground railway*	OIT	Organización Internacional de Trabajo, *International Labour Organisation*
m2	Metro cuadrado, *square metre*	OLP	Organización para la liberación de Palestina, *PLO*
Max.	máximo, *maximum*	O.M.	Orden Ministerial, *Ministerial order*
M.C.	Mercado Común, *Common Market*	OMS	Organiación Mundial de la Salud, *World Health Organisation*
MCCA	Mercado Común Centroamericano, *Central American Common Market*	ONU	Organización de las Naciones Unidas, *UN*
MCE	Mercado Común Europeo, *Common Market*	OPEP	Organización de Paises Exportadores de Petróleo, *OPEC*
Md.	Madrid	OTAN	Organización del Tratado del Atlántico Norte, *NATO*
MF	Ministerio de Fomento, *Ministry of Public Works and the Economy*	OVNI	objeto volante no indentificado, *UFO*
mg.	miligramo, *milligram*	p/	pagaré, *IOU, debt*
Mili	*military service*	PAC	Política Agrícola Común, *Common Agricultural Policy*
min.	mínimo, *minimum*		
ml.	mililitro, *millilitre*		
mm.	milímetro, *millimetre*		

pag., pags.	página, *page*; páginas, *pages*
p/cta.	por cuenta, *by account*
P.D., P.S.	posdata, *postscript*
PDC	Partido Democrata Cristiano, *Christian Democratic Union*
pdo.	pasado, *passed (last month)*
p.e., p.ej.	por ejemplo, *for example*
PED	Procesamiento Electrónico de Datos, *electronic data processing*
PIB	Producto Interior Bruto, *Gross Domestic Product*
Pl.	Plaza, *Square*
P.N.	peso neto, *net weight*
PNB	Producto Nacional Bruto, *Gross National Product*
p.o., P.O., p/o.	por orden, *by order*; Paseo, *walk/drive*
p.p., P.P.	porte pagado, *handling paid*; pronto pago, *prompt payment*
p.pdo.	próximo pasado, *last*
pral.	Principal
prof.	Professor
prol.	Prólogo, *Prologue*
prov.	Provincia, *province*
PS	Partido Socialista
pta., ptas.	Peseta, pesetas, *Spanish peseta(s)*
pte.	Presente
P.V.P.	Precio de Venta al Público, *retail price*
PYMES	Pequeñas y Medianas Empresas, *small and medium-sized companies*
Pzs.	Piezas, *pieces*
q.e.S.m.	que estrecha Su mano, *yours faithfully*
R.A.C.E.	Real Automóvil Club de Espana *(RAC/AA equivalent)*
ref., Rf.a	Referencia, Referencias
RENFE	Red Nacional de Ferrocarriles Españoles, *Spanish State railways*
RFF	Represión del Fraude Fiscal
R.O.	real orden, *Royal decree*
r.p.m.	Revoluciones por minuto, *revolutions per minute*
Rte.	Remite(nte), *sender*
rust.	en rústica, *paperbacked*
s., Sto., Sta.	San, santo, santa, *saint*
s/	Según, *according to*; Su, sus, *your*
SA	Sociedad Anónima, *corporation/limited company*
s/c.	su casa, *your house*
Sdad.	Sociedad, *Society*
sdo.	saldo, *balance, settlement, sale*
S.E.	Su Excelencia, *Excellency*
SE	sudeste, *south east*
S. en C.	Sociedad en Comandita, *limited partnership status of a company*
s.e.u.o.	Salvo error u omisión, *all errors and omissions excepted*
s.f.	sin fecha, *no date*
S.G.	Sin Gastos, *no outlay*
sgte	siguiente, *next, following*
SID	Servicio de Información Búrsatil, *Stock Exchange Information Service*
SIDA	Síndrome de immunidad deficiente adquirida, *AIDS*
S.I.M.	Servicio de Información Militar, *Military Intelligence*
SL	Sociedad de Responsabilidad Limitada, *limited liability company*
s.l. ni f	sin lugar ni fecha, *neither place nor date*
SME	Sistema Monetario Europeo, *European Monetary System*
s/n.	Sin número, *no number*
s/o	su orden *order*
SO	sudoeste, *south west*
s/p.	su pagaré, *debt/IOU*
Sr.	Señor, *Sir, Mr*
Sra.	Señora, *Madam, Mrs*
Sres., Srs.	Señores, *Sirs, Gentlemen*
Srta.	Señorita, *Miss*
SRC	Sociedad Regular Colectiva, *general partnership*
S.R.M.	Su Real Majestad, *his/her Royal Highness*
S.S.	Su Santidad, *His Holiness*
SS	Seguridad Social *(NI equivalent)*
ss., sigs.	siguientes, *following*
s.s.s.	Su seguro servidor, *Yours faithfully, your humble servant*
t.	tomo, *volume*
TEC	Tarifa o Arancel Exterior Comun
Tel., Telef.	teléfono, *telephone*
Tente.	Teniente, *Lieutenant*
TIR	Transporte Internacional por Carretera, *Road Haulage Association*
Tit.	título, *title*
Tlf.	teléfono, *telephone*

Tm.	tonelada metrica, *weight*	v.	*véase, see*
Tons.	toneladas, *weight*	Vda.	viuda, *widow, widowed*
Trav.	travesía, crossroads	V.E.	Vuestra Excelencia, *Your Excellency*
Ud., Uds.	Usted, Ustedes, *you*	v.g., v.gr.	verbigracia, *for example*
UEP	Unión Europea de Pagos, *European Payments Union*	V.I.	Vuestra Ilustrísima, *Your Grace*
ult.	Último, *last*	vol.	volumen, *volume*
UNICE	Unión de Industrias de la Comunidad Europea	VQRPD	Vinos de Calidad Provenientes de Regiones Determinadas *(wine classification normally applying to the produce of a particular local region)*
U.P.U.	Unión Postal Universal, *Universal Postal Union*		
URSS	Unión de Repúblicas Socialistas Sovieticas, *USSR*	vto.	vencimiento, *due, expiry*
		w.	watio, *watt*
V/	valor, *value*	Xp	Cristo, *Christ*

5 ITALIAN

Abreviazioni e sigle (Abbreviations and acronyms)

a	arrivo, *arrival*	AGM	assemblea generale annuale, *annual general meeting*
A.A.M.S.	Azienda Autonoma dei Monopoli di Stato, *Board of State Monopolies*	AIAC	Associazione Internazionale degli Agenti di Cambio, *International Stockbrokers' Association*
A.A.R.R.	Altezze Reali, *Royal Highness*		
AAT	Azienda Autonoma di Soggiorno, Cura e Turismo, *Local Tourist Board*	all	allegato, *enclosure, enclosed*
		alt	altitudine, *altitude*
ab	abitanti, *inhabitants, population*	amm.ne	amministrazione, *administration*
abb	abbonamento, *subscription*	ANAS	Azienda Nazionale Autonoma delle Strade, *National Road Board/Authority*
abbr	abbreviato, *abbreviated*; abbreviazione, *abbreviation*		
A.B.I.	Associazione Bancaria Italiana, *Italian Bankers' Association*	ANSA	Azienza Nazionale Stampa Associata *(an Italian news agency)*
a.c.	assegno corrente, *banker's draft*; anno corrente, *present year*; a capo, *new line/ paragraph*	app	appendice, *appendix*
		AR	Altezza Reale, *Royal Highness*; andata e riturno, *return ticket*
aC	avanti Cristo, *BC*	ARCE	Associazione per le Relazioni Culturali con l'Estero, *Association for Cultural Relations with Foreign Countries*
ACI	Automobile Club d'Italia *(Italian motoring organisation)*		
AD	Amministratore Delegato, *Managing Director*		
aD, AD	anno Domini, *AD*	arr	arrivo, *arrival*
AG	Alberghi per la Gioventù, *Youth Hostels*	ASST	Azienda di Stato per i Servizi Telefonici *(National Telephone State Board)*
AGI	Agenzia Giornalistica Italiana *(an Italian news agency)*	Avv	avvocato, *lawyer, solicitor, barrister*
AGIP	Azienda Generale Italiana Petroli *(Italian national oil company)*	az	azione, *share*
		BA	Belle Arti, *Fine Arts*

bim	bimestre, *a two-month period*; bimestrale, *bi-monthly*		Alberghi, *Italian Great Hotels Company*
BIRS	Banca Internazionale per la Riconstruzione e lo Sviluppo, *International Bank for Reconstruction and Development*	CIP	porto e assicurazione pagati, *carriage and insurance paid*
		CIT	Compagnia Italiana del Turismo *(an Italian Travel Agency)*
BM	Banca Mondiale, *World Bank*		
BR	Banco di Roma, *Bank of Rome*	cit	citado, *quoted*
brev	brevetto, *patent*	c.m.	corrente mese, *of this month*
bross	brossura, *paperback binding*	Com in Prov	Comune in provincia di, *township in the province of*
BT	bassa tensione, low voltage		
BU	Bollettino Ufficiale, *Official Gazette*	CONI	Comitato Olimpico Nazionale Italiano, *Italian Olympic Games Committee*
ca	circa, *approximately*; corrente alternata, *alternating current*	cons	consigliere, *councillor, director*
		cont.ssa	contessa, *countess*
CAA	Corte d'Assise d'Appello, *Criminal Court of Appeal*	corr	correlativo, *correlative*; corrispondenza, *correspondence*
cad	cadauno, *each*	CP	Casella Postale, *post office box*
CAI	Club Alpino Italiano, *Italian Alpine Club*	cp	cartolina postale, *post card*
		CPT	porto pagato, *carriage paid to*
cat	categoria, *category*; catalogo, *catalogue*	c.s.	come sopra, *as above*
		C.so	corso, *avenue/street*
Cav	Cavaliere, *Knight (title of nobility)*	CT	commissario tecnico, *coach*
c/c	conto corrente, *current account*	c.to	conto, *account*
CCI	Camera di Commercio Internazionale, *International Chamber of Commerce*	DAF	reso frontiera, *delivered at frontier*
		DC	Democrazia Cristiana, *Christian Democratic Party*
ccp	conto corrente postale, *current postal account*	dC	dopo Cristo, *AD*
		DD	direttissimo, *fast train*
CDF	Consiglio di Fabbrica, *Works Committee*	DDP	reso sdoganato, *delivered duty paid*
C d R	Cassa di Risparmio, *Savings Bank*	DDU	reso non sdoganato, *delivered duty unpaid*
CDS	Comitato di Difesa Nazionale, *National Defence Committee*	DES	franco bordo nave e destino, *delivered ex ship*
CEE	Comunità Economico Europea, *European Community*	dett	dettaglio, *detail*; dettagliante, *retailer*
CERP	Centro Europea di Relazioni Pubbliche, *European Centre of Public Relations*	DG	Direttore Generale, *General Manager*
		dipl	diploma, *degree*
CFR	costo e nolo, *cost and freight*	Dir	Direttore, *director/manager*; Direzione, *administrative office*
cfr	confronta, *compare*		
CI	Credito Italiano, *Italian Credit Bank*	Dir.ce	Direttrice, *Manageress, Directress*
C.ia	compagnia, *company*	Dir. Gen	Direttore Generale, *General Manager*; Direzione Generale, *Main Office*
CIF	costo, assicurazione e nolo, *cost, insurance and freight*		
CIG	Corta Internazionale di Giustizia, *International Court of Justice*	div.	divisione, *department*
		dott; dr	dottore, *doctor/Dr*
		dott.ssa	dottoressa, *lady doctor*
CIGA	Compagnia Italiana dei Grandi	dozz; dz	dozzina, *dozen*

EAM	Ente Autotrasporti Merci, *Freight Transport Board*		fob	franco a bordo, *free on board*
ecc	eccetera, *etc*		freq	frequenza, *frequency*
ECU	Unità di Conto Europea, *European Currency Unit*		FS/FFSS	Ferrovie dello Stato, *Italian State Railways*
ed	edizione, *edition/publication*		f.to	firmato, *signed*
Ed, edit	editore, *publisher*			
EE	Escursionisti Esteri *(licence plate for foreigners living temporarily in Italy)*		g.	giorno, *day*
			G.d.F	Guardia di Finanza, *Revenue Guard Corps*
EE.PP	Enti Pubblici, *Public Agencies*		gg	giorni, *days*
eff.	effetto, *bill/promissory note*; effettivo, *effective*		GI	Giudice Istruttore, *Examining Magistrate*
EFIM	Ente partecipazioni E Finanziamento Industria Manifatturiera *(one of the three powerful state holding companies)*		giorn.	giornale, *newspaper*; giornaliero, *daily*
			GV	Grande Velocità, *express goods service (trains)*
EFTA	Associazione Europea di Libero Scambio, *European Free Trade Association*		HF	alta frequenza, *high frequency*
Egr. Sig.	Egregio Signor, *Mr (in address)*		ICE	Istituto Italiano per il Commercio Estero, *Italian Institute for Foreign Trade*
ENEL	Ente Nazionale per l'Energia Elettrica, *National Electricity Board*		IGE	imposta generale sull'entrata, *purchase tax*
ENIT	Ente Nazionale Italiano per il Turismo, *Italian Tourist Authority*		ILOR	imposta locale sul reddito, *local income tax*
ERP	Programma di Ricostruzione Europea, *European Recovery Programme*		IMQ	Istituto del Marchio di Qualità, *Quality Standards Institute*
			ind	industria, *industry*
es.	esempio, *example*		ing	ingenere, *engineer*
EV	Eccellenza Vostra, *Your Excellency*; Era volgare, *in the year of the Lord/AD*		INPS	Istituto Nazionale di Previdenza Sociale, *National Institute of Social Insurance*
EXW	franco fabbrica, *ex works*		IRPEF	imposta sul reddito delle persone fisiche, *personal income tax*
FAS	franco sottobordo, *free alongside ship*		IRPEG	imposta sul reddito delle persone giuridiche *(corporate income tax, corporation tax)*
fatt	fattura, *invoice*			
FCA	franco vettore, *free carrier*		ISTAT	Istitute Centrale di Statistica, *Central Statistics Institute*
f.co	franco, *free*			
Fed	federale, *federal*		ITC	Istitute Tecnico Commerciale, *Business and Technical School*
FFS	Ferrovie Federali Svizzere, *Swiss Federal Railways*		IVA	Imposta sul Valore Aggiunto, *VAT*
FIA	Federazione Internazionale Automobilistica, *International Automobile Association*		L; Lit	Lira italiana, *Italian Lira*
			L/C	Lettera di Credito, *Letter of Credit*
F.igli	Figli, *sons*			
fil.	filiale, *branch office*		libr	libraio, *bookseller*; libreria, *bookshop*
F.lli	Fratelli, *Brothers/Bros*			
FMI	Fondo Monetario Internazionale, *International Monetary Fund*		locuz	locuzione, *phrase*
			L.st	lira sterlina, *pound (sterling)*

Ma	Maestra, *mistress, school teacher*	pr	per ringraziamento, *with thanks*
magg	maggiore, *major*	Prof	professore, *Professor*
MEC	Mercato Europeo Comune, *Common Market*	P.S.	Post Scriptum, *PS*
		PT	Poste e Telecomunicazioni, *Post Office*
mens	mensile, *monthly*		
Mil	militare, *military*	P.za	Piazza, *square*
mitt	mittente, *sender/from*		
mod	modulo, *form*	q.c.	qualche cosa, qualcosa, *something*
		q.v.	qualche volta, *sometimes*
n/; ns	nostro, *our(s)*		
no	numero, *number/no*	racc	raccomandata, *Registered (letter)*
NSGC	Nostro Signore Gesù Cristo, *Our Lord Jesus Christ*	RAI-TV	Radio Audizioni Italiane e Televisione, *Italian Radio and TV Broadcasting Corporation*
NU	Nazioni Unite, *United Nations*; Nettezza Urbana, *City Sanitation Department*	RAV	Rimessa Assegni e Vaglia, *draft and money order remittance*
		Rep	Republica, *Republic*
obb. mo	obbligatissimo, *your obedient servant (letters)*	Rev	Reverendo, *Reverend*
		rif	riferimento, *reference*
O. d. G.	Ordine del Giorno, *order of the day*	RINA	Registro Italiano Navale e Aeronautico, *Italian Air and Shipping Registry*
off	officina, *workshop, shop*	ripr. viet.	riproduzione vietato, *copyrighted*
OIL	Organizzazione Internationale del Lavoro, *International Labour Organisation*	Rrr	raccomandata con ricevuta di ritorno, *registered*
OMS	Organizzazione Mondiale della Sanità, *World Health Organisation*	S	Santo, *Saint*
		SA	Società Anonima, *joint stock company*
ONU	Organizzazione delle Nazioni Unite, *United Nations*	sa	sine anno, *no year*
		S. Acc	Società in Accomadita, *limited partnership (Ltd)*
P	partenza, *departure*	SapA, S.acc.p.a.	Società in accomandita per azioni *(similar to Sas but the partner's capital is represented by shares)*
p, pag	pagina, *page*		
pagg	pagine, *pages*		
parr	parrochia, *parish*; parroco, *vicar/priest*		
pe, p.es	per esempio, *for example*	Sas	Società in accomandita semplice, *limited liability partnership*
pers	persona, *person*; personale, *personal*		
p. est	per estensione, *by extension*	SC	Sede Centrale, *Head Office*
p.f.	per favore, *please*	SCV	Stato della Città del Vaticano, *Vatican City*
PG	Procuratore Generale, *Attorney-General*	sd	senza data, *no date*
PNL	Prodotto Nazionale Lordo, *GNP*	sdl	senza data o luogo, *no place or date*
PO	Posta Ordinaria, *first-class mail*		
PP	posa piano, *handle with care*; porto pagato, *carriage paid*	SDN	Società delle Nazioni, *League of Nations*
PP	pacco postale, *parcel post*; per procura, *pp*	SE	Sua Eccellenza, *His/Her Excellency*
		sec	secolo, *century*
PPP	più che piano, *extremely soft*	segg	seguenti, *following*
PPTT	Poste e Telecomunicazioni, *Post, Telephone and Telegraph Services*	segr	segretario, *secretary*
		SEO	slavo errori e omissioni, *errors and omissions excepted*

sg	secondo grandezza, *according to size*		TCI	Touring Club Italiano, *Italian Touring Club*
Sig	Signore, *Mr*		tel	telefono, *telephone*
Sig.a, Sig.ra	Signora, *Mrs*		telegr	telegrafo, *telegraph*
Sigg.	Signori, *Messrs*		TIR	Trasporti Internazionali su Strada, *International Transport of Merchandise by Road*
Sig.na	Signorina, Miss			
SIP	Società Italiana per l'esercizio telefonico, *Italian Telephone Company*		tosc	toscano, *Tuscan*
			TOTIP	Totalizzatore Ippico, *Horse-race Pools*
slm	sul livello del mare, *above sea level*		TOTO-CALCIO	Totalizzatore del (Gioco del) Calcio, *Football Pools*
SME	Sistema Monetario Europeo, *European Monetary System*		trad	traduttore, *translator*
Snc	Società in nome collettivo, *unlimited liability business partnership*		uff	ufficiale, *official*; ufficio, *office*
			UIL	Unions Italiana del Lavora, *Italian Federation of Trade Unions*
Soc	Società, *partnership/company*			
SpA	Società per Azioni, *Public limited liability company*		UPT	Ufficio Provinciale del Tesoro, *District Treasury Office*
Spett., Spett.le	Spettabile, *Dear Sirs*		US	Ufficio Stampa, *Press Agency*; Uscita di Sicurezza, *Emergency Exit*
Spett. Ditt.	Spettabile Ditta, *Messrs*			
SPQR	Senatus Populusque Romanus, *The Senate and the People of Rome*		u.s.	ultimo scorso, *last month*
			V	via, *street*
Srl	Società a responsabilità limitata, *Private limited liability company*		v/;vs	vostro, *Your(s)*
			Vat	Vaticano, *Vatican*
			VG	Vostra Grazia, *Your Grace*
S/S.ta	San(to)/Santa, *Saint*		vic	vicolo, *alley*
SS	Sua Santità, *His Holiness*		V.le	Viale, *avenue*
str.	strada, *street/road*		vp	vedi pagina, *see page*
			vr	vedi retro, *PTO, please turn over*
tav	tavola, *table*			
T/B	tratta su banche, *drafts drawn on banks*		vs	vedi sopra, *see above*
			VV, VU	Vigili Urbani, *city police*

Section 2 MULTILINGUAL GLOSSARY OF KEY BUSINESS VOCABULARY

English	French	German	Spanish	Italian
ability	capacité(f)	Fähigkeit(f)	capacidad(f)	capacità(f)
abroad	étranger(m)	Ausland(n)	extranjero(m)	estero(m)
abrupt	subit(e)	abrupt	súbito(a)	improvviso(a)
absent	absent(e)	abwesend	ausente	assente
absolutely	absolument	unbedingt	absolutamente	assolutamente
accent	accent(m)	Akzent(m)	acento(m)	accento(m)
acceptance	réception(f)	Annahme(f)	aceptación(f)	accettazione(f)
accommodation	logement(m)	Unterkunft(f)	hospedaje(m)	alloggio(m)
(to) accompany	accompagner	begleiten	acompañar	accompagnare
account	compte(m)	Konto(n)/ Rechnung(f)	cuenta(f)	conto(m)
accountant	comptable(m/f)	Bücherrevisor(m)	contable(m/f)	contabile(m)
acquaintance	ami(m)	Bekannter(m)	conocido(m)	conoscente(m)
actually	en fait	eigentlich	en realidad	in fondo
(to) add up	additionner	addieren	sumar	sommare
(to) adjust	régler	einstellen	ajustar	regolare
administration	administration(f)	Verwaltung(f)	administración(f)	amministrazione(f)
advantage	avantage(m)	Vorteil(m)	ventaja(f)	vantaggio(m)
advertisement	publicité(f)	Anzeige(f)	anuncio(m)	inserzione(f)
advertising	publicité(f)	Werbung(f)	publicidad(f)	pubblicità(f)
advice	conseil(m)	Rat(m)	consejo(m)	consiglio(m)
(to) agree upon	convenir de	vereinbaren	convenir	fissare
ahead	en avant	voraus	delante	avanti
(to) allow	permettre	erlauben/gestatten	permitir	permettere
already	déjà	bereits/schon	ya	già
amount	montant(m)	Betrag(m)	importe(m)	somma(f)
angry	fâché(e)	ärgerlich	enfadado(a)	arrabbiato(a)
(to) announce	annoncer	ansagen	anunciar	annunciare
(to) annul	annuler	annullieren	anular	annullare
(to) apologise	s'excuser de	entschuldigen, sich	disculparse	scusarsi
application	demande(f)	Antrag(m)	solicitud(f)	domanda(f)
(to) apply (job)	poser sa candidature	bewerben, sich	presentarse	concorrere
appointment	rendez-vous(m)	Verabredung(f)	cita(f)	appuntamento(m)
(to) approve	autoriser/ approuver	genehmigen/ billigen	permitir/aprobar	approvare
argument	argument(m)/ dispute(f)	Argument(n)/ Streit(m)	argumento(m)/ discusión(f)	argomento(m)/ disputa(f)
(to) arrange	arranger	arrangieren	organizar	arrangiare
article	article(m)	Artikel(m)	artículo(m)	articolo(m)
as a result of	par suite de	infolge	por	in seguito a
as far as	autant que	soweit	hasta tanto	sin dove
(to) assert	affirmer	behaupten	afirmar	affermare
asset	actif(m)	Aktiva(npl)	activo(m)	attivo(m)
as soon as	dès que	sobald	tan pronto como	non appena

English	French	German	Spanish	Italian
(to) assure	assurer	versichern	asegurar	assicurare
at first	d'abord	zuerst	primero	dapprima
at least	au moins	mindestens/ wenigstens	por lo menos	almeno
at the most	tout au plus	höchstens	a lo sumo	al massimo
attitude	attitude(f)	Einstellung(f)	actitud(f)	atteggiamento(m)
auditor	commissaire aux comptes	Wirtschaftsprüfer (m)	auditor(m)	revisore(m)
authorisation	autorisation(f)	Genehmigung(f)	permiso(m)	permesso(m)
authority	procuration(f)	Vollmacht(f)	poder(m)	delega(f)
available	en vente/ présent(e)	erhältlich/ vorhanden	que puede adquirirse/ presente	acquistabile/ disponibile
average	moyen(ne)	durchschnittlich	medio(a)	medio(a)
(to) avoid	éviter	meiden/ vermeiden	evitar	evitare
backwards	en arrière	rückwärts	marcha atrás	in dietro
bad luck	malchance(f)	Pech(n)	mala suerte(f)	sfortuna(f)
balance (sheet)	bilan(m)	Bilanz(f)	balance(m)	bilancio(m)/ saldo(m)
bank	banque(f)	Bank(f)	banco(m)	banca(f)
bank account	compte bancaire(m)	Bankkonto(n)	cuenta bancaria(f)	conto bancario(m)
banking system	système bancaire(m)	Bankwesen(n)	sistema bancario(m)	sistema bancario(m)
bankruptcy	faillite(f)	Konkurs(m)	quiebra (f) bancarrota(f)	bancarota(f)/ fallimento(m)
bank transfer	virement(m)	Banküber- weisung(f)	transferencia(f)	storno(m)
base	base(f)	Grundfläche(f)	base(f)	base(f)
basis	base(f)	Basis(f)	base(f)	base(f)
(to) be allowed	avoir le droit	dürfen	poder	potere
(to) be ashamed	avoir honte	schämen, sich	tener vergüenza	vergognarsi
(to) be astonished	s'étonner de	staunen	asombrarse	stupirsi
(to) become	devenir	werden	llegar	diventare
(to) be defeated	être vaincu par qn	unterliegen	sucumbir	soccombere
beginner	débutant(m)	Anfänger(m)	principiante(m)	principiante(m)
(to) be glad	être heureux(euse)	freuen, sich	alegrarse de	rallegrarsi
(to) behave	se comporter	benehmen, sich	comportarse	comportarsi
(to) be late	être en retard	verspäten	llevar retraso	ritardare
(to) be mistaken	se tromper	irren	equivocarse	sbagliare
(to) be noticeable	se faire remarquer	auffallen	llamar la atención	dare nell'occhio
(to) be on strike	faire grève	streiken	hacer huelga	scioperare
besides	en outre	außerdem	además	inoltre
(to) be silent	se taire	schweigen	callar	tacere
(to) betray	trahir	verraten	traicionar	tradire
between	entre	zwischen	entre	tra/fra
(to) be worth	valoir	gelten	valer	valere
bilingual	bilingue	zweisprachig	bilingüe	bilingue
bill (invoice)	facture(f)	Faktura(f)/ Rechnung(f)	factura(f)	fattura(f)/ effetto(m)

English	French	German	Spanish	Italian
bill of exchange	lettre de change(f)	Wechsel(m)	letra de cambio(m)	lettera di cambio(f)
(to) blame	reprocher	vorwerfen	echar en cara	rimproverare
Board (of directors)	conseil d'administration (m)	Aufsichtsrat(m)	junta directiva(f)	consiglio d'amministrazione (m)
book-keeping	comptabilité(f)	Buchhaltung(f)	contabilidad(f)	contabilità(f)
boring	ennuyeux(euse)	langweilig	aburrido(a)	noioso(a)
boss	patron(m)	Chef(m)	jefe(m)	capo(m)
branch	succursale(f)	Filiale(f)	sucursal(f)	filiale(f)
brand	marque(f)	Marke(f)	marca(f)	marca(f)
breach of contract	rupture de contrat(f)	Vertragsbruch(m)	incumplimiento de contracto(m)	rottura di contratto(f)
(to) broadcast	transmettre	senden	transmitir	trasmettere
brochure	prospectus(m)/ dépliant(m)	Prospekt(n)	prospecto(m)	opuscolo(m)
Bros (Brothers)	Frs.	Gebr.	Hnos.	F.lli
(to) build	construire	bauen	construir	costruire
business hours	heures d'ouverture(fpl)	Öffnungzeiten ((f)pl)	horario de oficina(m)	orario d'ufficio(m)
businessman	commerçant(m)	Kaufmann(m)	comerciante(m)	commerciante(m)
busy	occupé(e)	beschäftigt	ocupado(a)	occupato(a)
buyer	acheteur(m)	Käufer(m)	comprador(m)	acquirente(m)
by chance	par hasard	zufällig	por casualidad	per caso
bye!	salut!	tschüs!	¡hasta luego!	ciao!
(to) calculate	calculer	rechnen	calcular	fare i conti
calendar	calendrier(m)	Kalender(m)	calendario(m)	calendario(m)
(to) call off	annuler	abblasen	anular	disdire
(to) cancel	décommander	abbestellen	anular	annullare
capable	capable	fähig	hábil	capace
capital	capital social(m)	Kapital(n)	capital social(m)	capitale sociale(m)
capital increase	augmentation de capital(f)	Kapitalerhöhung(f)	ampliación de capital(f)	aumento di capitale(m)
career	carrière(f)	Karriere(f)	carrera(f)	carriera(f)
careful	soigneux(euse)	sorgfältig	cuidadoso(a)	accurato(a)
careless	imprudent(e)	unvorsichtig	descuidado(a)	imprudente
cash	espèces(fpl)	Bargeld(f)	dinero al contado(m)	contanti(mpl)
cash on delivery	remboursement(m)	Nachnahme(f)	cóbrese al entregar/ entrega contra reembolso(f)	pagamento contro assegno(m)
certain	certain(e)	gewiß	cierto(a)	certo(a)
(to) certify	attester	bescheinigen	atestiguar	attestare
chairman	président(m)	Vorsitzender(m)	presidente(m)	presidente(m)
Channel, The	Manche(f)	Ärmelkanal(m)	Canal de la Mancha(m)	Manica(f)
(to) chat	causer	plaudern	conversar	chiacchierare
(to) cheat	tromper	betrügen	engañar	ingannare
cheers!	santé!	prost!	¡salud!	salute!
cheque	cheque(m)	Scheck(m)	cheque(m)	assegno(m)
circumstances	circonstances(fpl)	Umstände(m)	circunstancias(fpl)	circostanze(fpl)

English	French	German	Spanish	Italian
(to) clear away	ranger	aufräumen	arreglar	mettere in ordine
(to) close an account	clôturer un compte	ein Konto schliessen	cancelar una cuenta	chiudere/liquidare un conto
c/o (care of)	a.b.s.	bei	a/c	presso
commission	commission(f)	Provision(f)	comisión(f)	provvigione(f)
(to) communicate	communiquer	in Verbindung stehen	comunicar	comunicare
communication	communication(f)	Mitteilung(f)	comunicación(f)	comunicazione(f)
company	firme/entreprise(f)	Firma(f)/Unternehmen(n)	empresa(f)	ditta(f)/impresa(f)
competent	compétent(e)	zuständig	competente	competente
competition (the)	concurrence(f)	Konkurrenz(f)	competencia(f)	concorrenza(f)
(to) complain	se plaindre	beschweren, sich	quejarse	lamentarsi
computer	ordinateur(m)	Computer(m)	ordenador(m)	computer(m)
conference	conférence(f)	Konferenz(f)	conferencia(f)	conferenza(f)
(to) confirm	confirmer	bestätigen	confirmar	confermare
congratulations	félicitations(fpl)	Glückwunsch(m)	felicitaciones(fpl)	auguri(mpl)
(to) connect	relier	verbinden	unir	unire
conscientious	consciencieux (euse)	gewissenhaft	concienzudo(a)	coscienzioso(a)
consumer	consommateur (trice)	Verbraucher(m)	consumidor(a)	consumatore(m)
contact	contact(m)	Kontakt(m)	contacto(m)	contatto(m)
(to) contain	contenir	enthalten	contener	contenere
contents	contenu(m)	Inhalt(m)	contenido(m)	contenuto(m)
contract	contrat(m)	Vertrag(m)	contrato(m)	contratto(m)
contract of employment	contrat de travail(m)	Arbeitsvertrag(m)	contrato de trabajo(m)	contratto di lavoro(m)
(to) contradict	contredire	widersprechen	contradecir	contraddire
contribution	contribution(f)	Beitrag(m)	contribución(f)	contributo(m)
(to) convey	transmettre	übermitteln	transmitir	trasmettere
corporate body	personne morale(f)	juristische Person(f)	personalidad jurídica(f)	organo sociale(m)
corporation tax	impôt sur les sociétés(m)	Korperschaftsteuer(f)	impuesto sobre la sociedad(m)	imposta sul reddito delle persone giuridiche(m)
(to) cost	coûter	kosten	costar	costare
(to) cover up	couvrir	zudecken	tapar	coprire
(to) create	réussir à faire	schaffen	crear	creare
credit	crédit(m)	Kredit(m)	crédito(m)	credito(m)
credit note	note de crédit(f)	Gutschriftsanzeige(f)	crédito(m)	nota di accreditamento
culture	culture(f)	Kultur(f)	cultura(f)	cultura(f)
currency	argent(m)/ monnaie(f)	Währung(f)	dinero(m)	valuta(f)
current account	compte courant(m)	Kontokorrent(n)/ Konto(n)	cuenta corriente(f)	conto corrente(m)
curriculum vitae	résumé/curriculum vitae(m)	Lebenslauf(m)	curriculum vitae(m)	curriculum vitae(m)
customs	douane(f)	Zoll(m)	aduana(f)	dogana(f)
customs duty	droits de douanes(mpl)	Zoll(m)	derechos de arancelarios(mpl)	dazio doganale(m)

English	*French*	*German*	*Spanish*	*Italian*
daft	bête	doof	tonto(a)	scemo(a)
daily	quotidien(ne)	täglich	cotidiano(a)	quotidiano(a)
dangerous	dangereux(euse)	gefährlich	peligroso(a)	pericoloso(a)
dated	antique	alterümlich	antiguo(a)	antico(a)
day after tomorrow	après-demain	übermorgen	pasado mañana	dopodomani
day before yesterday	avant-hier	vorgestern	anteayer	l'altro ieri
dealer	commerçant(m)	Händler(m)	comerciante(m)	commerciante(m)
debt	dette(f)	Schulden(fpl)	deudas(fpl)	debiti(mpl)
decision	décision(f)	Entschluß(m)/ Entscheidung(f)	decisión(f)	decisione(f)
(to) dedicate	dédier	widmen	dedicar	dedicare
deed	action(f)	Tat(f)	acción(f)	azione(f)
definitely	certainement	bestimmt	ciertamente	certamente
delay	retard(m)	Verspätung(f)	retraso(m)	ritardo(m)
deliberate	délibéré(e)	bewußt	intencionado(a)	intenzionale
delighted	ravi(e)	entzückt	encantado(a)	affascinato(a)
delivery	livraison(f)	Lieferung(f)	suministro(m)	fornitura(f)
(to) demonstrate	démontrer	demonstrieren	demostrar	dimostrare
demonstration	démonstration(f)	Demonstration(f)	demostración(f)/ manifestación(f)	dimostrazione(f)
(to) deny	nier	leugnen	negar	negare
department store	grand magasin(m)	Kaufhaus(n)	grandes almacenes(mpl)	grande magazzino(m)
departure	départ(m)	Ausreise(f)/Ab- farht(f)/Abreise(f)	salida(f)	partenza(f)
(to) deplore	se plaindre de	beklagen	quejarse	lamentare
(to) deposit	déposer	hinterlegen	depositar	depositare
detailed	détaillé	ausführlich	detallado(a)	dettagliato(a)
(to) develop	développer	entwickeln	desarrollar	sviluppare
diary	agenda(m)	Tagebuch(n)	agenda(f)	agenda(f)
difficult	difficile	schwierig	difícil	difficile
diligent	travailleur(euse)	fleißig	diligente(a)	diligente
director	directeur(m)	Direktor(m)	director(m)	direttore(m)
discussion	discussion(f)	Aussprache(f)	discusión(f)	discussione(f)
dissatisfied	mécontent(e)	unzufrieden	descontento(a)	scontento(a)
(to) distribute	distribuer	austeilen	distribuir	distribuire
distrust	méfiance(f)	Mißtrauen(n)	desconfianza(f)	sfiducia(f)
dividend	dividende(m)	Dividende(f)	dividendo(m)	dividendo(m)
document	document(m)	Urkunde(f)	documento(m)	documento(m)
documentary credit	crédit documentaire(m)	Akkreditiv(n)	crédito documentario(m)	credito documentario(m)
doubtful	douteux(euse)	zweifelhaft	dudoso(a)	dubbioso(a)
doubtless	sans doute	zweifellos	sin duda	senza dubbio
drawing	dessin(m)	Zeichnung(f)	dibujo(m)	disegno(m)
driving licence	permis de conduire(m)	Führerschein(m)	permiso de conducir(m)	patente(f)
during the week	en semaine	wochentags	entre semana	nei giorni feriali
each time	chaque fois	jedesmal	cada vez	ogni volta
economical	économe	sparsam	económico	parsimonioso(a)

English	*French*	*German*	*Spanish*	*Italian*
effective	efficace	wirksam	eficaz	efficace
either . . . or	ou . . . ou	entweder . . . oder	o . . . o	o . . . o
(to) elect	élire	wählen	elegir	eleggere
elsewhere	ailleurs	woanders	en otra parte	altrove
employment	emploi(m)	Beschäftigung(f)	empleo(m)	impiego(m)
enemy	ennemi(m)	Feind(m)	enemigo(m)	nemico(m)
engineer	mécanicien(m)	Mechaniker(m)	mecánico(m)	meccanico(m)
(to) enjoy o.s.	s'amuser	amüsieren, sich	divertirse	divertirsi
(to) enlarge	agrandir	vergrößern	agrandar	ingrandire
enough	assez	genug	bastante	abbastanza
envelope	enveloppe(f)	Umschlag(m)	sobre(m)	busta(f)
environment	environnement(m)	Umwelt(f)	medio ambiente(m)	ambiente(m)
(to) erase	effacer	ausradieren	borrar	cancellare
especially	surtout	besonders	sobre todo	particolarmente
(to) estimate	estimer	schätzen	estimar	stimare
european	européen(ne)	europäisch	europeo(a)	europeo(a)
everyday life	vie quotidienne(f)	Alltag(m)	vida cotidiana(f)	vita quotidiana(f)
everywhere	partout	überall	por todas partes	dappertutto
exact	exact(e)	genau	exacto(a)	preciso(a)
exciting	énervant(e)	aufregend	emocionante	eccitante
expenses	frais(mpl)/ coûts(mpl)	Kosten(fpl)/ Spesen(fpl)/ Unkosten(fpl)	costas(mpl)/ gastos(mpl)	spese(fpl)
(to) export	exporter	ausführen	exportar	esportare
export	exportation(f)	Ausfuhr(f)/ Export(m)	exportación(F)	esportazione(f)
extra charge	supplément(m)	Zuschlag(m)	suplemento(m)	supplemento(m)
fact	fait(m)	Tatsache(f)	hecho(m)	fatto(m)
factory	usine(f)	Fabrik(f)	fábrica(f)	fabbrica(f)
failure	échec(m)	Mißerfolg(m)	fracaso(m)	insuccesso(m)
fake	imité(e)	unecht	falso(a)	falso(a)
famous	célèbre	berühmt	famoso(a)	famoso(a)
fashion	mode(f)	Mode(f)	moda(f)	moda(f)
fault	culpabilité(f)	Schuld(f)	culpa(f)	colpa(f)
fax	télécopie(m)	Fax(n)	telefax(m)	fax(m)
feeling	sentiment(m)	Gefühl(n)	sentimiento(m)	sensazione(m)
few	peu	wenige	pocos(as)	pochi
file	porte- documents(m)	Aktenmappe(f)	cartera(f)	cartella(f)
finances	finances(fpl)	Finanzen(pl)	finanzas(fpl)	finanze(fpl)
(to) find	trouver	finden	encontrar	trovare
firm	entreprise(f)	Firma(f)	empresa(f)	ditta(f)
first of all	pour l'instant	zunächst	en primer lugar	dapprima
fiscal	fiscal	fiskalisch	fiscal	fiscale
(to) fit out	aménager	einrichten	equipar	arredare
following	suivant(e)	folgend	siguiente	seguente
forbidden	interdit(e)	verboten	prohibido(a)	vietato(a)
foreigner	étranger(m)	Ausländer(m)	extranjero(m)	straniero(m)
foreign language	langue étrangère(f)	Fremdsprache(f)	idioma extranjero(m)	lingua straniera(f)

English	French	German	Spanish	Italian
(to) form a company	fonder/constituer une société	eine Gesellschaft gründen	constituir una sociedad	costituire una società
fraud	tromperie(f)	Betrug(m)	engaño(m)	inganno(m)
free trade	libre échange(m)	Freihandel(m)	librecambio(m)	libero scambio(m)
freight	fret(m)	Fracht(f)	flete(m)	carico(m)
fully booked	complet(ète)	ausgebucht	completo(a)	esaurito(a)
gap	lacune(f)	Lücke(f)	espacio(m)	lacuna(f)
general	général(e)	allgemein	general	generale
generous	généreux(euse)	großzügig	generoso(a)	generoso(a)
genuine	vrai(e)	echt	verdadero(a)	vero(a)
gifted	doué(e)	begabt	dotado(a)	dotato(a)
(to) give in one's notice	donner sa démission	aufgeben	dimitir	licenziarsi
(to) give up	abandonner	aufgeben	renunciar	rinunciare
glad	content(e)	froh	contento(a)	lieto(a)
(to) go ahead	marcher devant	vorangehen	pasar adelante	andare adelanti
goal	but(m)	Ziel(n)	meta(f)	meta(f)
(to) go along with	accompagner	mitgehen	acompañar	accompagnare
(to) go away	s'en aller	weggehen	marcharse	andare via
goods	marchandise(f)	Ware(f)	mercancía(f)	merce(f)
government	gouvernement(m)	Regierung(f)	gobierno(m)	governo(m)
guarantee	garantie(f)	Gewähr(f)	garantía(f)	garanzia(f)
guide	guide(m)	Reiseführer(m)	guía(m)	guida(f)
habit	habitude(f)	Gewohnheit(f)	costumbre(f)	abitudine(f)
(to) hand over	remettre/présenter	übergeben/ überreichen	transmitir/entregar	consegnare
(to) happen	arriver	geschehen/ passieren	occurrir/pasar	accadere/ succedere
hardly	à peine	kaum	apenas	appena
heading	titre(m)	Überschrift(f)	título(m)	titolo(m)
headline	manchette(f)	Schlagzeile(f)	títular(m)	titolo(m)
healthy	sain(e)	gesund	sano(a)	sano(a)
hectic	trépidant	hektisch	agitado(a)	nervoso(a)
(to) hesitate	hésiter	zögern	vacilar	esitare
(to) hinder	empêcher	hindern	impedir	impedire
hint	indication(f)	Hinweis(m)	indicación(f)	indicazione(f)
hopefully	espérons	hoffentlich	espero que	speriamo que
host	hôte(m)	Gastgeber(m)	anfitrión(m)	ospite(m)
hotel	hôtel(m)/ auberge(f)	Hotel(n)/ Gasthaus(n)	hotel(m)/posada(f)	osteria(f)/albergo
hourly	toutes les heures	stündlich	cada hora	ogni ora
however	cependant	jedoch	sin embargo	tutta via
(to) hurry	se dépêcher	eilen	darse prisa	andare in fretta
idea	idée(f)	Idee(f)/Vorstellung(f)	idea(f)	idea(f)
illegal	illégal(e)	gesetzwidrig	ilegal	illegale
immediately	immédiatement	sofort	en seguida	subito
impatient	impatient(e)	ungeduldig	impaciente	impaziente
import	importation(f)	Einfuhr(f)/ Import(m)	importación(f)	importazione(f)

English	French	German	Spanish	Italian
English	*French*	*German*	*Spanish*	*Italian*
impression	impression(f)	Eindruck(m)	impresión(f)	impressione(f)
improvement	amélioration(f)	Besserung(f)	mejora(f)	miglioramento(m)
inaccurate	inexact(e)	ungenau	inexacto(a)	impreciso(a)
in addition	supplémentaire	zusätzlich	adicional	supplementare
in a muddle	pêle-mêle	durcheinander	en desorden	sottospora
inappropriate	mal à propos	unpassend	inadecuado(a)	sconveniente
income	revenu(m)/ revenus(mpl)	Einkommen(n)/ Verdienst(m)	ingresos(mpl)/ ganancia(f)	entrate(fpl)/ guadagno(f)
(to) increase	augmenter	vermehren	aumentar	aumentare
inflation	inflation(f)	Inflation(f)	inflación(f)	inflazione(f)
information	renseignement(m)	Auskunft(m)	información(f)	informazione(f)
information technology	informatique(f)	Informationstech- nologie(f)	informática(f)	informatica(f)
inspired	enthousiaste	begeistert	entusiasta	entusiasta
instalment	quote-part(f)	Rate(f)	plazo(m)	rata(f)
instead	en échange	dafür	en su lugar	invece
insult	offense(f)	Beleidigung(f)	ofensa(f)	offesa(f)
insurance	assurance(f)	Versicherung(f)	seguro(m)	assicurazione(f)
intelligent	intelligent(e)	intelligent	inteligente	intelligente
intention	intention(f)	Absicht(f)	intención(f)	intenzione(f)
intentionally	exprès	absichtlich	adrede	apposta
interest	intérêt(m)	Interesse(n)	interés(m)	interesse(m)
interference	trouble(m)	Störung(f)	molestia(m)	disturbo(m)
(to) interrupt	interrompre	unterbrechen	interrumpir	interrompere
interview	interview(m)	Interview(n)	entrevista(f)	intervista(f)
(to) introduce	présenter	vorstellen	presentar	presentare
invitation	invitation(f)	Einladung(f)	invitación(f)	invito(m)
itinerary	itinéraire(m)	Reiseroute(f)	itinerario(m)	itinerario(m)
jealousy	jalousie(f)	Eifersucht(f)	celos(mpl)	gelosia(f)
(to) joke	plaisanter	spaßen	bromear	scherzare
journey	voyage(m)	Fahrt(f)	viaje(m)	viaggio(m)
keen	zélé(e)	eifrig	diligente	diligente
(to) know one's way about	s'y connaitre	auskennen, sich	conocer a fondo	conoscere
landlord	patron(m)	Wirt(m)	dueño(m)	oste(m)
language	langage(m)	Sprache(f)	lengua(f)	lingua(f)
late	tard	spät	tarde	tardi
lately	récemment	kürzlich	reciente	recente
(to) laugh at	rire de qn	auslachen	reirse de	deridere
law	loi(f)/droit(m)	Gesetz(n)	ley(f)/derecho(m)	legge(f)/ giurisprudenza(f)
lawyer	avocat(m)	Rechtsanwalt(m)	abogado(m)	avvocato(m)
leader	guide(m)	Führer(m)	guía(m)	guida(f)
legislation	législation(f)	Gesetzgebung(f)	legislación(f)	legislazione(f)
(to) lend	prêter	ausleihen/leihen	prestar	prestare
letter	lettre(f)	Brief(m)	carta(f)	lettera(f)
letterbox	boîte aux lettres(f)	Briefkasten(m)	buzón(m)	cassetta postale(f)

English	French	German	Spanish	Italian
liabilities	passif(m)	Passiva(pl)	pasivo(m)	passivo(m)
like this	ainsi	so	así	così
likewise	aussi	ebenfalls	tambien	altrettanto
(to) listen	écouter	zuhören	escuchar	ascoltare
(to) load	charger	verladen	cargar	caricare
long-distance call	communication interurbaine(f)	Ferngespräch(n)	llamada interurbana(f)	telefonata interurbana(f)
loss	perte(f)	Verlust(m)	pérdida(f)	perdita(f)
low season	basse saison(f)	Vorsaison(f)	pretemporada(f)	bassa stagione(f)
luck	chance(f)	Glück(n)	suerte(f)	fortuna(f)
lunch	déjeuner(m)	Mittagessen(n)	comida(f)	pranzo(m)
luxury	luxe(m)	Luxus(m)	lujo(m)	lusso(m)
machine	machine(f)	Maschine(f)	máquina(f)	macchina(f)
mainly	surtout	hauptsächlich	principalmente	principalmente
(to) make up for	réparer	wiedergutmachen	subsanar	riparare
manager	gérant(m)	Geschäftsführer(m)	gerente(m)	gerente(m)
managing director	directeur général	Direktor(m)	director(a) general(m/f)	amministratore delegato(m)
manufacturer	producteur(m)	Hersteller(m)	productor(m)	produttore(m)
market	marché(m)	Markt(m)	mercado(m)	mercato(m)
market value	valeur marchande(f)	Marktwert(m)	valor de mercado(m)	valore di mercato(m)
meanwhile	entretemps	inzwischen	mientras tanto	frattanto
meeting	séance(f)/ rencontre(f)	Sitzung(f)/ Treffen(n)	reunión(F)/ encuentro(m)	seduta(f)/ incontro(m)
member	membre(m)	Mitglied(n)	miembro(m)	membro(m)
memorandum	note(f)	Memorandum(n)	nota(f)/memorandum(m)	memorandum(m)
menu	menu(m)	Speisekarte(f)	lista de platos(f)	menu(m)
message	message(m)/ information(f)/ nouvelle(f)	Botschaft(f)/ Nachricht(f)	mensaje(m)/ comunicación(f)/ noticia(f)	messaggio(m)/comunicazione(f)/ notizia(f)
migraine	migraine(f)	Migräne(f)	jaqueca(f)	emicrania(f)
mistake	faute(f)/erreur(f)	Fehler(m)/ Irrtum(m)	falta(f)/error(m)	sbaglio(m)/ errore(m)
misunderstanding	malentendu(m)	Mißverständnis(n)	malentendido(m)	equivoco(m)
monthly	mensuel(le)	monatlich	mensual	mensile
mortgage	hypothèque(f)	Hypothek(f)	hipoteca(f)	ipoteca(f)
(to) move out	déménager	ausziehen	mudarse	sloggiare
namely	à savoir	nämlich	a saber	cioè
narrow	étroit(e)	eng	estrecho(a)	stretto(a)
national	national(e)	national	nacional	nazionale(f)
nationality	nationalité(f)	Nationalität(f)	nacionalidad(f)	nazionalità(f)
native language	langue maternelle(f)	Muttersprache(f)	lengua materna(f)	lingua materna(f)
nearly	presque	beinahe	casi	circa/quasi
need	besoin(m)	Bedürfnis(n)	necesidad(f)	bisogno(m)
needy	nécessiteux	dürftig	escaso(a)	misero(a)
(to) neglect	négliger	vernachlässigen	descuidar	trascurare
neither	ni	weder	ni	né

English	French	German	Spanish	Italian
never	ne . . . jamais	niemals	jamás	mai
night club	boîte de nuit(f)	Nachtlokal(n)	local nocturno(m)	night(m)
nonsense	bêtises(fpl)	Unsinn(m)	absurdo(m)	nonsenso(m)
no parking	défense de stationner(f)	Parkverbot(n)	estacionamiento prohibido(m)	divieto di parcheggio(m)
notary	notaire(m)	Notar(m)	notario(m)	notaio(m)
not at all	pas du tout	keineswegs	en modo alguno	non affatto
not binding	sans engagement	unverbindlich	sin compromiso	non impegnativo(a)
numerous	nombreux(euse)	zahlreich	numeroso(a)	numeroso(a)
(to) obey	obéir	gehorchen	obedecer	ubbidire
(to) oblige	obliger	verpflichten	obligar	obbligare
occasion	occasion(f)	Gelegenheit(f)	oportunidad(f)	occasione(f)
off!	allons-y!	los!	¡adelante!	avanti!
offer	offre(f)	Angebot(n)	oferta(f)	offerta(f)
office	bureau(m)	Amt(n)/Buro(n)	oficio(m)/oficina(f)	ufficio(m)
often	souvent	oft	a menudo	spesso
one after another	l'un derrière l'autre	hintereinander	uno detrás de otro	uno dopo l'altro
one-sided	partial(e)	einseitig	unilateral	unilaterale
on one hand	d'une part	einerseits	por un lado	da un lato
on the other hand	d'autre part	andererseits	por otra parte	d'altra parte
(to) order	commander	bestellen	pedir	ordinare
(to) organise	organiser	organisieren/ veranstalten	organizar	organizzare
outline	esquisse(f)	Entwurf(m)	proyecto(m)	abbozzo(m)
(to) overestimate	surestimer	überschätzen	sobrevalorar	sopravvalutare
overnight stay	logement pour une nuit(m)	Übernachtung(f)	pernoctación(f)	pernottamento(m)
owner	propriétaire(m)	Eigentümer(m)	propietario(m)	proprietario(m)
page	page(f)	Seite(f)	página(f)	pagina(f)
pair of scissors	ciseaux(mpl)	Schere(f)	tijeras(fpl)	forbici(fpl)
panic	panique(f)	Panik(f)	pánico(m)	panico(m)
paper	papier(m)	Papier(n)	papel(m)	carta(f)
parent company	maison mère(f)	Muttergesell- schaft(f)	casa matriz(f)	casa madre(f)
parking place	parking(m)	Parkplatz(m)	plaza de aparcamiento(f)	parcheggio(m)
partly	en partie	teilweise	en parte	in parte
(to) pass by	passer	vergehen	pasar	passare
passing through	passage(m)	Durchreise(f)	paso(m)	transito(m)
(to) pass on a message	transmettre	ausrichten	comunicar	riferire
passport	pièce d'identité(f)/ passeport(m)	Ausweis(m)/ Paß(m)/ Reise- paß(m)	documento de identidad(m)/ pasaporte(m)	documento d'identità(m)/ passaporto(m)
(to) pay attention	faire attention	aufpassen	prestar atención	fare attenzione
(to) pay back	rembourser	zurückzahlen	devolver	rimborsare
payment	paiement(m)	Zahlung(f)/ Bezahlung(f)	pago(m)	pagamento(m)

English	French	German	Spanish	Italian
(to) pay off	finir de payer	abbezahlen	pagar a plazos	pagare a rate
penniless	fauché(e)	ohne Geld	sin dinero	fallito(a)
pensioner	retraité(m)	Rentner(m)	pensionista(m)	pensionato(m)
per cent	pour cent	Prozent(n)	por ciento(m)	percentuale(f)
permanent	permanent	ständig	permanente	fisso(a)
permissible	permis(e)	zulässig	permitido(a)	permesso(a)
phone call	communication téléphonique(f)/ coup de téléphone(m)	Telefon- gespräch(n)/ Telefonanruf(m)	conversación telefónica(f)/ llamada tele- fónica(f)	conversazione telefonica(f)/ telefonata(f)
phone number	numéro de téléphone (m)	Telefonnummer(f)	número de teléfono(m)	numero telefonico(m)
photocopy	photocopie(f)	Fotokopie(f)	fotocopia(f)	fotocopia(f)
(to) pick up	aller chercher	abholen	recoger	andare a prendere
pledge	gage(m)	Pfand(n)	prenda(f)	pegno(m)
pointless	inutile	zwecklos	inútil	inutile
point of view	point de vue(m)	Standpunkt(m)	punto de vista(m)	punto di vista(m)
politician	politicien(m)	Politiker(m)	político(m)	politico(m)
possession	propriété(f)	Besitz(m)	posesión(f)	proprietà(f)
postage	port(m)	Porto(n)	franqueo(m)	affrancatura(f)
post office	bureau de poste(m)	Postamt(n)	oficina de correos(f)	ufficio postale(m)
president	président(m)	Präsident(m)	presidente(m)	presidente(m)
(to) prevent	empêcher	verhinden	evitar	impedire
previous	précédent(e)	vorig	precedente	precedente
price	prix(m)	Preis(m)	precio(m)	prezzo(m)
private	privé(e)	privat	privado(a)	privato
profession	profession(f)	Beruf(m)	profesión(f)	professione(f)
profit	gain(m)	Gewinn(m)	ganancia(f)	guadagno(m)
profitable	rentable	rentabel	rentable	profittevole
(to) pronounce	prononcer	aussprechen	pronunciar	pronunciare
publicity(advertis- ing)	publicité(f)	Werbung(f)	publicidad(f)	pubblicità(f)
purpose	but(m)	Zweck(m)	finalidad(f)	scopo(m)
(to) put in order	ordonner	ordnen	ordenar	ordinare
quality	qualité(f)	Eigenschaft(f)/ Qualität(f)	atributo(m)/ cualidad(f)	qualità(f)
question	question(f)	Frage(f)	pregunta(f)	domanda(f)
quick	rapide	rasch	impulsivo(a)	rapido(a)
quite	assez	ziemlich	bastante	affatto/abbastanza
(to) raise	augmenter/lever	erhöhen/erheben	elevar	alzare/aumentare
rank	grade(m)/rang(m)	Grad(m)	título(m)	grado(m)/ rango(m)
rate	tarif(m)	Tarif(m)	tarifa(f)	tariffa(f)
rate of interest	taux d'intérêt(m)	Zinsfuß(m)	tipo de interés(m)	tasso de interesse(m)
rate per cent	pourcentage(m)	Prozentsatz(m)	tanto por ciento(m)	percentuale(f)
rather	mieux	lieber	más bien	piuttosto

English	French	German	Spanish	Italian
raw material	matière première(f)	Rohstoff(m)	materia prima(f)	materia prima(f)
(to) reach	atteindre	erreichen	alcanzar	raggiungere
ready	prêt(e)	bereit/fertig	dispuesto(a)/listo(a)	pronto(a)
(to) realise (bring about)	réaliser	verwirklichen	llevar a cabo	realizzare
receipt	acquit(m)/ quittance(f)	Quittung(f)	recibo(m)	ricevuta(f)
recently	l'autre jour	neulich	recientemente	recentemente
(to) recognise	reconnaître	erkennen	reconocer	riconoscere
recorded delivery	lettre recom- mandé(f)	Einschreibe- brief(m)	carta certificada(f)	lettera raccomandata(f)
(to) reduce	diminuer	verringern	disminuir	diminuire
redundancy	licenciement(m)	Entlassung(f)	despido(m)	licenziamento(m)
redundancy payment	indemnité(f)/ prime de licenciement(f)	Abfindung(f)	indemnización por despido(f)	trattamento di fine rapporto(m)
refreshment	rafraîchissement (m)	Erfrischung(f)	refresco(m)	rinfresco(m)
refund	remboursement(m)	Rückerstattung(f)	reembolos(m)	rimborso(m)
region	région(f)	Gebiet(n)/ Gegend(f)	zona(f)/región(f)	regione(f)
registered head office	siège social(m)	Firmensitz(m)	sede social(f)	sede legale(f)
registration taxes	droits d'en- registrement(m)	Anmeldungs- eintragungs- gebuhr(f)	tasas de registro(f)	imposta di registro(f)
(to) reject	refuser	ablehnen	rehusar	rifiutare
related	parent(e)	verwandt	emparentado(a)	imparentado(a)
relationship	relation(f)	Beziehung(f)	relaciones(f)	rapporto(m)
reliable	sûr(e)	zuverlässig	de confianza	affidabile
(to) remember	souvenir/se souvenir de	erinnern/ gedenken	recordar/ acordarse de	ricordare
(to) renew	renouveler	erneuern	renovar	rinnovare
(to) replace	remplacer	ersetzen	sustituir	sostituire
(to) report	faire un rapport/ annoncer	berichten/melden	informar/declarar	riferire/ annunciare
report	rapport(a)	Bericht(m)	relación(f)	relazione(f)
(to) represent	représenter	vertreten	representar	rappresentare
request	demande(f)	Bitte(f)	ruego(m)	domanda(f)
reservation	réserve(f)	Vorbehalt(m)	reserva(f)	riserva(f)
(to) resign	cesser d'appartenir/ demissionner	zurücktreten	(darse) de baja/ dimitir	dimettersi
responsibility	responsabilité(f)	Verantwortlich- keit(f)	responsabilidad(f)	responsabilità(f)
result	résultat(m)	Ergebnis(n)	resultado(m)	risultado(m)
retirement	retraite(f)	Ruhestand(m)	descanso(m)	pensione(f)
revenge	vengeance(f)	Rache(f)	venganza(f)	vendetta(f)
revenue	revenu(m)	Einkommen(n)	ingresos(mpl)	entrate(fpl)
risk	risque(m)	Risiko(n)	riesgo(m)	rischio(m)
roadway	chaussée(f)	Fahrbahn(f)	calzada(f)	carreggiata(f)

English	French	German	Spanish	Italian
English	*French*	*German*	*Spanish*	*Italian*
round trip	circuit(m)	Rundfahrt(f)	gira(f)	giro(m)
route	itinéraire(m)	Reiseroute(f)	itinerario(m)	itinerario(m)
safety	sécurité(f)	Sicherheit(f)	seguridad(f)	sicurezza(f)
salary	salaire(m)	Gehalt(n)	sueldo(m)	stipendio(m)
sale	vente(f)	Verkauf(m)	venta(f)	vendita(f)
salesman	vendeur(m)	Verkäufer(m)	vendedor(m)	venditore(m)
(to) save	épargner	sparen	ahorrar	risparmiare
savings bank	caisse d'épargne(f)	Sparkasse(f)	caja de ahorros(f)	cassa di risparmio(f)
(to) say goodbye to	prendre congé de	verabschieden	despedirse de	congedare
(to) say thanks	remercier	bedanken	agradecer	ringraziare
scandal	scandale(m)	Skandal(m)	escándulo(m)	scandolo(m)
secretary	secrétaire(f)	Sekretärin(f)	secretaria(f)	segretaria(f)
(to) see again	revoir	wiedersehen	volver a ver	rivedere
seemingly	apparemment	anscheinend	aparentamente	apparentamente
(to) seize	tenir ferme/saisir	festhalten/greifen	sujetar/coger	tener fermo/afferrare
self assured	sûr(e) de soi	selbstsicher	seguro de sí mismo	sicuro di sé
self service	libre-service(m)	Selbstbedienung(f)	autoservicio(m)	self-service(m)
(to) send	envoyer	schicken/über-senden	mandar/enviar	inviare/spedire
sensible	raisonnable	vernünftig	razonable	ragionevole
settlement	accord(m)/convention(f)	Vereinbarung(f)	convenio(m)	accordo(m)
share (stock)	action(f)	Aktie(f)	acción(f)	azione(f)
shareholder	actionnaire(m/f)	Aktionär(m)	accionista(m/f)	azionista(m/f)
shipment	embarquement(m)	Einschiffung(f)	embarque(m)	imbarco(m)
shop	magasin(m)	Geschäft(n)/Laden(m)	tienda(f)	negozio(m)
(to) sign	signer	unterschreiben	firmar	firmare
signature	signature(f)	Unterschrift(f)	firma(f)	firma(f)
simultaneous	en même temps	gleichzeitig	a la vez	contemporaneo(a)
situation (business cycle)	conjoncture(f)	Konjunktur(f)	coyuntura(f)	congiuntura(f)
small change	monnaie(f)	Kleingeld(n)	cambio(m)	spiccioli(mpl)
small package	petit paquet(m)	Päckchen(n)	paquetito(m)	pacchetto(m)
sold out	épuisé(e)	ausverkauft	vendido(a)	esaurito(a)
so much	tant	soviel	tanto	quanto/tanto
soon	bientôt	bald	pronto	presto
souvenir	souvenir(m)	Andenken(n)	recuerdo(m)	ricordo(m)
(to) speak	parler	sprechen	hablar	parlare
(to) speculate	spéculer	spekulieren	especular	speculare
splendid	magnifique	prächtig	magnífico(a)	meraviglioso(a)
(to) spoil	gâter	verwöhnen	mimar	viziare
(to) spread	propager	verbreiten	difundir	diffondere
(to) stand by somebody	assister	beistehen	asistir a	assistere
stationery shop	papeterie(f)	Schreibwaren-handlung(f)	papelería(f)	cartoleria(f)

English	French	German	Spanish	Italian
statistics	statistique(f)	Statistik(f)	estadística(f)	statistica(f)
stock	réserves(fpl)	Vorrat(m)	provisión(f)	scorte(fpl)
Stock Exchange	Bourse de valeurs(f)	Börse(f)	Bolsa de Valores(f)	Borsa (Valori)(f)
strike	grève(f)	Streik(m)	huelga(f)	sciopero(m)
stuff	truc(m)	Zeug(n)	cosa(f)	cose(fpl)
subsidiary	filiale(f)	Tochtergesell-schaft(f)	subsidiaria(f)	succursale(f)
successful	avec succès	erfolgreich	afortunado(a)	pieno(a) di successi
suitable	approprié(e)/ assorti(e)	geeignet/passend	indicado(a)/ apropriado(a)	adatto(a)
(to) support	soutenir	unterstützen	apoyar	assitere
(to) switch off	éteindre/arrêter	abschalten/ ausschalten/ ausmachen	desconectar/ apagar	spegnere
(to) switch on	allumer	einschalten	conectar	accendere
table of contents	table de matières(f)	Inhalts-verzeichnis(n)	índice(m)	indice(m)
(to) take notice of	observer	beachten	prestar atención a	osservare
(to) take place	avoir lieu	stattfinden	tener lugar	avere luogo
task	tâche(f)	Aufgabe(f)	tarea(f)	incarico(m)
telegram	télégramme(m)	Telegramm(m)	telegrama(m)	telegramma(m)
telephone	téléphone(m)	Fernsprecher(m)	teléfono(m)	telefono(m)
television set	poste de télévision(m)	Fernseher(m)	televisor(m)	televisore(m)
tense	tendu(e)	gespannt	tenso(a)	teso(a)
through train	express(m)	D-Zug(m)	tren expreso(m)	direttissimo(m)
timetable	horaire(m)	Fahrplan(m)	horario(m)	orario(m)
tourist	touriste(m)	Tourist(m)	turista(m)	turista(m)
town centre	centre ville(m)	Innenstadt(f)	centro de ciudad(m)	centro citta(m)
trade union	syndicat(m)	Gewerkschaft(f)	sindicato(m)	sindacato(m)
train	train(m)	Zug(m)	tren(m)	treno(m)
training	formation(f)	Schulung(f)/ Ausbildung(f)	formación(f)	formazione(f)
(to) transfer	virer/transborder	überweisen/ umladen	transferir/ transbordar	trasferire/ trasbordare
transport	transport(m)	Transport(m)	transporte(m)	trasporto(m)
travel agency	agence de voyages(f)/bureau touristique(m)	Reisebüro(n)/ Verkehrsbüro(n)	oficina de viajes(f)/oficina de turismo	agenzia turistica(f)/ ufficio turistico(m)
trouble	détresse(f)	Not(f)	dificultad(f)	miseria(f)
(to) turn over (page)	tourner la page	umblättern	volver la hoja	voltare pagina
(to) type	taper à la machine	tippen	escribir a máquina	battere a macchina
typewriter	machine à écrire(f)	Schreibmaschine(f)	máquina de escribir	macchina da scrivere(f)
unable to make it	empêché(e)	verhindert	impedido(a)	impedito(a)

English	French	German	Spanish	Italian
underground	métro(m)	U–Bahn(f)	metro(m)	metropolitana(f)
unemployed	en chômage	arbeitslos	desempleado(a)	disoccupato(a)
unemployment	chômage(m)	Arbeitslosigkeit(f)	desempleo(m)	disoccupazione(f)
unexpected	inattendu(e)	unerwartet	inesperado(a)	inatteso(a)
unwelcome	inopportun(e)	unerwünscht	indeseado(a)	indesiderato(a)
useful	utile	nützlich	útil	utile
useless	inutile	nutzlos	inútil	inutile
vacation	vacances(fpl)	Urlaub(m)	vacaciones(fpl)	vacanze(fpl)
validity	validité(f)	Gultigkeit(f)	validez(f)	validità(f)
valuable	précieux(euse)	wertvoll	valioso(a)	prezioso(a)
value	valeur(f)	Wert(m)	valor(m)	valore(m)
vending machine	distributeur auto-matique(m)	Automat(m)	ditribuidor automático(m)	distributore automatico(m)
vice versa	*vice versa*	umgekehrt	contrario(a)	inverso(a)
visitor	visiteur(m)	Besucher(m)	visitante(m)	visitatore(m)
voice	voix(f)	Stimme(f)	voz(f)	voce(f)
voucher	bon(m)	Gutschein(m)	vale(m)	buono(m)
(to) warn	déconseiller/ exhorter/ prévenir de	abraten/mahnen/ warnen	desaconsejar/ notificar/ advertir	sconsigliare/ ammonire
willingly	avec plaisir	gern	con gusto	volentieri
(to) wind up a company	dissoudre/liquider une société	eine Gesellschaft liquidieren	liquidar una sociedad	liquidare una società
working day	jour ouvrable(m)	Werktag(m)	día laborable(m)	giorno feriale(m)
workshop	atelier(m)	Werkstatt(f)	taller(m)	officina(f)
world language	langue internationale(f)	Weltsprache(f)	lengua universal(f)	lingua mondiale(f)
(to) wrap up	envelopper	einwickeln	envolver	avvolgere
yesterday	hier	gestern	ayer	ieri
(to) yield	céder	nachgeben	ceder	cedere
zip	fermeture(f)	Reißverschluß(m)	cremallera(f)	chiusura lampo(f)

Section 3 INTERNATIONAL BUSINESS INFORMATION SOURCES

Sources of information in common use and names, addresses and telephone numbers of related organisations.

CHAMBERS OF COMMERCE

In France

Association of French Chambers of Commerce, 45 avenue d'Iena, 75116 Paris. T: 40 69 37 00.

Franco-British Chamber of Commerce, 8 rue Cimarosa, 75116 Paris. T: 44 05 32 88.

International Chamber of Commerce, 38 Cours Albert 1er, 75003 Paris. T: 49 53 28 28.

International Chamber of Commerce – French Committee, 9 boulevard Malesherbes, 75008 Paris. T: 42 65 12 66.

Paris Chamber of Commerce, 27 rue de Friedland, 75382 Paris Cedex 08. T: 42 89 70 00.

Paris Chamber of Commerce International Department, Bourse de Commerce, 2 rue de Viarmes, 75001 Paris. T: 45 08 35 00.

Chambre Franco-Allemande de Commerce & Industrie, 18 rue Balard, 75015 Paris. T: 40 58 35 35.

Chambre de Commerce Italienne pour la France, 134 rue du Fg St Honoré, 75008 Paris. T: 42 25 41 88.

Chambre de Commerce d'Espagne, 32 avenue de l'Opéra, 75002 Paris. T: 47 42 45 74.

In Germany

British Chamber of Commerce in Germany, Heumarkt 14, 5000 Köln 1. T: 0221 234284.

Central Office of the German Chambers of Industry and Commerce, Adenauerlle 148 Postfach 14 46, 5300 Bonn 1. T: 0288 1040.

German Group of International Chambers of Commerce, Kolumbe Str 5, Postfach 10 04 47, 5000 Köln. T: 0221 21 95 31.

In Spain

Association of Spanish Chambers of Commerce, Claudio Coello, 19, 28001 Madrid. T: 5 75 34 00.

Madrid Provincial Chamber of Commerce, Cámara de Comercio e Industria de Madrid, Huertas 13, 28012 Madrid. T: 538 3677 (has an international department: Departmento de Relaciones Internacionales, which can be consulted on most subjects).

Cámara de Comercio Británica, Plaza de Santa, Bárbara 10-1er piso, 28004 Madrid. T: 308 3082.

Cámara Francese de Comercio e Industria, R. Alarcón 7, 28014 Madrid. T: 522 0349.

Cámara de Comercio Alemana para España, Paseo de la Castellana 42, 28046 Madrid. T: 575 4000.

Cámara de Comercio Italiana, Cristobal Bordiu 3, 28003 Madrid. T: 534 0423.

In Italy

Camera di Commercio Britannica per L'Italia, Via Agnello 8, 20121 Milano. T: 02 876981.

Camera di Commercio e Dell'Industria Francese in Italia, Via Cusani 5, 20121 Milano. T: 02 8053890.

Camera de Commercio Italo-Germanica, Via Napo Torriani 29, 20124 Milano. T: 02 66988351.

Camera di Commercio Ufficiale Spagnola in Italia, Via Rugabella 1, 20122 Milano. T: 02 861137.

Camera Commercio Industria Artigianato E Agricoltura Di Milano, Via Meravigli 9/11, 20121 Milano. T: 02 85151.

In the UK

Association of British Chambers of Commerce, Sovereign House, 212A Shaftesbury Avenue, London WC2H 8EB. T: 071-240 5831/222 1555.

French Chamber of Commerce, Knightsbridge House, 197 Knightsbridge, London SW7 1RB. T: 071-225 5250.

German Chamber of Commerce, 16 Buckingham Gate, London SW1E 6LB. T: 071-233 5656.

The International Chamber of Commerce, ICC UK, Centre Point, 103 New Oxford Street, London WC1A 1QB. T: 071-240 5558.

Italian Chamber of Commerce, Walmar House, 296 Regent Street, London W1R 6AE. T: 071-637 3062.

London Chamber of Commerce, 69 Cannon Street, London EC4N 5AB. T: 071-248 4444.

Spanish Chamber of Commerce, 5 Cavendish Square, London W1M 0DP. T: 071-637 9061.

CONFERENCES

Exhibitions and Conferences from A to Z by S Black, Modino

Exhibition Bulletin (monthly) for when and where conferences take place: London Bureau, 266–72 Kirkdale, Sydenham, London SE26 4RZ.

Exhibition and Conference Fact Finder (monthly) from Pembroke, Campsbourne House, Hornsey, London N8 7PT.

Assistance and information for conference organisers:
Fairs and Promotion Branch, British Overseas Trade Board, Department of Trade, Dean Bradley House, 52 Horseferry Road, London SW1T 2AG. T: 071-276 3000.

British Exhibition Venues Association, Mallards, Five Ashes, Mayfield, East Sussex, TN20 6NN. T: 0892 33442.

International Conference and Exhibitions Limited, 29 Dering Street, London W1. T: 071-499 7774.

Venue Helpline: 0891 515466 – for a service of venues including theatres, galleries, conference centres, ships and boats.

CULTURAL ORGANISATIONS/BRIEFINGS

Cultural attachés at the embassies listed below can be approached for assistance, along with British Council offices and Institutes of Culture in major European cities.

In Italy

At Home in Florence, Via della Pergola 36, 50121 Firenze. T: 055-234 2580.

Centro Studi Italiani, 61049 Urbania (Pesaro e Urbino).

In the UK

Alliance Française, Goethe Institute, Italian Cultural Institute, Institut Français, Hispanic and Luso Brazilian Council (*see* **Language training** for further details).

Hints to Exporters Booklets for individual countries give advice to business executives travelling abroad – obtainable from DTI Export Publications, PO Box 55, Stratford-on-Avon, CV37 9GE.

Language Export (LX) Centres (*see* **Language training** for further details).

The Centre for International Briefing, Farnham Castle, Farnham, Surrey. T: 0252 721 1911.

Directory of European Professional and Learned Societies, CBD Research Ltd (written in English, French and German).

Live and Work in France by Mark Hempshell, published by Vacation Work.

EMBASSIES

In France

British	35 rue du Fg St Honoré, 75008 Paris. T: 42 66 91 42.
German	13 avenue Franklin D Roosevelt, 75008 Paris. T: 42 99 78 00.
Spanish	22 avenue Narequ, 75008 Paris. T: 44 43 18 00.
Italian	47 rue de Varenne, 75007 Paris. T: 45 44 38 90.

In Germany

British	Friedrich-Ebert-Allee 77B, W-5300, Bonn 1. T: 49 228 234061.
French	Kapellenweg 1A, W-5300, Bonn 2. T: 49 228 362031.
	Consular department: Rheinstrasse 52, W-5300, Bonn 2, T: as above.

Spanish	Schloss Strasse 4, W-5300, Bonn 1. T: 49 228 217094.
Italian	Karl-Finkelmburg-Strasse 51, W-5300, Bonn 2. T: 49 228 820060.

In Spain

British	Embajada Británica, Fernando el Santo 16, 28010 Madrid. T: 306 0618/319 2630.
	Avda. Miraflores 23, 28035 Madrid. T: 373 7244.
French	Ambassade de France en Espagne, Paseo de la Castellana 30, 28046 Madrid. T: 431 5321.
	Embajada de Francia, S. Olozaga 9, 28001 Madrid. T: 435 6655.
German	Embajada de la Republica Federal de Alemania, calle Fortuny 8, 28010 Madrid. T: 319 9100.
Italian	Embajada de Italia, calle Lagasca 98, 28006 Madrid. T: 577 6529.

In Italy

British	Ambasciata Gran Bretagna, Via Venti Settembre 80/A, 00187 Roma. T: 06 4825441.
	British Consulate, Via S Paolo 7, 20121 Milano. T: 392 8693442.
French	Ambasciata Di Francia, Piazza Famese 67, 00186 Roma. T: 06 686011.
German	Ambasciata Germania Repubblica, Via Po 25/C, 00198 Roma. T: 06 884741.
Spanish	Ambasciata Spagna, Largo Fontanella di Borghese 19, 00186 Roma. T: 06 6878264.
Italian	Ambasciata D'Italia, c/o Santa Sede, Via Flaminia 166, 00196 Roma. T: 06 3201801.

In the UK

Belgian	103 Eaton Square, London SW1W 9AB. T: 071-235 5422.
Danish	55 Sloane Street, London SW1X 9SR. T: 071-235 1255.
French	58 Knightsbridge, London SW1X 7JT. T: 071-235 8080.
German	23 Belgrave Square, London SW1X 8QB. T: 071-235 5033/0282/0165.
Greek	1a Holland Park, London W11 3TP. T: 071-727 8860.
Irish	17 Grosvenor Place, London SW1X 7HR. T: 071-235 2171.
Italian	14 Three Kings Yard, Davies Street, London W1Y 2EH. T: 071-629 8200.
Luxembourg	27 Wilton Crescent, London SW1X 8SD. T: 071-235 6961.
The Netherlands	38 Hyde Park Gate, London SW7 5DP. T: 071-584 5040.
Portuguese	11 Belgrave Square, London SW1X 8PP. T: 071-235 5331.
Spanish	24 Belgrave Square, London SW1X 8QA. T: 071-235 5555.

THE EUROPEAN UNION

Addresses and reference sources

The European Commission's Headquarters are at:
rue de la Loi 200, B-1049 Brussels. T: 322 299 1111.

The Commission has information offices at:
8 Storey's Gate, London SW1P 3AT. T: 071-222 8122.

The information office of the Court of Justice of the European Communities is at:
Palais de la Cour de Justice, L2925, Luxembourg. T: 352 430 31.

Bureau Européen Des Unions de Consommateurs (Consumer Protection), 36 avenue de Tervuren Bte 4, B-1040 Brussels. T: 322 7353110.

Council of Europe, Palais de L'Europe, F-67006 Strasbourg, Cedex, France. T: 33 88 614961.

The Council of Ministers, rue de la Loi 170, B-1048 Brussels. T: 322 234 6111.

The Economic and Social Committee, 2 rue Ravenstein, B-1000 Brussels. T: 322 519 9011.

European Investment Bank, 100 boulevard Konrad Adenauer, Kirchberg, Luxembourg. T: 352 43791.

European Commission, Serrano, 41 Quinta Planta, 28001 Madrid. T: 4 35 17 00.

European Parliament Headquarters, L-2929 Luxembourg. T: 352 43001.

European Parliament (UK office), 2 Queen Anne's Gate, London SW1H 9AA. T: 071-222 0411.

Centre for European Business Information, Small Firms Service, 2nd Floor, 11 Belgrave Road, London SW1V 1RV. T: 071-828 6201.

European Business Institute, 1 St Mary's Place, London W5 5HA. T: 081-579 4688.

European Communities Encyclopedia and Directory, Europa

European Year Book, Europa

European Municipal Directory, European Directories Ltd (written in nine official EC languages)

Directory of the Commission, HMSO

Europe sans Frontières – CBI (an information pack is obtainable from CBI, Centre Point, 103 New Oxford Street, London WC1A 1DU. T: 071-379 7400; also obtainable from the CBI's office in Brussels at 40 rue Joseph 11, Bte 14, 1040 Brussels. T: 322 231 0465.

European Report – a twice-weekly news publication on political, economic and industrial matters published by Europe Information Service, 46 Avenue Albert Elisabeth, 1200 Brussels.

Agence Europe – a daily news-sheet about general European matters available from 10 boulevard Saint-Lazare, 1210 Brussels.

Business methods and marketing opportunities

Chapmans European Directory by Peter Kaye, Chapmans Publishers Ltd

Doing Business in Europe, CCH Editions Ltd

Doing Business in the European Community, Kogan Page

The Single Market (Financial Services), DTI

The Single Market (A Guide to Public Purchasing), DTI

Guide to Exporting, BOTB

How to sell to Europe by Danton de Rauffignac, Pitman Publishing

Selling in the Single Market (A Guide for Exporters), DTI

Marketing without Frontiers, RMI

Government Contacts for Specific Sectors of EC Legislation, DTI

Euro Manual, DTI and CCH Editions Ltd: Outlines: (1) Framework within which business must work in the EC and (2) EC measures which will affect companies

Note DTI address: Department of Trade and Industry, 1 Victoria Street, London SW1 0ET. T: 071-215 7877.
Business in Europe Hotline: 071-215 4782/4786 – open 24 hours, 7 days a week.

Publications giving information on companies in the EU

European Company Information, London Business School

Kompass: Contact Europe, Kompass

Europe's 15 000 largest companies, ELC International (written in English, French and German)

Wer Liefert Was? Who Supplies What?, BDE (written in English, French, German, Italian and Spanish)

Who Owns Whom: Continental Europe, Dun and Bradstreet

Directory of European Industrial and Trade Associations, CBD Research (written in English, French and German)

Directory of European Community Trade and Professional Associations, Delta

European information centres

The Centre for European Business Information, Small firms, 11 Belgrave Road, London SW1. T: 071-828 6201; *or* The European Information Centre, The London Chamber of Commerce and Industry, 69 Cannon Street, London EC4W 5AB. T: 071-489 1992.

EICs are based at centres throughout Europe establishing a network to help locate local suppliers or find partners in Europe. They have access to a wide range of databases such as INFO 92 on the implementation of single market measures and CELEX on EC law and preparatory documents. Many of the EICs are located at libraries.

Grants from the EU

Grants from Europe: How to get money and influence policy by A Davidson, Bedford Square Press

EU legislation

Butterworth Guide to the European Communities, Butterworth–Heinemann

Croner's Europe, a loose-leaf updating service, Croner

EEC Brief: A handbook of EEC Law and Policy by G Myles, Locksley Press Ltd

The Single Market – Company Law Harmonisation, DTI

The EEC: A guide to the maze, Kogan Page

European Community Law by P Kent (M+E Handbooks) Pitman Publishing

Members of the European Parliament, Commissioners and officials

The Times Guide to 1992

Vacher's European Companion

Statistics

Eurostat: *Europe in Figures* (a range of statistics on economic, industrial, financial and social situations in EC member states).

The Statistical Office of the European Communities, BP 1907, rue Alcide de Gasperi, L-2929 Luxembourg. T: 43011.

European Marketing Data and Statistics, Euromonitor

Statistics Europe, CBD Research Ltd

EXAMINATIONS FOR EXECUTIVE SECRETARIES

In Europe

European Diploma for Business Administration – Secretarial

The development of this diploma is a joint project which the Royal Society of Arts is undertaking in association with the Chambers of Commerce in Paris, Dusseldorf and Cologne. It is designed to be recognised in all three countries and has the French title *Diplôme européen d'assistant de direction* and the German title *Europaïsches Diplom für Wirtschaft und Verwaltung Sekretariat*.

The aim is to assess the ability to apply the knowledge and skills required in the performance of a range of administrative and senior secretarial tasks within a European context. This will involve the use of both a main and a subsidiary foreign language, thus enabling the candidate to achieve mobility within the European Community. Possible units include the European framework for business and trade; Background to business; European law; European financial systems; Applied foreign languages and Business Administration – secretarial practice and skills. A period of 12 months' work experience is an essential element of the course.

The chambers of commerce will carry information regarding any language and secretarial courses/qualifications they offer in their countries.

In France

French Ministry of Education Brevet de Technicien Supérieur for Trilingual Secretaries

A two-year full-time post-Baccalauréat qualification consisting of French language; Economics and law; Foreign languages; Administration and management techniques; Shorthand transcription including composition in a foreign language, and a Business Case Study using a foreign language. Training periods in commerce and work experience abroad are featured in the training programme.

Other examinations are offered for executive secretaries and commercial bilingual secretaries.

In Germany

See European Diploma (above).

In Italy

Istituto Sempionne 2000, Corso Sempione 65, 20149 Milano. T: 02 3319422.

Istituto Dardi, Via Raffaello Sanzio 4, 20149 Milano. T: 02 4692570.

Istituto Monteceneri, Viale Monteceneri 78, 20155 Milano. T: 02 39215969.

In the UK

Business and Technology Education Council, Central House, Upper Woburn Place, London WC1H 0HH. T: 071-387 4141 (offers a range of NVQ, GNVQ, National and Higher National Awards).

London Chamber of Commerce and Industry Examinations Board, Marlowe House, Station Road, Sidcup, Kent DA15 7BJ. T: 081-302 0261 (offers a range of awards, including the Private and Executive Secretary's Diploma).

Private and Executive Secretary's Diploma

This diploma examination is intended for senior private secretaries wishing to be employed by top-level management and capable of holding a senior appointment involving secretarial or information-based aspects of management.

The examination consists of Use of English; Meetings (from a video recording); Shorthand transcription or audio transcription (a recording); Secretarial administration; Management appreciation and an interview. The examination structure stresses equal importance of the secretarial role in administration and management and requires the candidate to accept the executive secretary's role as a part of the management team.

Pitman Examinations Institute, Catteshall Manor, Godalming, Surrey GU7 1UU. T: 0483 415311 (offers a range of awards, including Administration and Secretarial Procedures Level 3).

Administration and Secretarial Procedures Level 3

This three-hour, single-subject, written examination tests the candidate on the concepts, competences and responsibilities associated with office administration and the provision of a full secretarial service. Emphasis is placed on problem-solving and decision-making, and an awareness of current developments in equipment, systems and technology is expected. The syllabus covers the knowledge requirements of the UK Administration (Secretarial) NVQ at Level 3 which includes Organisation and supervision; Personnel functions; Communication; Administrative support services and Secretarial support services.

Royal Society of Arts Examination Board, Westwood Way, Coventry CV4 8HS. T: 0203 470033 (offers a range of awards including NVQ Administration and the European Diploma, *see* above).

NVQ (National Vocational Qualification) Administration Level 3

National vocational qualifications are set at different levels of competence, e.g. Level 3 recognises competence in skilled areas that involve performance of a broad range of work activities including many that are complex, non-routine and may be of a supervisory nature. These qualifications are based on employment-led standards set by a lead body of employers for each sector; in the case of administration the lead body is administered from the offices of the Institute of Chartered Secretaries and Administrators, 16 Park Crescent, London W1N 4AH.

NVQ schemes are based on continuous appraisal of candidates' performance while carrying out tasks at their place of learning or within the workplace. Accreditation may also be given for prior qualifications, learning and experience.

The Level 3 units for assessment of administrators including secretaries are included in this book.

BTEC, LCCI, PEI and RSA (as referred to above) all offer programmes for NVQ qualifications.

Institute of Linguists, Mangold House, 24A Highbury Grove, London N5 2EA. T: 071–359 7445 (holds language examinations at five levels and promotes the learning and use of modern languages).

INTERNATIONAL ORGANISATIONS

Organisation	Headquarters	Telephone Nos
The Commonwealth	Marlborough House, Pall Mall, London SW1 5HY	071-930 3783
Council of Europe	Palais de l'Europe, 67006, Strasbourg, Cedex, France	33 88 614961
European Union	200 rue de la Loi, 1049, Brussels, Belgium	322 299 1111
European Free Trade Association	9–11 rue de Varembe, 1211 Geneva 20, Switzerland	749 11 11
European Trade Union Confederation	Rue Montagne aux Herbes Potagères 37, 1000 Brussels	218 3100
Food and Agriculture Organisation of the United Nations	Via della Terme di Caracalla, 00100 Rome, Italy	57 971
General Agreement on Tariffs and Trade	Centre William Rappard, 154 rue de Lausanne, 1211 Geneva 21, Switzerland	739 5111
International Atomic Energy Agency	Vienna International Centre, PO Box 100, A-1400 Vienna, Austria	2630
International Bank for Reconstruction and Development	1818 H St. NW, Washington DC, 20433, USA London office: New Zealand House, Haymarket, SW1Y 4TQ	477 1234
International Civil Aviation Organisation	1000 Sherbrooke Street West, Montreal, Quebec, Canada PQ H3A 2R2	285 8219
International Confederation of Free Trade Unions	37–41 rue Montagne aux Herbes Potagères, Brussels 1000, Belgium	217 80 85
International Federation of Commercial, Clerical, Professional and Technical Employees (FIET)	15 Avenue de Balexert, Chatelanine, 1219, Geneva, Switzerland	21 96 2733

Organisation	Headquarters	Telephone Nos
International Federation of Stenography and Typewriting (INTERSTENO)	Postfach 12 02 69 D 5300, Bonn 1, Germany	25 15 09
International Fund for Agricultural Development	107 Via del Serafico, 00142 Rome, Italy	54 591
International Labour Organisation	CH-1211, Geneva 22, Switzerland	799 6214
International Maritime Organisation	4 Albert Embankment, London SE1 7SR	071-735 7611
International Monetary Fund	700 19th St, NW, Washington DC, 20431, USA	623 7000
International Telecommunication Union	Place des Nations, 1211, Geneva 20, Switzerland	730 51 11
North Atlantic Treaty Organisation	1110 Brussels, Belgium	728 41 11
Organisation for Economic Co-operation and Development	2 Rue André Pascal, 75775 Paris, Cedex 16, France	45 24 8200
Travel and tourism	Bureau International du Tourisme Social, rue de la Loi 63, 1040 Bruxelles	2 230 7530
United Nations	Palais des Nations, 1211, Geneva 10, Switzerland	734 6011
United Nations Educational, Scientific and Cultural Organisation	UNESCO House, 7 Place de Fontenoy, Paris	45 68 1000
Universal Postal Union	Weltpoststrasse 4, 3000, Berne 15, Switzerland	43 2211
Western European Union	9 Grosvenor Place, London SW1X 7HL	071-235 5351
World Council of Churches	PO Box 2100, 150 route de Ferney, 1211 Geneva 2, Switzerland	791 61 11
World Federation of Clerical Workers	Beggaardenstraat 1, B 2000, Antwerpen, Belgium	32 3 234 1500
World Health Organisation	Headquarters: 1211 Geneva 27, Switzerland	791 21 11
World Intellectual Property Organisation	Headquarters: 34 Chemin des Colombettes, 1211 Geneva 20, Switzerland	730 91 11
World Meteorological Organisation	Headquarters: Case postale 5, CH-1211, Geneva 2, Switzerland	730 81 11
World Trade Centre	Europe House, East Smithfield, London E1 9AA	071-488 2400
Pan European Associations	CBD Research Ltd	
Principal International Businesses	Dunn and Bradstreet	

LANGUAGE TRAINING

In France

British Institute, 9 rue Constantine, 75007 Paris. T: 4 55 57 19 9 (linked to View of London Language Courses)

Alliance Française, 101 boulevard Raspail, 75006 Paris. T: 4 54 43 82 8 (French language, literature and economics)

Cours de Civilisation Française de la Sorbonne, 47 rue des Ecoles, 75005 Paris. T: 40 46 26 72 (French language and civilisation courses)

European Institute of Languages, 1 Place du Republique, F-75003, Paris

In Germany

Linguothek Institut, Schluterstr 18, D-2000, Hamburg 18. T: 4940 459520 (offers general German courses and specialist training for executives)

In Spain

Instituto Británico, Almagro 5, 28010 Madrid. T: 337 3500

Institut Français, c/Marqués de la Ensenada 12, 28004 Madrid, T: 319 4956

In Italy

Centro Pontevecchio, Piazza del Mercato Nuovo 1 (Loggia del Porcellino), 50123 Firenze. T: 055 294511.

Centro Studi Italiani, 61049 Urbania (Pesare e Urbino).

International School of Milan, Via Osoppo 4, 20148 Milano. T: 02 40092180.

Oxford Institutes Italiani, Via Senato 28, 20121 Milano. T: 02 76013836.

Scuola Toscana, Via de Benci 23, 50122 Firenze. T: 055 244583.

In the UK

BBC Language Courses, BBC Education Information, Villiers House, London W5 2PA. T: 081-991 8031 (TV and radio series, books, cassettes, software and tutors notes).

Berlitz School of Languages Ltd, Wells House, 79 Wells Street, London W1A 3B7. T: 071-580 6482.

BLISS, Business Language Information Services, 76 Colesbourne Drive, Downhead Park, Milton Keynes MK15 9AP. T: 0908 607739 (consultancy and support service for companies, individuals and organisations needing to develop language skills for business).
Publications such as *Making your Mark: Effective Business Communication in German* and *Franc Exchange: Effective Business Communication in France* are available as part of the language learning courses.

Association of Language Excellence Centres, PO Box 178, Manchester M60 1LL. T: 061-228 1366 (provides language services, training and consultancy for business needs).

The European Centre, Oxford House, 16 Oxford Street, Manchester M1 5EH T: 061-236 6090 (provides training and consultancy services for business in Europe).

Centre for Information on Language Training and Research (CILT), Regent's College, Inner Circle, Regent's Park, London NW1 4NS. T: 071-486 8221 (An independent organisation sponsored by the government to help improve language competence in the UK. CILT helps to analyse the language needs of companies and find suitable suppliers. It publishes many books on language learning and teaching. The CILT library collects and distributes information on language training. Netword is a network of local self-help groups co-ordinated by CILT and aimed at providing easier access to language training data and encouraging contact within the language training/teaching world.)

UK Lingua Unit, Seymour Mews House, Seymour Mews, London W1H 9PE. T: 071-224 1477. Offices also in Edinburgh and Belfast. (Lingua is an EC Action Programme to support the teaching and learning of foreign languages throughout the EC member states. It can provide grants for the training of teachers and trainers, grants for the assistance of certain students in higher education and for the language needs of small and medium-sized businesses and exchanges for young people.)

Alliance Française, 1 Dorset Square, London NW1 6PU. T: 071-723 0020 (provides lectures, telephone language courses, legal French, courses in France and French teaching in companies).

Euro Training Consortium. This consists of the University of Westminster, the University of North London, South Bank University and Thames Valley University. Consortium members design and deliver language training programmes. Project Director: University of North London, 1 Prince of Wales Road, London NW5 3LB. T: 071-753 5106.

Goethe-Institut, Ridgefield House, 14 John Dalton Street, Manchester M2 6JR. T: 061-834 4635 (Courses in Germany and at London, Glasgow and Manchester branches providing access to German culture and civilisation).

Hispanic and Luso Brazilian Council, 2 Belgrave Square, London SW1X 8PJ. T: 071-235 2303.

Institute Cervantes (formerly Spanish Institute), 102 Eaton Square, London SW1W 9AN. T: 071-235 1484.

Institut Français, 14 Cromwell Place, London SW7. T: 071-581 2701 (official French Government Centre of Language and Culture; training given in language and bilingual secretarial skills).

Italian Cultural Institute, 39 Belgrave Square, London SW1X 8NX. T: 071-235 1461.

Kingston Language Export Centre, Millenium House, 21 Eden Street, Kingston upon Thames, Surrey KT1 1BL. T: 081-547 2623.

Language Export (LX) Centres Co-ordinating Unit, Regent's College, Inner Circle, Regent's Park, London NW1 4NS. T: 071-224 3748 (This is a network of language export centres involving universities and colleges set up with government help to provide language courses and cultural briefings tailor-made to specific business needs of individual companies).

Linguaphone, Business Sales Department, 50 Poland Street, London W1V 4AX. T: 071-734 0574.

NVQ Languages Lead Body Secretariat, 20 Bedfordbury, London WC2N 4LB. T: 071-379 5134.

Central Bureau for Educational Visits and Exchanges, Seymour Mews House, Seymour Mews, London W1H 9PE. T: 071-486 5101.

Reference books

Business Companions for France, Germany, Spain and Italy, by Karsta Neuhaus and Margaret Haltern, Cassell

Collins range of dictionaries and phrasebooks

Hamlyn pocket dictionaries and phrasebooks

Harrap pocket dictionaries and vocabularies

The Multilingual Business Handbook – a guide to international correspondence, Macmillan

Multilingual Commercial Dictionary, Pan

Bilingual Guide to Business and Professional Correspondence: Italian (Harvard and Miletto) and Spanish (Harvard and Ariza), Pergamon

MAGAZINES, JOURNALS AND NEWSPAPERS FOR BUSINESS

In Europe

The Bulletin, Monique Ackroyd, 329 Ave Mohere, 1060 Brussels – weekly newsletter of the capital of Europe

In France

FUSAC – bi-monthly contacts publication for the American and British community in France

In Germany

Der Erfolg (*Office Administration*), Hans Halzmann Verlag, Gewerbestrasse 2, 8939 Bad Worishofen. T: 8247-35401.

Top Business, Verlag Moderne Industrie AG, Ingolstaedter Strasse 22, 8000 Munchen 45. T: 89 350 930.

In Italy

Gente Money, Rusconi Editore SpA, Viale Sarca 235, 20126 Milano. T: 02 66191.

L'Espresso, Via Giovanni de Alessandri 11, 20144 Milano. T: 02 4818350.

Economia & Management, Arnoldo Mondadori Editore, 20090 Segrate, Milano. T: 02 75421.

Il Giornale del Dirigente, Via Compagnoni 1, 20129 Milano. T: 02 76111064.

Il Mondo, Rcs Rizzoli Periodici SpA, Via Rizzoli 2/4/6, 20132 Milano. T: 02 25843173.

Il Sole 24 Ore, Via Lomazzo 52, 20154 Milano. T: 02 31031.

Mondo Economico, Via Lomazzo 57, 20154 Milano. T: 02 331211.

In Spain

Expansión, calle Alcalde Sainz de Baranda 35, 28009 Madrid. T: 574 3650.

La Gaceta de los Negocios, calle ODonnell 12-1, 28009 Madrid. T: 586 3300.

Actualidad Económica, calle Recoletos 1, 28001 Madrid. T: 431 0917.

In the UK

Administrative Management, 40 Chatsworth Parade, Petts Wood, Orpington, Kent BR5 1RW. T: 0689 875555.

Business Education Today, Pitman Publishing Periodicals Division, 128 Long Acre, London WC2E 9AN. T: 071-379 7383.

Business Equipment Digest, IML Group plc, Blair House, High Street, Tonbridge, Kent TN9 1BQ. T: 0732 359990.

Business News, British Telecommunications plc, Telephone House, Temple Avenue, London EC4Y 0HL. T: 0800-800851.

City, PA Publishing Consultancy Services, Blue Barn Farm Cottages, Goudhurst, Kent TN17 2PD. T: 0580 211153.

Computing Equipment, IML Group plc, The Coach House, Didsbury Park, Manchester M20 0LJ. T: 061-445 7729.

The Economist, 25 James's Street, London SW1A 1HG. T: 071-839 7000.

Executive PA, Harmsworth Magazines, 175-9 St John's Street, London EC1V 4RP. T: 071-490 1166.

Executive Woman, Saleworld Publishing, 2 Chantry Place, Harrow, Middlesex HA3 6NY. T: 081-420 1210.

The Financial Times, 1 Southwark Bridge, London SE1. T: 071-873 3000.

Focus on Business Education, The Society of Teachers in Business Education, Saffron Hill, Uplands Road, Totland Bay, Isle of Wight PO39 0DY. T: 0983 755391.

Management Today, 30 Lancaster Gate, London W2 3LP. T: 071-413 4542/4566.

Office Lifestyle, Whitehall Press Ltd, Warwick House, Azalea Drive, Swanley, Kent BR8 8HY. T: 0322 660070.

Office Secretary Magazine for Senior and Executive Secretaries, Trade Media Ltd, Brookmead House, Two Rivers, Station Lane, Witney, Oxon OX8 6BH. T: 0993 775545.

Systems and Networking, Inmac (UK) Ltd, Market Street, Bracknell, Berks RG12 1BS. T: 0344 301144.

Today's PA, Corporate Image Publications, 16th Floor, Station House, 1 Harrow Road, Wembley, Middx HA9 6DE. T: 081-903 9633.

Girl about Town and *Executive PA Magazine*, GAT Publishing, 141-3 Drury Lane, London WC2B 5TS. T: 071-836 4433.

MARKETING AND PUBLIC RELATIONS

In France

Association Nationale pour le Developpement des Techniques de Marketing (French Marketing Association), 30 rue d'Astorg, 75008 Paris. T: 42 66 51 13.

In Germany

Absatzwirtschaftliche Gesellschaft eV (Distribution and Marketing), Josephsplatz 20, 8500 Nurnberg 1. T: 0911 22 12 57.

Deutsche Marketing – Vereinigung eV (German Marketing Association), Orangeriestrasse 6, 4000 Dusseldorf. T: 0211 32 00 78.

Deutsche Public Relations Gesellschaft eV (German Public Relations Society), Berufsuerband Offentlichkeitsarbeit, Rhenusallee 20, 5300 Bonn 3. T: 0228 46 70 81.

In Italy

Associazione Italiana per gli Studi di Marketing, Via Olmetto 3, I-20123 Milano. T: 02 863293.

Federazione Italiana della Pubblicità, Via M Gonzaga, I-20123 Milano. T: 02 865262/8055081.

Jeanne Perego Relazioni Publiche Srl, Via Maria Teresa 8, 20123 Milano. T: 02 72021363.

SI Comunicazione E Marketing Srl, Via Carroccio 16, 20123 Milano. T: 02 58103755.

SIPR Studio Italiano Public Relations Srl, Via Tomassetti 5, 00161 Roma. T: 06 8555874/8551613.

Cronopac Srl, Via Abbondio Sangiorgio, 00145 Milano. T: 02 33600396.

Makrotest Srl, Via Carducci 22, 20123 Milano. T: 02 874854.

Atesia Spa, Via Silvio D'Amico 53, 00145 Roma. T: 06 543951.

Utenti Pubblicità Associati, Via Larga 13, I-20122 Milano. T: 02 861951.

In Spain

AC Neilsen Company SA, Pl Descubridor Diego Ordás 3, 28003 Madrid. T: 91 592 11 00.

Alef-Millward Brown SA, Maldonado, 55 Edificio C, 28006 Madrid. T: 91 564 44 33.

Intergallup SA, Hermosilla, 23 3° Dcha, 28001 Madrid. T: 91 431 93 36.

Sofemasa, Princesa, 1 Torre Madrid 10-6, 28008 Madrid. T: 91 248 96 08.

Guía del Marketing en España, Ediciones y Estudios SA, Enrique Larreta 7, 7° A, 28036 Madrid. T: 315 7419.

In the UK

Institute of Marketing, Moor Hall, Cookham, Maidenhead, Berks SL6 9QH. T: 0628 524 922.

Institute of Public Relations, The Old Trading House, 15 Northburgh Street, London EC1V 0PR. T: 071-253 5151.

International Marketing Strategy by F Bradley, Prentice-Hall.

Marketing Consumer Goods: Western Europe, British Overseas Trade Board.

Marketing: International, ed. by Bovel and Thill, McGraw-Hill.

Public Relations Consultants Association, Willow House, Willow Place, London SW1P 1JH. T: 071-233 6026.

Tips for Exhibitors Handbook, Academy Expo.

Introduction to Public Relations by S Black, Modino.

Selecting and Employing a PR Consultancy, Institute of Public Relations.

PERSONNEL AND TRAINING

In Europe

European Association of Personnel Management, c/o IPM, IPM House, Camp Road, Wimbledon, London SW19 4UW. T: 081-946 9100.

European Trade Union Confederation, 37 rue Montagne aux Herbes Potagères, 1000 Brussels, Belgium. T: 218 3100.

Union of Industrial and Employers' Confederations of Europe, 40 rue Joseph II, 1040 Brussels. T: 237 6511.

In France

Fédération Européenne des Conseils en Ressources Humaines, rue Fabert, 30, 75007, Paris. T: 45 55 25 81.

In Germany

Social and Labour Central Placement Office of Federal Employment Institute, Zentralstelle Für Arbeitsvermittlung, Feuerbachster 42-46, 60325 Frankfurt-am-Main. T: 69 71110, Fax: 69 7111555.

In Italy

Athena Research, Via Serbelloni 4, 20122 Milano. T: 02 76014561.

Sintex SRL, Via Frua 24, 20146 Milano. T: 02 4691417.

Studio Vittorio Anfossi
Ricerca & Selezione
Dirigenti E Quadri } Via Castelvetro 9, 20154 Milano
Marketing E Vendite

Daniela Rossi & Associati SRL, Via Sardegna 43, 20146 Milano. T: 02 48011813.

In Spain

TEA CEGOS, Fray Bernadino de Sahagun, 28036 Madrid. T: 345 7026.

In the UK

Department for Education, Elizabeth House, York Road, London SE1 7PH. T: 071-934 9000.

Department of Employment, Caxton House, Tothill Street, London SW1H 9NF. T: 071-213 3000.

Department of Training, Moorfoot, Sheffield S1 4PQ. T:. 0742 753275.

Equal Opportunities Commission, Overseas House, Quay Street, Manchester M3 3HN. T: 061-833 9244.

Trade Union Congress, Congress House, Great Russell Street, London WC1. T: 071-636 4030.

Federation of Recruitment and Employment Services (FRES), 36-8 Mortimer Street, London W1N 0ET. T: 071-323 4300 (the trade body for the recruitment industry with European contacts and listings of recruitment consultancies for specific sectors).

The Industrial Society, Peter Runge House, 3 Carlton House Terrace, London SW1Y 5DG. T: 071-839 4300. (The Society runs training courses and conferences aimed at helping organisations to become more effective, productive and profitable. Consultancy and in-house training are available along with an information service, publications, surveys and audits. The country's largest independent advisory and training body and leading authority in the development of people in the workplace.)

Institute of Administrative Management, 40 Chatsworth Parade, Petts Wood, Orpington, Kent BR5 1RW. T: 0689 875555.

Institute of Personnel Management, IPM House, 35 Camp Road, London SW19 4UW. T: 081-946 9100.

Management and Skills Training (MAST), Hermitage House, Bath Road, Taplow, Maidenhead, Berks SL6 0AR. T: 0628 784062 (an international training and development business wth services available for personal, team and company performance development).

National Council for Vocational Qualifications, 222 Euston Road, London NW1 2BZ. T: 071-387 9898.

National Advisory Centre on Careers for Women, 8th Floor, Artillery House, Artillery Row, London SW1P 1RT. T: 071-401 2280.

Spanish Embassy, 20 Peel Street, London W8 7PD; Education Office. T: 071-727 2462; Labour Office. T: 071-221 0098.

Personnel and Training Management Year Book and Directory

Careers Information and Careers Libraries by E J Summerson, Career Consultants Ltd

Careers Research and Advisory Council (CRAC) compile books (published by Hobsons) and organise courses on career choice and development. *Job Book*, a handbook of employment and training for secretarial leavers, is a CRAC publication.

Great British Conference Destinations Directory, BACT.

GO – Graduate Opportunities, The Newpoint Publishing Co. Ltd.

ROGET – Register of Graduate Employment and Training, CSU.

Occupations, Careers and Occupational Information Centre.

Working Abroad – The Daily Telegraph Guide to Working and Living Overseas (including a country by country listing) by Godfrey Golzen, Kogan Page.

World of Learning (includes a listing of educational establishments), Europa.

Yearbook of Recruitment and Employment Services, Longman.

British Qualifications, Kogan Page.

POSTAL SERVICES CONTACT NUMBERS

In France La Poste 010-33 1 43 35 60 00 (Paris). Numero vert – Parcel services: toll free 050 74074.

In Germany Generaldirektionen 010-49 228 1830 (Bonn). Toll free: 0130-804141.

In Italy Post and Telecommunications 010-39 6 700 4417 (Rome).

In Spain Post Office and Telecommunications 010 34 1 33 75400 (Madrid).

In the UK Royal Mail Information line 0800-224466.

Royal Mail Services *Mailguide* and leaflets
Parcelforce Services *UK User Guide*
International User Guide

British Rail Red Star
Delivery Services: *Red Star Services and Price Guide*
Courier services offered by private delivery companies

PROFESSIONAL ASSOCIATIONS FOR SECRETARIES AND NETWORKING OPPORTUNITIES

In Europe

European Association of Professional Secretaries, Maison de L'Europe, Hôtel de Coulanges, 35 rue des Francs Bourgeois, 75004 Paris, France. T: 42 72 94 06.

European Women's Management Development Network, European HQ: rue Washington 40, B-1050 Brussels, Belgium. T: 648 0385, Fax: 646 0768.

International Federation of Commercial, Clerical, Professional and Technical Employees, 15 avenue de Balexert, Chatelanine, 1219 Geneva, Switzerland. T: 41 21 96 27 33.

In France

European Association of Professional Secretaries, Dominique Charmes, 18 rue Violet, F-75015, Paris.

In Germany

European Association of Professional Secretaries, Helga Glatzel, Endersbacher Str 10, D-7307, Aichwald 2.

Deutscher Sekretärinnen Verband ev, Lagewiesenstr 1a, 6700 Ludwigshafen 14.

International Federation of Stenography and Typewriting, Postfach 12 02 69, D5300, Bonn 1.

In Spain

Asociación de Secretarias Profesionales de Madrid, Paseo de la Castellana 62, 28046 Madrid. T: 563 8885.

Asociación Española de Secretarias, calle Fray Bernardino de Sahagún 24, 28036 Madrid. T: 458 8311.

European Association of Professional Secretaries, Zulema Perez Tapia, Air France, Gran Vía 57-4, ES-28013, Madrid.

In Italy

European Association of Professional Secretaries, Luisa Dondina, Universita Luigi Bocconi, Via Sarfatti 25, I-20136, Milano.

In the UK

Association of Medical Secretaries, Practice Administrators and Receptions (AMSPAR), Tavistock House North, Tavistock Square, London WC1H 9LN. T: 071-387 6005.

Association of Personal Assistants and Secretaries Ltd (APAS), 14 Victoria Terrace, Leamington Spa, Warwickshire CV31 3AB. T: 0926 424 794.

Barbican Secretary Club, Barbican Centre, London EC2Y 8DS. T: 071-638 4141 (The Club is aimed primarily at senior secretaries and PAs and its purpose is to help secretaries meet the demands and challenges of personal and professional life).

European Association of Professional Secretaries, Heathrow Business Centre, Terminal 2, Heathrow Airport, Hounslow, Middlesex TW6 1EU. T: 071-371 2443.

European Women's Management Development Network: Ms Lyn Bicker, 21 Essex Street, Whitstable, Kent CT5 4HP. T: 0227 265969.

Institute of Agricultural Secretaries, National Agricultural Centre, Stoneleigh, Kenilworth, Warwickshire CV8 2LZ. T: 0203 696592.

Institute of Qualified Private Secretaries Ltd, 68 Longmoor Road, Long Eaton, Nottingham NG10 4FP. T: 0602 733235.

The Industrial Society, Peter Runge House, 3 Carlton House Terrace, London SW1Y 5DG. T: 071-839 3398; Secretarial Development Department T: 071-839 4300; Network Helpline: 071-454 6769. (The Industrial Society campaigns for the development of the secretarial and administrative function by providing a variety of courses aimed at developing the potential of secretaries. Courses and workshps cover topics such as 'The Secretary in the Single Market'; 'Assertiveness for Secretaries'; 'Time Management' and 'Networking for Secretaries').

National Alliance of Women's Organisations, 279 Whitechapel Road, London E1 1BY. T: 071-247 7052.

The Pepperell Network Membership Department, The Industrial Society, 49 Calthorpe Road, Edgbaston, Birmingham, B15 1TH. T: 071-262 2407 (focuses on women's training and career options).

The Institute of Linguists, 24a Highbury Grove, London N5 2EA. T: 071-359 7445 (Conferences and courses of interest to secretarial linguists are organised by the Institute of Linguists).

UK Federation of Business and Professional Women, 23 Amsdell Street, London W8 5BN. T: 071-938 1729 (The Federation is open to working women from all sectors and at all levels and has strong international affiliations).

Women in Enterprise, 62 Bond Street, Wakefield, WF1 2QP. T: 0924 361 789.

Women in Management, 64 Marryat Road, Wimbledon, London SW19 5BN. T: 071-495 5040.

Working Mothers' Association, 77 Holloway Road, London N7 8JZ. T: 071-700 5772.

Conferences, seminars and exhibitions such as the Secretary and Office Management Show in London, the London Language Show and other regional exhibitions in the UK provide secretaries with good networking opportunities. Involvement with the Chambers of Commerce through company membership can also be fruitful. alongside contact with organisations such as the French Institute, Hispanic and Luso Brazilian Council and the Goethe Institute.

Facilitator, 2 Chantry Place, Harrow, Middlesex. T: 081-420 1210; Information Line: 081-420 1270. (A service enabling unaccompanied female business guests to meet, dine and network in hotels which are part of the Facilitator Group/service.

RECRUITMENT AGENCIES AND CONSULTANCIES

In France

Sheila Burgess International, 62 rue Saint-Lazare, 75009 Paris. T: 44 63 02 57.

EGOR SA, 8 rue de Berri, 75008 Paris. T: 42 25 71 07.

GR Intérim, 12 rue de la Paix, 75001 Paris. T: 42 61 82 11

PA Consulting Group, 3 rue des Graviers, 92521 Neuilly, Cedex. T: 40 88 79 79.

Plus Intérim, Champs Elysées, 57 rue Pierre Cnarron, 75008 Paris. T: 42 25 77 15 (with many branches in Paris and its environs).

Selective Executive Assistants, 91 Faubourg St Honoré, 75008 Paris.

In Germany

The secretarial recruitment process in Germany does not have a strong agency culture. Most companies advertise directly.

In Holland

Europool, the European Graduate Resource Office Centre, Jozef Israelskade 48, 1072 SB Amsterdam, The Netherlands. T: 20 76 70 56.

In Spain

Alta Gestión, Avenida Pío XII, No 21, 28016 Madrid. T: 91 457 50 50.

AYUDIR, Instituto Europeo de Ciencias Secretariales, Glorieta López de Hoyos 5, 1 Dcha, 28002 Madrid. T: 1 564 65 98.

Euro Head Hunter SA, Calle Campomanes No 3, 1° Dcha, 28013 Madrid.

Euro Tempo SA, Gran Vía 60, 28013 Madrid. T: 542 76 91.

Intergrupp Service SA, Calle Villanueva 2, despacho 24, Madrid.

Leaders Consulting, Montevideo 33, 28020 Madrid.

Mercuri Urval SA, Fernadex de los Rios 59, 28015 Madrid.

In Italy

As in Germany, agencies do not proliferate as in the UK. Personal recommendations are important. Companies advertise direct and speculative applications are common.

International Secretary Centre, Torre 5, Centro Commerciale, 20090 San Felice Segrate. T: 02 7534258.

Mercuri Urval, Centro Direzionale Colleoni, Palazzo Astrolabio, 20041 Agrate Brianza, Milano.

PA Consulting Group, Via Turati 40, 20121 Milano.

In the UK

Angela Mortimer International Division, 37 Golden Square, London, W1R 4AH. T: 071-287 7788.

Appointments by Language, 3 Princes Street, London W1R 7RA. T: 071-734 3380.

Bilingual People, 8 Golden Square, London W1R 3AF. T: 071-287 1688.

Bilinguasec, Suite 1, 49 Maddox Street, London W1R 9LA. T: 071-493 6446.

Boyce Bilingual, Liberty House, 222 Regent Street, London W1R 5DE. T: 071-287 6060.

Cavell Bilingual Recruitment, 26 Goodge Street, London W1P 1FG. T: 071-255 3277.

CLC Language Services, 6 Buckingham Street, London WC2N 6BU. T: 071-839 3365.

Crone Corkhill, Victory House, 99–101 Regent Street, London W1R 7HB. T: 071-434 4512.

DSA, Garden Studios, 11–15 Betterton Street, London WC2H 9BP. T: 071-379 0344.

Drake International Recruitment Consultants, 57 Brompton Road, Knightsbridge, London SW3 1DP. T: 071-589 5898.

Euro London Appointments, Hare Place, 47 Fleet Street, London EC4Y 1BJ. T: 071-583 0180.

Euro Secretaries, 2 Beechworth Close, London NW3 7UT. T: 071-435 0718.

The Language Business, 5 Denmark Street, London WC2H 8LP. T: 071-379 3189.

Language Matters, 5th Floor, Carrara House, 20 Embankment Place, London WC2N 6NN. T: 071-930 1811.

Language Recruitment Services, 54–62 Regent Street, London W1R 5PJ. T: 071-287 0424.

Link Language Appointments, 10 South Molton Street, London W1Y 1DF. T: 071-408 2150.

Merrow, 73 New Bond Street, London W1Y 9DD. T: 071-499 3939.

Multilingual Services, 22 Charing Cross Road, London WC2H 0HR. T: 071-836 3794.

Sheila Burgess International Recruitment Consultants, 4 Cromwell Street, London SW7 2JE. T: 071-584 6446.

REFERENCE LIBRARIES AND SOURCES OF INFORMATION FOR BUSINESS

In Europe

European Association of Information Services, 9A High Street, Calne, Wilts, SN11 0BS, UK. T: 0249 814584.

European Society for Press and Information Services, Kurfurstendamm 102, W-1000 Berlin 31, Germany. T: 49 892 4028.

In France

European Businesses Institute, 49 Rue Ponthieu, F-75008 Paris. T: 42 25 22 22.

In Italy

Business information libraries are attached to Chambers of Commerce (*see* page 271).

In Germany

Oeckl Taschenbuch des Öffentlichen Lebens, published by Festland Verlag, Bonn.

In Spain

Instituto de la Pequeña y Mediana Industrial, Castellana 141, 28046 Madrid. T: 582 9300.

Marcial Pons Libreros, Economia y Gestión, Paseo de las Salesas 10, 28004 Madrid. T: 308 5649.

Marcial Pons Libreros, Libros Jurídicos, calle Bárbara de Braganza 8, 28004 Madrid. T: 319 4250.

Castiñeira Libreria, Santiago Rusiñol 4, 28040 Madrid. T: 533 8201.

Agoza Nexum, Bravo Murillo 95, 28003 Madrid. T: 534 9352.

In the UK

British Library Reference Division, Great Russell Street, London WC1B 3DG. T: 071-636 1544 (general switchboard).

Business Information Unit, Scottish Council for Development and Industry, 17 Park Circus Place, Glasgow, G3 6AH. T: 041-332 9119.

City Business Library, Gillett House, 55 Basinghall Street, London EC2V 5BX. T: 071-638 8215.

City University Business School Library, Frobisher Crescent, Barbican, London EC2Y 8HB. T: 071-920 0111.

Federal Office for Foreign Trade Information, Mecklenburg House, 16 Buckingham Gate, London SW1E 6LB. T: 071-630 1807 (specialises in providing business information to German companies).

Industrial Development Board for Northern Ireland, Business Information Centre, 64 Chichester Street, Belfast BT1 4JX. T: 0232 233233.

LCCI Research and Information Department, 69 Cannon Street, London EC4N 5AB. T: 071-248 4444.

London Business School, Sussex Place, Regent's Park, London NW1 4SA. T: 071-262 5050; Library and information service: 071-724 2300.

The British Library Official Publications and Social Service Library, Great Russell Street, London WC1B 3DG. T: 071-636 1544.

Walford's *Guide to Reference Material*.

Whitaker's *British Books in Print* (microfiche).

HMSO publications from HMSO Publications Centre, PO Box 276, London SW8 5DT.

Catalogue of British Official Publications (not those published by HMSO), Chadwyck-Healey.

Certain reference libraries form information networks offering fast access to technical and business information held by organisations local to a particular area. HATRICS is an example of such a network in the south of England with its headquarters at 81 North Walls, Winchester, Hants SO23 8BY. T: 0962 846064.

SECRETARIAL TRAINING

In France

Ecole Commerciale de Jeunes Filles, 39 avenue Trudaine, 75009 Paris. T: 42 30 23 23.

La Femme Secrétarire, 101 rue de Lille, 75007 Paris. T: 45 55 02 00.

In Germany

Social and Labour Central Placement Office of Federal Employment Institute, Zentralstelle Für Arbeitsvermittlung, Feuerbackster 42–46, 60325 Frankfurt-am-Main. T: 69 71110.

In Spain

CEU, Colegio Mayor Vasco de Quiroga, P° de las Moreras s/n, 28021 Madrid. T: 449 38 00.

Escuela Especial de Secretariado, Maria Borkowska, Nuñez de Balboa 47, 28001 Madrid. T: 275 97 19.

Escuela Superior de Secretarias, Lagasca 65, 28001 Madrid. T: 431 17 65.

Centro Internacional Sampere, Castelló 50, 28001 Madrid. T: 276 82 64.

Euro Aula, Rambla del Prat 2, 08012 Barcelona. T: 93-217 00 60.

Escuela de Secretariado Aloya, Couto 2, 36204 Vigo. T: 986-41 08 57.

Escuela Superior de Secretariado, Montessori, Pedro IV 12, 50009 Zaragoza. T: 976-56 15 00.

Escuela de Secretariado Arriaca, Barrionuevo 2, 19001 Guadalajara. T: 22 70 61.

Centro De Estudios de Secretariado, San Jacinto 28, 46008 Valencia. T: 96-382 01 30.

Berkley Business College, Uria 30-3°, 33007 Oviedo. T: 985-22 44 97.

Escuela de Secretariado Europeo, Cervantes 19-3°, 33004 Oviedo. T: 985-25 45 85.

Centro Nuevas Profesiones, Pl Conde Valle Suchil 4, 28015 Madrid.

In the UK

Details of all public-funded colleges offering courses for secretaries and personal assistants are listed in the *Education Authorities Directory and Annual*, published by School Government Publishing Ltd, Darby House, Bletchingley Road, Mersthan, Redhill, Surrey. T: 0737 42223.

The Independent Guide to Secretarial Colleges provides an analysis of courses and facilities compiled and edited by Angela Mortimer: published by Angela Mortimer Ltd and First Formula Publishing.

Brookside Secretarial College, 2 Brookside, Cambridge CB2 1JE. T: 0223 64539.

Caroline King Training Centre, 87 New Bond Street, London W1. T: 071-409 1188.

Cranbrook Training plc, 5–9 Headstone Road, Harrow HA1 1PL. T: 081-863 0621 and at 20 Artillery Lane, Bishopsgate, London E1 7LS. T: 071-375 0333.

French Institute, 14 Cromwell Place, London SW7 2JR. T: 071-494 3851.

Guildford Secretarial College, Woodbridge Road, Guildford, Surrey GU1 4RF. T: 0483 64835.

London Business College, 60 South Molton Street, London W1. T: 071-493 3401.

Marlborough Secretarial Colleges in Oxford, Cambridge and Leeds. T: Oxford: 0865 249484; Cambridge: 0223 76016; Leeds: 0532 453073.

Mid-Kent College of Higher and Further Education, Oakwood Park, Tonbridge Road, Maidstone, Kent ME16 8AQ. T: 0622 691555 (A Euro PA Course is offered)

Office Skills, 20 Bedford Street, Covent Garden, London WC2. T: 071-836 3901.

Pitman Education and Training Ltd, Pitman Central College, 154 Southampton Row, London WC1B 5AX. T: 071-837 4481 (colleges also in Cambridge, Oxford and Leeds).

Purley Secretarial and Language College, 14 Brighton Road, Purley, Surrey CR8 3AB. T: 081-660 2568.

Queen's Secretarial College, 22–24 Queensberry Place, London SW7 2DS. T: 071-589 8583.

Sight and Sound Education Ltd, 118–120 Charing Cross Road, London WC2H 0JR. T: 071-379 0691.

Speedwriting, 60 South Molton Street, London W1X 2AY. T: 071-493 3401.

St Aldates Secretarial and Business College, Rose Place, Oxford OX1 1SB. T: 0865 240963.

St James Secretarial College, 4 Wetherby Gardens, London SW5. T: 071-373 3852.

Wolverhampton University (*see* Language training).

SELF-IMPROVEMENT

In the UK

CareerTrack, Department No 986, Winterhill, Milton Keynes, MK6 1HQ. T: 0908 669346 (organises seminars on different aspects of improving communication and business skills, time management and career development).

Colourflair, 188 Warren Road, Brighton, BN2 6DD. T: 0273 605540.

First Impressions Colour Coding, 1 Dover Street, Cambridge CB1 1DY. T: 0223 462700.

International Stress and Tension Control Society, The Priory Hospital, Priory Lane, Roehampton, London SW15 5JJ. T: 081-876 8261.

Lancashire College, Southport Road, Chorley PR7 1NB. T: 0257 276719 (offers training courses in developing management skills ranging from interpersonal skills to IT; foreign language training; negotiating; public speaking and assertiveness training).

Lifelink Ltd, 14 Wimpole Street, London W1M 7AB. T: 071-436 2074 (provides health assessment and advice).

Personal Style Image Development, 10 Southcote, Woking, Surrey GU21 4QX. T: 0483 740407.

Positive Health Centre, 101 Harley Street, London W1N 1DF. T: 071-935 1811.

Stressbusters, Garden Studios, 11–15 Betterton Street, London WC2H 9BP. T: 071-379 0344 (on-site massage and stress release).

The Hale Clinic, 7 Park Crescent, London W1N 3HE. T: 071-631 0156.

The One-Minute Manager by Kenneth Blanchard and Spencer Johnson, Fontana.

The Complete Spokesperson by P Bartram and C Coulson-Thomas, Policy Publications Ltd.

TELECOMMUNICATIONS

In the UK

Telephone directories (*Phone books* and *Yellow Pages*) for different areas of the country.

Talking Pages – a British Telecom service for selected parts of Britain in which specially-trained operators help callers to find information from Yellow Pages. The Talking Pages operators have access to up-to-date information on businesses, such as opening hours, credit card acceptance, telephone, fax and telex numbers, products and brands stocked, etc.

Business Pages – seven British Telecom classified business directories giving details of some 420 000 potential businesses with their names, addresses, telephone numbers and products/services covering the major industrial and commercial regions of Britain.

Thomson Local Directories

UK Telex and Answerback Directory, British Telecom

Fax Directory, British Telecom

TELETEXT SERVICES

In the UK

BBC Ceefax – TV Channels 1 and 2: BBC Television Centre, Wood Lane, London W12 7RJ. T: 081-743 8000.

ITV Teletext – TV Channels 3 and 4. Teletext Ltd, Craven House, 25-32 Marshall Street, London W1V 1LL. T: 071-434 3121.

Prestel – British Telecom (an interactive system linked to the telephone): Prestel Viewdata Service Headquarters, Telephone House, Temple Avenue, London EC4Y 0HL. T: 071-822 1122.

A special financial information service, called Citiservice, is provided by BT for investors, traders, financial advisers and business executives who require access to immediate market conditions.

Private viewdata systems supply specialised information to restricted user groups, e.g. farming, travel, stock exchange.

TRADING AND INDUSTRIAL ORGANISATIONS

Europe

Kompass Contact Europe, Kompass
Major Companies of Europe, Graham and Trotman

France

Ministry of Industry, 101 rue de Grenelle, 75007 Paris. T: 1 45 56 36 36.

Institut National de la Propriété Industrielle, 26 Bis rue de Leningrad, 75800 Paris. T: 1 42 94 52 52.

Délégations du Territoire et de l'Action Régionale (DATAR), 1 Avenue Charles Floquet, 75007 Paris. T: 1 47 83 61 20.

France 30,000, Dun and Bradstreet

Kompass France

Germany

Handbuch der Grossunternehmen, Hoppenstedt

Kompass Germany

Spain

Confederación Española de Organizaciones Empresariales, Diego de Léon 50, 28006 Madrid. T: 262 4410.

Dun's 15,000: Principales Empresas Espanolas, Dun and Bradstreet

Kompass Spain

Fomento de la Producción: España 30,000, Casanova 57, 08011 Barcelona.

Italy

Dun and Bradstreet, Via Valtorta 48, 20127 Milano. T: 02 284551.

Kompass Italy

UK

Companies

Dun and Bradstreet's *Who Owns Whom*

Kelly's Business Directory

Key British Enterprises: Britain's Top 50,000 Companies, Dun and Bradstreet

UK's 10,000 Largest Companies, ELC International

Handbook of Market Leaders, Extel

British Business Rankings

The Times 1000 Leading Companies in Britain and Overseas

Confederation of British Industry (CBI), Centre Point, 103 New Oxford Street, London WC1A 1DU. T: 071-379 7400.

National Federation of the Self-Employed and Small Businesses Ltd, 32 St Anne's Road, West Lytham, St Annes, Lancs FY8 1NY. T: 0253 720911.

Directors of companies

International Stock Exchange Official Year Book

Directory of Directors

Institute of Directors, 116 Pall Mall, London SW1Y 5ED. T: 071-839 1233.

British Institute of Management, Management House, Cottingham Road, Corby, Northants, NN17 1TT. T: 0536 204222.

TRANSLATION AND INTERPRETER SERVICES

In France

Société Internationale de Traduction, 19 rue de la Paix, 75001 Paris. T: 47 42 79 59.

In Germany

European Translators College, PO Box 1162, W-4172 Straelen. T: 49 2834 10 68.

Vereilnigung der Sprachmittler der DDR beim VDJ (German Translators and Interpreters Association), Ackerstrasse 17, 1040 Berlin.

Verband der Ubersetzungsburos eV (German Association of Translation Bureaux), Heerstrasse 33, 5300 Bonn. T: 0228 63 24.

In Spain

Escuela de Traductores, Calle Castelló 42, 28001 Madrid. T: 575 9790.

In Italy

Associazione Nazionale Interpreti di Congresso Professionisti (Assointerpreti), Viale Caterina da Forli 50/3, 20146 Milano. T: 02 4088867.

Centro Mitec Impresa Individuale, Via Vittoria Colonna 49, 20149 Milano. T: 02 48195750/4390383.

International Business Centre Sr1, Corso Europa 12, 20122 Milano. T: 02 76013821.

ABC Traduzioni Impresa Individuale, Via R Lanciani 74, 00162 Roma. T: 06 8323512.

In the UK

Association of Translation Companies, 7 Buckingham Gate, London SW1E 6JS. T: 071-630 5454.

Interlingua Ltd, Rothschild House, Whitgift Centre, Croydon CR9 3QJ. T: 081-688 3852 (member of ALPNET, the largest translation network in the world).

Institute of Translating and Interpreting, 318a Finchley Road, London NW3 5HT. T: 071-794 9931.

Directory of Translators and Translating Agencies in the UK, edited by P Morris and G Weston, Bowker-Saur.

TRAVEL

In Europe

European Travel Commission, 2 rue Linois, F-75015 Paris. T: 45 75 62 16.

In France

French Government Tourist Board, 178 Piccadilly, London W1V 9DB. T: 071-499 6911.

Icotour: guide des vols, bateaux, routes, hotels, tour operateurs, visas, vaccins, etc.

In Germany

Deutsche Zentrale für Tourismus eV (German National Tourist Board), Beethovenstrasse 69, W-6000 Frankfurt. T: 49 69 75720.

German National Tourist Office, 65 Curzon Street, London W1Y 7PE. T: 071-495 3990.

In Spain

Oficina de Turismo, Plaza Mayor 3, 28012 Madrid. T: 366 5477.

Secretaria General de Turismo, Instituto de Turismo de España, Maria de Molina 50, 28006 Madrid. T: 411 6011/4014.

Spanish Tourist Office, 57 St James' Street, London SW1A 1LD. T: 071-499 0901.

Guía Renfe (Rail Guide)

Guía de los Hoteles (Hotel Guide)

In Italy

Italian Tourist Board, 1 Princes Street, London W1R 8AY. T: 071-408 1254.

Italy – The Best Guide, Piazzale Italia 285, 55100 Lucca. T: 0583 584818.

Michelin Guide, Michelin Italia SpA, Servizio Turismo, Corso Sempione 66, 20154 Milano. T: 02 3882305.

In the UK

General

Royal Mail International Business Travel Guide

ABC Guide to International Travel

Air services

ABC World Airways Guide

Hotels and restaurants

AA Members' Handbook and *RAC Members' Handbook*

ABC UK Holiday Guide

ABC Worldwide Hotel Guide

Daily Mail Guide to UK Hotels

Hotels and Restaurants in Great Britain

Financial Times World Hotel Directory

Good Food Guide

Michelin Guides

Harden's London Restaurants Guide published by Great Wen Publications

Time Out Guide to Restaurants (London) Restaurant Services. T: 081–888 8080.

Location of places, names of towns, etc.

Ordnance Survey Gazetteer of Great Britain

Chambers World Gazetteer

Motoring information

AA Members' Handbook and *RAC Members' Handbook*

AA and RAC Guides for motoring in Europe

Passports

Regional Passport Offices

Shipping services

ABC Passenger Shipping Guide

Lloyd's International List

Train times

ABC Rail Guide

British Rail Timetables

Travel information

Travel Trade Directory

Hints to Exporters (DTI)

ABC Guide to International Travel

APPENDIX

French Ministry of Education Brevet de Technicien Supérieur for Trilingual Secretaries, 1992 examinations

CASE STUDY: ADMINISTRATIVE AND MANAGEMENT TECHNIQUES

Time allowed: 4 hours

Documents given to candidates
Examination text

Annexes
Annex 1: List of tasks to be completed in order to take part in the PAAS Show and diary extracts of the second and third quarters of 1992.
Annex 2: Press file
Annex 3: Breakdown of costs incurred and turnover achieved at the PAAS Show.
Annex 4: Order form: standard conditions of sale
Annex 5: Bill of exchange

Allocation of marks
Part One: 8 marks
Part Two: 16 marks
Part Three: 10 marks
Part Four: 6 marks

Introduction to the Company

Company Name:	LES SOLEILS DE PROVENCE
Legal entity:	SARL – Limited Company
Registered Office:	81 rue Joliot-Curie
	ZI des Milles
	13850 Aix-en-Provence Cedex
Business activity:	Preparation and marketing of natural products from Provence (soaps, toilet waters, bath products, perfumes, pots-pourris)
Start-up date:	1986
Total number of staff:	12
Managing director:	Madame Marie-Laure Deylet
Export manager:	Monsieur Xavier Verkhove
1991 turnover:	3 million French francs
Major export markets:	USA
	Canada
	Switzerland
	Belgium
	Germany
	Great Britain
	Denmark

It was through a love of natural beauty preparations that, in 1986, Madame Deylet created her own company, with the name 'MARIE-L SENTEURS' and launched a range confined to household soaps.

Her market grew rapidly, sales extended outwards, not only in the south-east and Paris areas, but also abroad through the use of agents from Paris.

Once the company had become a 'Limited' concern, it continued to grow: turnover has increased more than ten-fold in five years. The name Marie-L has been retained as its trademark, the name under which it became well known, and the company enjoys a very good reputation thanks to good product branding and the choice within the 'produits de Provence naturels' range.

In 1990 and 1991 the company confirmed its intention of becoming more international by taking part in international exhibitions.

You have just been recruited as Export Assistant and various administrative tasks have been entrusted to you.

Part One

Madame Marie-L Deylet has decided to take part in the next PAAS International Show (Paris – Ateliers d'Arts – Show) which will take place from Friday 4th to Tuesday 8th September inclusive, 1992, at Parc des Expositions in Paris, Porte de Versailles.

This show is solely for those in the business, who come from all over the world to plan and order their stock. Exhibitors have the opportunity to build up often very useful contacts with the top European and North American companies.

Taking part in this show requires very detailed planning and you decide to put together a schedule from which the order of priority for the tasks to be completed will emerge.

To do

From Annex 1 (List of tasks, with lead times and 1992 diary) show, by means of a PERT network analysis (Programme Evaluation and Review Technique), the sequence of these events and determine the start date for operations. Show the critical path analysis. Which tasks could be delayed without jeopardising successful participation in the Show?

Part Two

In order to put together the list of exhibitors brochure, which is made available to visitors, each exhibitor must provide the organisers with introductory and follow-up literature about their company. At the same time, a letter of invitation will be sent to overseas customers.

To do

1 Making use of the documents in Annex 2, draft the text of the literature for insertion in the exhibitors brochure. The piece of about ten lines must inform visitors about the company exhibiting, its products, its unique qualities, etc.

2 Draft and set out the letter to be sent to overseas customers. This letter must motivate them to go to the show and emphasise, in particular, the related benefits of such a visit.

Part Three

After the show has finished, the manager asks you to carry out an appraisal of the costs of the project.

To do

From the information contained in Annex 1 and 3:

1 Calculate the cost of taking part in the PAAS Show.

2 Determine whether the company's involvement has been profitable.

Part Four

You temporarily take the place of the accountant. You must prepare the invoices and bills of exchange to be sent to various customers. These documents are drawn up on the day of delivery.

After close examination of the order form filled in for Printemps-Haussmann and of the standard conditions of sale for 'Marie-L' (Annex 4), you fill out the documents to be sent to the customer.

To do

1 Show the calculations giving you the total amount for the bill of exchange (preparation of the invoice itself is not requested).

2 Raise the bill of exchange number 543 (Annex 5).

3 Record the accounts:

3.1 The invoice addressed to Printemps-Haussmann.

3.2 The bill of exchange after acceptance.

Annex 1
List of tasks to be completed with the intention of taking part in the PAAS Show

Tasks	Symbol	Length (in days)	Task directly before
1 General			
– Decision to exhibit			
– Budget preparation	A	2	
2 Stand and equipment			
– Request for stand hire and await confirmation	B	10	A
– Choice of merchandise to exhibit and to be transported	C	2	A
– Pitch for fitters, wait	E	15	B and C
– Choice of fitter	F	1	E
– Preparation (packaging) of exhibit merchandise and documentation	D	2	B and C
– Transportation of merchandise	H	4	F and D
– Setting up and decoration of stand (the day before the show begins)	I	1	H, G and K
– Taking down the stand (the day after the show finishes)	Q	1	P
3 Staff			
– Staff selection and training	J	3	B
– Travel (two days before the show starts, in evening)	K	1	J

Tasks	Symbol	Length (in days)	Task directly before
4 Promotion			
– Confirmation and advertising schedule	L	2	B and C
– Preparation of copy for insertion in exhibitors brochure and send off	G	3	B
– Order invitations	M	5	L
– Formulate letters, translation, send out with cards	N	3	M
– Press release (the day before show)	O	1	L
– Show	P	5	I, O and N

NB For the tasks before the show, Saturdays, Sundays and public holidays are not working days.

1992

AVRIL	MAI	JUIN	JUILLET	AOUT	SEPTEMBRE
Les jours augmentent de 1 h 34	Les jours augmentent de 1 h 16	Les jours augmentent de 13 mn	Les jours diminuent de 58 mn	Les jours diminuent de 1 h 35	Les jours diminuent de 1 h 42
1 M Hugues	1 V F. DU TRAVAIL	1 L Justin 23	1 M Thierry	1 S Alphonse	1 M Gilles
2 J Sandrine	2 S Boris	2 M Blandine	2 J Martinien	2 D Julien	2 M Ingrid
3 V Richard	3 D Jacques/Philippe	3 M Kévin	3 V Thomas		3 J Grégoire
4 S Isidore		4 J Clotilde	4 S Florent	3 L Lydie 32	4 V Rosalie
5 D Irène	4 L Sylvain 19	5 V Igor	5 D Antoine-Marie	4 M J.-M. Vianney	5 S Raissa
	5 M Judith	6 S Norbert		5 M Abel	6 D Bertrand
6 L Marcellin 15	6 M Prudence	7 D PENTECÔTE	6 L Marietta 28	6 J Transfiguration	
7 M J.-B. de la Salle	7 J Gisèle		7 M Raoul	7 V Gaëtan	7 L Reine 37
8 M Julie	8 V VICTOIRE 1945	8 L Médard 24	8 M Thibaut	8 S Dominique	8 M Nativité de N.-D.
9 J Gautier	9 S Pacôme	9 M Diane	9 J Amandine	9 D Amour	9 M Alain
10 V Fulbert	10 D F. Jeanne d'Arc	10 M Landry	10 V Ulrich		10 J Inès
11 S Stanislas		11 J Barnabé	11 S Benoît	10 L Laurent 33	11 V Adelphe
12 D Rameaux	11 L Estelle 20	12 V Guy	12 D Olivier	11 M Claire	12 S Apollinaire
	12 M Achille	13 S Antoine de P.		12 M Clarisse	13 D Aimé
13 L Ida 16	13 M Rolande	14 D Elisée	13 L Henri/Joël 29	13 J Hippolyte	
14 M Maxime	14 J Matthias		14 M F. NATION.	14 V Evrard	14 L Sainte Croix 38
15 M Paterne	15 V Denise	15 L Germaine 25	15 M Donald	15 S ASSOMPTION	15 M Roland
16 J Benoît Labre	16 S Honoré	16 M J.-F. Régis	16 J N.-D. Mt Carmel	16 D Armel	16 M Edith
17 V Vendr. St	17 D Pascal	17 M Hervé	17 V Charlotte		17 J Renaud
18 S Parfait		18 J Léonce	18 S Frédéric	17 L Hyacinthe 34	18 V Nadège
19 D PAQUES	18 L Eric 21	19 V Romuald	19 D Arsène	18 M Hélène	19 S Emilie
	19 M Yves	20 S Silvère		19 M Jean Eudes	20 D Davy
20 L Odette 17	20 M Bernardin	21 D F. Dieu/F. Pères	20 L Marina 30	20 J Bernard	
21 M Anselme	21 J Constantin		21 M Victor	21 V Christophe	21 L Matthieu 39
22 M Alexandre	22 V Emile	22 L Alban 26	22 M Marie-Madel.	22 S Fabrice	22 M Maurice
23 J Georges	23 S Didier	23 M Audrey	23 J Brigitte	23 D Rose	23 M Constant
24 V Fidèle	24 D Donatien	24 M Jean-Baptiste	24 V Christine		24 J Thècle
25 S Marc		25 J Prosper	25 S Jacques le M.	24 L Barthélemy 35	25 V Hermann
26 D Souv. Déportés	25 L Sophie 22	26 V Sacré-Cœur	26 D Anne et Joachim	25 M Louis	26 S Côme/Damien
	26 M Bérenger	27 S Fernand		26 M Natacha	27 D Vincent de Paul
27 L Zita 18	27 M Augustin de C.	28 D Irénée	27 L Nathalie 31	27 J Monique	
28 M Valérie	28 J ASCENSION		28 M Samson	28 V Augustin	28 L Venceslas 40
29 M Catherine de S.	29 V Aymar	29 L Pierre/Paul 27	29 M Marthe	29 S Sabine	29 M Michel/Gabriel
30 J Robert	30 S Ferdinand	30 M Martial	30 J Juliette	30 D Fiacre	30 M Jérôme
	31 D Fête des Mères		31 V Ignace de L.	31 L Aristide 36	
Printemps le 20 mars à 8 h 49		Eté le 21 juin à 3 h 15			Automne le 22 sept à 18 h 43

Annex 2
Technical details

Marie-L specialises in household soaps, Provence perfumes, a light eau-de-Cologne: 'Déa' eau-de-Provence.

Marie-L as a company wants to retain the theme of the South and Provence with very natural, authentic, sophisticated products and above all a strong, unique style: the new Provençal style.

Range

Perfumes
Refreshing and revitalising eau-de-Cologne, 80 per cent natural plant extracts from Provence.

Scents and Bath products
- Household soap
- 100 per cent vegetable soap tablets
- Bath salts and grains
- Gift packs
- Pots-pourris

Customers
USA through the buying agent EBO (Paris)

Who is Marie-L?
Marie-L or Marie-Laure Deylet was born in Aix-en-Provence. She grew up there surrounded by her grandmothers, one a florist, the other a laundress. Her love of scents, perfumes and bath products was influenced by this 1950s' background.

Through her own personality, Marie-L has created a style of her own. The company Marie-L was born out of this background in 1986, specialising in natural bath products and based at the very heart of Provence in its ancient capital: Aix-en-Provence.

Marie-L, the company, has great 'know-how' and experience within it. It brings together the talents of ten people with the same vocation: the quest for quality through respect for the environment, the quest for well-being.

A great achievement for a woman who chose household soap as the foundation of her product range and her route to expansion.

Today, Marie-L continues to surprise us, reaffirming her very genuine, sophisticated designer style.

Why do we notice Marie-L?
Quite simply because Marie-L has great powers of creativity – at the product level, all her creations are original and refined.

Does Marie-L have a code of ethics?
The Marie-L company was created by a woman whose belief it was that a company can *only* exist through a code of ethics.

Marie-L's code of ethics is based as much on harmony and balance as on moral and intellectual well-being.

This code of ethics affects all those who work at Marie-L and also its customers.

It is the code of ethics rather than turnover which steers the company's development.

Respect for the individual, the ability to listen, intellectual rigour, calling everything into question and concern about progress have now become more than a project for Marie-L: they have become a way of life.

This is how Marie-L has managed to avoid falling into the mould of other companies and has remained unique.

How did she arrive at this code of ethics?
Marie-L's *raison d'être* is to sell a range of natural perfumes, scents and soaps from Provence,

but in an original style, with vivid colours and all closely associated with Provence.

By bringing together tradition and design, Marie-L stands out from the competition.

How did she establish herself?

Marie-L wanted it to be known that household soap always occupies an important place as a caring quality product. Up to now, it has all too often been sold and used as an everyday product.

Marie-L overcame this challenge and transformed it into an up-market product.

How did she develop further?

By developing a range of products:

'Les "savoureuses" savonnettes cocktails', with Provençal fruitiness and elegant packaging in bright Provençal colours.

'Les Galets': a special care range, very gentle with pure extracts of clay, wheatgerm, seaweed and honey.

'Les Petits Pierre': delightfully presented as little coloured boxes.

'Les Provençales': finely edged little blocks, made with pure extract of verbena and bitter almond.

Marie-L is planning to launch even more products such as Déa: sophisticated Provençal eau-de-fraîcheur, a highly concentrated product with a base of 80 per cent natural plant extracts from Provence which deserves a whole page to itself.

Marie-L also means pot-pourris: you must try them!

They are energising and come perfumed with essential oils of peach, rose or hillside aromas.

Let us not forget Marie-L's 'Surprises Provençales' either: much sought-after beautiful gift boxes containing a variety of different yet complementary products all in tune with one another and decorated with a Provençale border.

Does Marie-L have any specialities?

Of course, above all 'Déa', eau-de-Provence. 'Déa' is the encapsulation of all the richness of the natural perfumes of Provence concentrated in a bottle the dusky-brown colour of Provençale lime.

A real eau-de-fraîcheur, it is a melodious balance of Provençal scents not only for its typical fragrances but also for the richness of its many ingredients such as lavender from the southern Alps, lime, peppermint and basil.

Moreover, it contains the subtle shades of fragrance of the peppery carnation, a scent which suits men as well as women.

But the secret of 'Déa' lies in the 80 per cent natural extracts from those Provençal plants, either in the form of essential oils or absolutes (essence of savory, basil, absolute of thyme and of lavender).

This all comes together to create a very sophisticated perfume with fresh, exotic notes, and a sparkling, warm perfume contributing to a sense of well-being.

It is more than an eau-de-toilette, it is an eau-de-fraîcheur, an eau vivifiante to be applied as much after the morning shower as after playing sport.

That is not all: the bottle designed by Pierre Dinan conjures up images of the Provençal Earls' coats of arms authentically sculpted into the glass. Once opened, it is impossible to do without this feeling of well-being emanating from this eau-de-fraîcheur, steeped in history and developed by Francis Bocris.

On sale in department stores: Printemps, Galeries Lafayette, certain gift shops, of interest to perfumeries as well.

Annex 3
Breakdown of costs incurred during involvement in the PAAS Show

- Hire of Stand: FF 1400,00
- Insertion in exhibitors catalogue: FF 1500,00
- Sundries (printing invitations, letters, etc.): valued at 60 per cent of the above catalogue costs
- Return journey Marseille–Paris through Air Inter: FF1400 per person. (Three people taking part in the show, one managed to secure a 30 per cent discount.)
- Hotel accommodation: three rooms at FF 275,00 per person, including breakfast. The three participants will return to Marseille the day after the show finishes. (On this day, the two meals are paid for by the company.)
- Meals: FF120 per meal.
- Despatch of exhibition items: FF 600,000.

All costs are quoted net of TVA.

Turnover net of TVA achieved during the show (in FF)

Italy:	45 000
Germany:	28 500
'La Paix' Parfumerie, Paris:	10 750
Netherlands:	15 550
Belgium:	17 860
Galeries Lafayette, Paris:	24 780
Canada:	22 830
Parfumerie Flamande, Lille:	9 780
Drugstore du Midi, Toulouse:	5 200

Mark-up for France: 40 per cent of T/O net of TVA
Mark-up for exports: 22 per cent of T/O net of TVA

Annex 4
Order form

FRANCE

LES SOLEILS DE PROVENCE
81 rue Joliot Curie, Z. 1. des Milles
13850 Aix en Provence cedex 3, France
Tel 42 56 71 73   Fax 33/42 29 87 70
AC 90 B 654 Siret 338 373 632 012

BON DE COMMANDE
NO 453

Facturer à:

PRINTEMPS HAUSSMANN
102 Rue de Provence
75009 PARIS

Livrer à: *Printemps*
9 quài du Chàtelier
93450 Ile St Denis

Période: *entre le 11 et*
le 16 mai 1992

Code	Désignation	Quantité	Prix Unit HT	Observations
2223	Sav. de Marseille 322g boîte bois naturel	24	15.95	
2224	Sav. de Marseille 322g boîte bois olivier	24	16.95	
2013	Savon Cocktail fruit Mûre	48	9.50	
2016	Savon Cocktail fruits Avocat	48	9.50	
2261	Savon Galet Argile	48	12.50	
2235	Etui Cocktail fruits 3 savons	60	29.00	
2236	Pochette Cadeau	60	24.20	
2260	Corbeille 3 coloris assortis 1 sachet pot pourri 1 savon cocktail fruits 1 savon Petit Pierre	72	48.50	
2253	Coffret 2 savons cocktail 4 savons Petit Pierre sur paille et pot pourri	36	48.20	

TOTAL PRIX HT: 10 720.80

Livraison le 16 mai
Remise 6%
TVA taux normal
ML

Conditions de paiement: *30 jours fin de mois par traite à partir date livraison domiciliation:*
Crédit Lyonnais Agence HP, Paris

Date: *9 mars 1992*   Signature du client: *A Blanc*

Annex 4 (paraphrased)
Standard Conditions of Sale

Applicable from 1 January 1991

Price

Our prices are exclusive of TVA. Prices quoted are those in effect at the date of delivery. The Company reserves the right to increase or reduce prices if a change in rate is necessary between placing an order and taking delivery.

Delivery

The delivery time quoted on the order form or confirmation is an indication only and not the essence of the contract. Prices are carriage paid for metropolitan France only, for orders over 3000 francs excluding TVA. For stock orders, carriage paid is from 1500 francs excluding TVA. For orders of less than 3000 francs excluding TVA or 1500 francs stock order, 120 francs will automatically be requested from the customer for transportation.

Complaints are accepted 48 hours after receipt of the goods. They must be addressed to the delivery company by registered letter with acknowledgement of receipt. A copy must be sent to us.

In the case of refusal to accept goods, whether returned to the sender or not, transportation costs will be billed automatically to the customer. The sum of 10 per cent of the order excluding TVA will also be payable to indemnify the seller against handling and administration costs.

Terms of payment

The first order is due for settlement in cash in the ten days following delivery of the goods. All invoices amounting to less than 3000 francs excluding TVA are payable in cash. All other invoices are payable either in cash or, at 30 days, by banker's draft. If, however, a banker's draft payment for 30 days at end of the month has been agreed by the Seller, this must be shown on the order form signed by the customer.

Any other form of late payment will incur a 2 per cent increase for each month's delay.

Default on any payment due date will immediately render all accounts due whether due or not and will result in suspension of deliveries. In such cases, 20 per cent interest will be charged . . . Any costs incurred in recovering unpaid monies will be charged to the customer.

Title

In accordance with Law 80335 of 12 May 1980, the property in the goods shall not pass to the Purchaser until the whole of the price of the goods has been paid. In the event of the Purchaser failing to honour any invoices, we reserve the right to retake possession of the merchandise and may enter any premises for such purpose.

Any attempt to copy or reproduce Marie-L goods will be met with legal action.

Orders

Products may not be returned or exchanged . . . Customers must inform us if they cease trading so that the Seller can make contact with the Purchaser's replacement.

Proper Law

The contract of which these Conditions form part shall only be governed by the Aix-en-Provence courts. By entering into an agreement with our Company, the Purchaser, by implication, accepts our Conditions: these cannot be changed without prior agreement on our behalf.

Signature of customer preceded by 'read and approved'

Read & approved

Notes to Order form

Bon de Commande	Order form
Facturer à	Billing address
Livrer à	Delivery address
Période	Delivery time
Désignation	Description
Quantité	Amount
Prix unit	Unit price
Observations	Comments
Total prix	Total cost

Livraison le 16 mai	Deliver on 16 May
Remise 6%	6% discount
TVA taux normal	Normal rate of VAT
Conditions de paiement	Payment conditions
30 jours fin de mois par traite à partir date livraison domiciliation: Crédit Lyonnais . . .	30 days after the end of the month of delivery by transfer to Crédit Lyonnais.

Annex 5
Bill of exchange

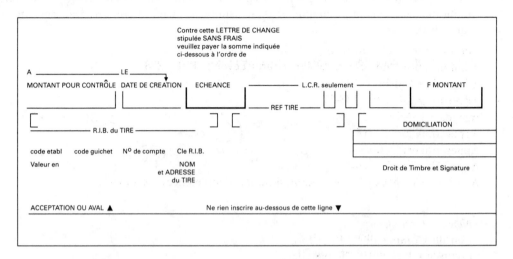

Notes:

Contre cette LETTRE DE CHANGE stipulée SANS FRAIS veuillez payer la somme indiquée ci-dessous à l'ordre de:

Echéance
Montant

Please pay the sum shown below against this bill of exchange stated WITHOUT CHARGES to the order of:

Due date
Total amount

INDEX